Welcome to Junior's!

Welcome to Junior's!

Remembering Brooklyn with Recipes and Memories from Its Favorite Restaurant

Marvin and Walter Rosen

with Beth Allen

Historical text by Judith Blahnik

William Morrow and Company, Inc. / New York

Library of Congress Cataloging-in-Publication Data

Rosen, Marvin.
    Welcome to Junior's! : remembering Brooklyn with recipes and memories from its favorite restaurant / Marvin and Walter Rosen, with Beth Allen ; historical text by Judith Blahnik—1st ed.
      p.   cm.
    ISBN 0-688-15900-1
      1. Cookery, American.   2. Cookery—New York (State)—New York.
3. Junior's (Restaurant)   4. Brooklyn (New York, N.Y.)—Social life and customs.   I. Rosen, Walter.   II. Allen, Beth.   III. Blahnik, Judith.   IV. Title.
TX715.R8344   1999
641.5'09747'23—dc21   98–38877
                                                                                                        CIP

Printed in the United States of America

First Edition

        1   2   3   4   5   6   7   8   9   10

BOOK DESIGN BY RICHARD ORIOLO

www.williammorrow.com

A tribute to Ruth and Harry Rosen

Contents

Welcome to Junior's!

CHAPTER ONE

1930s—In Brooklyn, the Art of Survival!

1930s—PUSHCARTS & SODA SHOPPES

Wine from Water . . . Matzoh Ball Soup . . . Split Pea Soup . . . White Meat Tuna Fish Salad . . . White Meat Chicken Salad à la Junior's . . . Challah Bread . . . Reuben Sandwich . . . Lemon Meringue Pie . . . Cherry Pie . . . Pie Pastry . . . Skyscraper Chocolate Ice Cream Soda . . . Skyscraper Broadway Ice Cream Soda . . . Chocolate Egg Cream . . . Mountain High Fresh Fruit Strawberry Sundae . . . Mountain High Vanilla Sundae . . . Never-Fail Whipped Cream

CHAPTER TWO

1940s—When Brooklyn Was . . . Everything

1940s—STAND-UP SNACK BARS & STEAK HOUSES

Jumbo Shrimp Cocktail . . . Crock of Baked Fresh Onion Soup Gratinee . . . New England Clam Chowder . . . Mashed Potatoes . . . Charbroiled Steak Smothered with Peppers and Onions . . . Prime Ribs of Beef with Fresh Mushroom Sauce . . . Hungarian Beef Goulash with Egg Noodles . . . Fresh Brisket of Beef with Delicious Gravy . . . Smothered Onions . . . Roasted Spring Chicken . . . Spanish Rice . . . Yellow Rice . . . Russian Dressing . . . Apple Pie . . . Pound Cake . . . Sponge Cake . . . Junior's Famous Fresh Strawberry Shortcake . . . Fresh Strawberry Sauce . . . Rice Pudding

Pure Cream Cheesecake—The Best of the Best! ... Thin Sponge Cake Layer for Cheesecake ... Fresh Strawberry Cheesecake ... Blueberry Cheesecake ... Pineapple Cheesecake ... Chocolate Swirl Cheesecake ... Apple Crumb Cheesecake ... Pumpkin Cheesecake

CHAPTER SIX

1980s—When Brooklyn . . . Came Back!

1980s—BAKE SHOPPE

Tea Biscuits ... Danish Dough ... Almond Cinnamon Danish ... Smear ... Cigars ... Apple Turnovers ... Fresh Peach Pie ... Fresh Blueberry Pie ... Pumpkin Pie ... Lemon Coconut Cake ... Chocolate Fudge Layer Cake ... Chocolate Fudge Frosting ... German Chocolate Layer Cake ... Carrot Cake with Cream Cheese Frosting ... Brownies ... Pure Butter Cookies ... Chocolate Chip Cookies ... Coconut Macaroons

CHAPTER SEVEN

1990s—Brooklyn! Still the World!

1990s—BROOKLYN FOOD

Homemade Cheese Blintzes ... Belgian Waffles ... Buffalo Wings with Bleu Cheese Sauce ... Chicken Fingers ... Honey Mustard Sauce ... Manhattan Clam Chowder ... Homemade Black Bean Soup ... BAR-B-Q Baby Back Ribs ... BAR-B-Q Sauce ... Broiled Shrimp Scampi ... Scampi Butter ... Broiled Fresh Sea Scallops with Garlic Butter ... Chicken on a Bun ... Yam Fries ... Spicy Fries ... Something Different ... Red Potato Salad ... Sweet Potato Pie ... Junior's Banana Royal ... Cookie Monster

Heading to Brooklyn
on the D-Train

IT IS SEVEN in the morning on a late-March day in

New York City. One of those days that says spring on the

calendar, but somehow feels more like the dead of winter.

My navy coat is not keeping out the cold breezes very well

as I stand on the Manhattan subway platform waiting, not

so patiently, for the D-Train.

Once again I look down at the piece of paper in my

hand—now wrinkled from my clutching it so hard that I can

barely read it. The instructions written by my assistant are simple enough: "Take the D-Train through all of the stations in lower Manhattan and over the Manhattan Bridge. Get off at the first stop in Brooklyn—DeKalb Avenue. Walk out of the subway, look for Junior's (you can't miss it!), walk in, and ask for Alan Rosen." The directions seem clear enough, except for that "can't miss it" part. This usually means trouble.

The D-Train comes. Once I'm on the subway, Manhattan is familiar territory for me. For I have lived in this exciting big city for many years and have grown to love it (even though there will always be a soft place in my heart for my Southern heritage of Houston, Texas, and its warm March days filled with flowering azaleas instead of icy breezes). This morning, as the subway makes its way along dark underground tracks, no one pays much attention to anything except his newspaper, coffee cup, or briefcase. But suddenly, as we approach Brooklyn, the D-Train gives us all a pleasant surprise. It climbs its way from belowground onto elevated tracks over the waterways into Brooklyn, in full view of the stately Brooklyn Bridge. As it chugs along, all my fellow passengers, even those who I thought were asleep, look up to enjoy the view—a golden sun exploding over the East River against a panoramic scene of Manhattan (equal to any wish-you-were-here postcard I have seen).

Approaching DeKalb and Flatbush

The D-Train screeches to a stop at DeKalb. Walking up the subway steps, I look up and immediately see what I came to Brooklyn for—Junior's restaurant, right across the street from where I'm standing. It's true, one really *can't* miss it, for Junior's *is* the whole corner of DeKalb Avenue and Flatbush Extension (naturally there are buildings on the other three corners, but nothing else seems to stand out). The restaurant beckons to everyone—with its orange-and-white Junior's neon sign rising high above the sidewalk and Junior's smiling face, topped with his chef's hat, on the side of the building, welcoming everyone passing by. The canopy, also orange and white in bold bright stripes, circles the building on both sides, stretching one way up Flatbush, and the opposite way down DeKalb. The look of the restaurant hasn't changed much (I would learn later) since Junior's opened in the 1950s. Everything seems the same. Except for one thing. Year after year, Junior's just keeps getting better—the food, the service, the surroundings.

Along Flatbush, the windows are so spotless that I get the feeling that someone has just polished them. As I peer into Junior's, I can clearly see inside to the rows and rows of cookies, strawberry cheesecakes, coconut layer cakes, and towering lemon meringue pies. They're so mouthwatering and tempting that they draw one in. Along DeKalb, in the other direction, I peek through a window and watch pancakes cooking on the griddle, alongside a dozen eggs sizzling sunny-side up. Further down the way, I see a glassed-in sidewalk café, with tables ready, set, and waiting.

Not many folks are on the streets at this hour, but those who are seem to all be heading into Junior's through the great big glass doors. Many smile, nod, or greet one another, as if they are friends. In fact, I am about the only person who doesn't know someone to say "good morning" to. But that doesn't matter. For some reason, I feel like I have just come *home*. Strange, for I have never before been on the D-Train, never before stepped out onto the corner of DeKalb and Flatbush, never before walked inside Junior's—until today.

All You Want, As You Want, at Junior's

As I walk inside, the sweet smells envelop me . . . so much that I want to just stop and savor them. They're coming from the bakery cases and shelves on my right, overflowing with pans of warm coffee rings stuffed with cherries and nuts, Danish filled with colorful fruits, muffins so big I can't imagine eating one at a single sitting. Through the glass cases I see some of the tallest cakes I can remember (I find out later that many have at least three layers, some four!): chocolate with swirls of fudge ganache and dark chocolate crumbs, coconut with swirls of lemon filling peeking out, and strawberry shortcakes frosted with whipped cream and crowned with fresh berries.

Everywhere I look, something's happening—everyone seems to be wide awake and very busy. One baker is neatly placing individual strawberry cheese pies on the top shelf of one of the glistening cases. Another is stacking up swirls of almond-cinnamon Danish on a sparkling glass plate—the delicious aromas tell me he just brought them out of the oven. Down at the other end of the counter, still another baker is cutting a piece of German chocolate cake that looks like it's at least eight inches high. Someone else is whirling down a rack from the bake shoppe right in front of me, filled with four dozen of Junior's famous cheesecakes—some plain and creamy, others crowned with strawberries, blueberries, or cherries, all finished off with crumbs (I now know it's their famous macaroon crumb topping).

The glass cases are already overflowing with rows and rows of perfect cookies (these are the only items I see that are dainty and small) . . . cherry pies, blueberry pies, and apple pies (I can see the fruit through the hole in the center) . . . oversized brownies frosted with fudge and a walnut on top . . . stacks of rugelach (I've read that's one of their specialties) . . . baskets of onion rolls, twisted rolls, and braided Challah . . . apple strudels, cheese strudels, and every kind of muffin you can imagine. This is no ordinary bakery counter. Most items look extra-high and extra-large, overstuffed with filling, towering with mounds of whipped cream or frosting, and professionally decorated to perfection. *All you want* . . . and much much more.

To the left, at the take-out deli counter, there are already folks standing in line for the morning special—coffee and an oversized muffin (today's special is blueberry; it says so right there on the handwritten sign). The waitress behind the counter, in an orange-and-white outfit, is busy taking breakfast orders: "Two scrambled with sausage walking on a roll . . . one special with OJ . . . a short stack with a rasher." The orders keep coming in as I walk by.

Past the deli is the soda-fountain counter that sparkles, with a large replica of Junior's restaurant perched on top. And beyond the counter I see two more rooms (Junior's extends around the corner into the bar and restaurant area, bordered by the glassed-in sidewalk café). Each room is shiny, spotless, and inviting, with brass chandeliers, Naugahyde-upholstered booths and chairs in the "signature orange," and waiters in white shirts and black slacks, vests, and bow ties—all making me think I just stepped back into the glorious fifties. There are framed press clippings on the walls, telling me that this place is a favorite eating spot of presidents, mayors, baseball heroes, and movie stars—from near and far. And here's Junior again, this time standing at attention as a two-foot-high statue with his chef's coat and smiling face, crowned with his high white hat. Now he's on one of the wood counters, welcoming me as I walk past and offering me a perfectly sculptured cheesecake, strawberry, of course.

I am early, so I climb up on one of the stools at the shiny curvy counter. Fred my waiter (I find out later he's been with Junior's over twenty-five years) greets me with a sincere smile. Recognizing I'm a newcomer, he hands me a menu. But menus aren't usually needed for breakfast: the policeman on my left is poured coffee, followed by Virginia ham and grits (which I haven't seen look this good since I left the South); the gentleman on my right, given a poached egg and corned beef hash; the lady across the way, cheese blintzes with strawberry sauce and sour cream; the businessman reading *The New York Times*, a stack of griddle cakes with a slab of butter melting on top. The food just keeps coming (no one else gets a menu), for these are "Regulars," I learn later, having "the regular" as they do morning after morning.

Now it's my turn: French toast that comes out crisp and crunchy on the outside, puffy and moist on the inside, with warm homemade apple and raisin preserves on the side. I'm quietly thanking my lucky stars that I arrived early as I savor each forkful. The orange juice is fresh, frosty, and frothy; the coffee is steaming and arrives in a bottomless cup; the rolls that just appear (without my ordering them) are freshly baked and still warm. I mentally make a note to come back the same time next week for the same thing.

Only the Best!

I soon discover that this is what Junior's is all about. Good food, good cooking, and good people, doing what they like to do best—pleasing other good people and giving them a good meal and a good time at the same time. Giving them *All You Want, as You Want*. This is the foundation that Harry Rosen built Junior's on in the fifties; that his sons, the Juniors themselves, Marvin and Walter Rosen, have spent their lifetimes keeping alive; and that now their sons Alan and Kevin Rosen maintain meticulously. In fact, Alan and Kevin are expanding beyond DeKalb and Flatbush—taking phone orders, sending cheesecakes across the country through overnight mails, giving press interviews, getting the word out about Junior's. Alan's even a "Regular" on one of the home-shopping networks. It's all of this that keeps folks coming back day after day.

And this is why I'm here at Junior's, and will keep coming time and again—to capture the history of Brooklyn from the 1930s until today, the story of how Junior's came to be, the homey surroundings, the down-home and ethnic flavors, and the recipes for Harry's delicious food still being served today. For Junior's represents Brooklyn at its bustling best in the 1950s—when folks came to meet their friends for an overstuffed deli sandwich and an egg cream for lunch and then back again with their families at the end of the day for fresh beef brisket or turkey, dressing, and all the trimmings. Junior's remains what it has become famous for throughout the years—a neighborhood restaurant filled with ethnic flavors, homey surroundings, and hometown folks.

All of these memories, recipes, and reminiscences I'm here to collect, by talking with the Rosens, the chefs, the bakers, the customers, and the waiters, too. By standing next to the short-order cook flipping the pancakes; watching the deli expert slice, stack, and fill sandwich after sandwich; working alongside the chef as he barbeques racks and racks of ribs; helping scoop out giant slabs of ice cream as the soda jerk whips up another chocolate malted; and observing the bakers carefully as they weigh out, whip up, bake out, and decorate hundreds of cheesecakes in the giant bakery upstairs. I am here to do all of this, so I can tuck the sights, smells, and tastes inside this book for you to read, to cook from, and to enjoy. And most of all, to feel at home with. *For this is what Junior's is all about.*

—BETH ALLEN

Acknowledgments

My thanks to . . .

Rebecca Goodhart—my editor at William Morrow and Company, Inc., who believed in Junior's, the Rosens, and their story, and my abilities to uncover the story, collect the recipes, record it all, and even bake a cake or grill a steakburger the Junior's Way. She was always as close as my telephone with her never-ending enthusiasm and support, her willingness to track down a map or help make my job easier, her guidance of top professionalism and highest editorial standards. And the whole staff at Morrow who were always willing to taste yet another cake, muffin, or cookie from our test kitchens.

The Copyediting and Production Staff at William Morrow—Ann Cahn, special projects production editor at Morrow, who contributed her valuable cookbook expertise from manuscript to bound book, making this book perfect in every way. Richard Oriolo, the designer, who turned my manuscript and photography collection into a visual masterpiece, capturing all the nostalgia and memories of Junior's. And Karen Lumley in the Production Department, who oversaw the book all the way through print production, which resulted in a top-quality professional book for readers to treasure.

All of the Rosens—Marvin, Walter, Alan, and Kevin for their many hours of sharing their family memories, treasured memorabilia, Junior's story as it has evolved over the years, daily restaurant experiences, menu memories, lessons learned, insights into the Junior's Way, and especially their never-faltering patience for answering my endless questions. Just when they thought they had given me everything they had collected, knew, or remembered, I would hand them a list of "things to look for and think about" before my next visit. Miraculously, the next time I returned, I was always welcomed once again, with sincere smiles, an unfaltering eagerness to help, and often with gems from old photo albums, menus, letters, recipe files, news clippings, even old framed pictures with menus tucked in back. And my thanks especially for their sharing wonderful food secrets, such as how to keep blueberries from sinking to the bottom of muffins, and digging out many facts, such as how many strawberries they use in a year.

The Staff at Junior's—the bakers at Junior's who let me bake alongside as they whipped up a cheesecake, shaped another batch of Danish, or frosted another cake; the short-order chefs who eagerly taught me how to grill a steakburger, cook an omelette, or stack up a sandwich the Junior's Way. The chef, his sous-chefs, and cooks in the kitchen who let me help, and patiently explained, as he and his professional kitchen staff roasted briskets of beef, basted turkeys, glazed hams, barbequed ribs, broiled steaks, simmered cauldrons of stocks and soups, broiled fish, stuffed shrimps, spiced up rice, whipped up gravies, fried up onion rings, battered up chicken, and whisked out plates and plates of scrumptious foods to hungry customers. The soda jerk who whipped up every ice cream soda on the menu, whirled up every malted, stirred up every egg cream, and scooped up every sundae—all so patiently so I could takes notes, ask questions, snap a photo. The hostesses, waiters, waitresses, line managers, cooks, busboys, and everyone else who always had a smile, a willingness to help, a moment to share their love of Junior's.

Judith Blahnik—who helped make this book much more than either one of us had ever envisioned, with the months of tedious research and even more hours of copywriting to gather the memories of Junior's and Brooklyn over the years—hours and hours, days and days as we interviewed anyone we could catch for a few moments in every corner of Junior's. Plus, her endless trips, tenacious determination, unending reading, and determined searching anyone, anything, anywhere, that might uncover the story: libraries, historical museums, history books, microfiches, old photo albums, old journals and letters, tattered postcards, newspaper clippings yellowed from age, videotapes, folks with memories of Junior's from interviews on sidewalks, street corners, and telephones, and numerous other meetings, day trips, and treasure hunts to anywhere priceless gems might be hidden.

Tom Thornton—a top professional in the food industry, who never tired of sorting out a food question, guiding me to the right source, and supporting me at every turn as we created this living history of Junior's.

To all who have ever experienced or would like to discover Junior's—from the "Regulars" who dine every day, to their loyal customers who return again and again, cheesecake lovers, deli lovers, mail-order recipients, celebrities, movie stars, congressmen, presidents, journalists, neighbors, out-of-town visitors, famous people and those not so famous, experienced cooks, armchair readers who know, love, and value what Junior's stands for, has always stood for—only the best—the best in service, food, and quality, just as Harry Rosen always said.

—BETH ALLEN

T

HIS BOOK, a work that interested me because of

my love for Brooklyn and passion for one of its landmark

restaurants, is not meant to be *the* factual history of either

Brooklyn or The Most Fabulous Junior's Restaurant. "No one

can know Brooklyn," says Brooklyn-born playwright Arthur

Miller, "because Brooklyn *is the world*." In the same way, no

one can know Junior's. A thriving family-owned business,

Junior's is a complex world with thousands of evolutionary

details, many of which passed away with founder Harry Rosen, who died at the age of ninety-two in 1996. It was Harry Rosen who spent fifty years turning a downtown Brooklyn sandwich shop into what would become an internationally known cheese-cake dynasty. Unfortunately, his death preceded the idea for this book by one year.

Depositories of records and memorabilia prior to 1981 were lost in a devastating fire which nearly took down the whole restaurant. The details about Junior's which we were able to piece together come from individuals' reminiscences, a few documents that escaped destruction, oral histories, and records saved since 1981.

Who's Telling This Story, Anyway?

What we have here is the history of Junior's as told to us, sifted from memory. We intend for you, the reader, to feel as if you are listening to Marvin and Walter Rosen (Harry's sons) tell everything they remember and have come to know as the second generation to operate the famous restaurant. We intend for the reader to feel what we felt as we sat with them at their favorite table in Junior's and listened to their stories. Even today, this is where you might find them during the early morning. Although the senior brothers have passed the reins of the restaurant to the younger Kevin and Alan Rosen, it was the older generation who gave us hours of taped interviews and oral histories right there in the restaurant. It was also Walter and Marvin who took my unpredictable phone calls with requests for details such as what happened at Junior's during the first New York City blackout, or what the Enduro bar was like on VJ Day.

The search for details was relentless and we know sometimes annoying for the Rosens; we felt like Peter Falk's character Colombo as we returned again and again for minutiae upon minutiae. So, we are grateful to the senior Rosens for their time, patience, effort, and memories. Because of them, we have been able to tell the story as they told it. The chapters are written in their voices, as if they are talking to us over coffee at Junior's, just as they did many times.

We are also grateful to the younger Rosens, Alan and Kevin, for shepherding the process of investigation and for making sure that all concerned read drafts as we went along. Also to Alan Rosen, thanks for unearthing boxes of priceless memorabilia, photos, news clippings, and videotapes which have been collected since Junior's devastating fire in 1981. His instinct for letting nothing go to waste, hiding it away somewhere, allowed for hundreds of colorful details to emerge.

We want to thank the staff of Junior's for their stories and memories, too—especially Camille Russo, who's been at the cash register and behind the bakery counter since 1960, Mary Blevins, who has expertly waited on customers at the counter since 1962, and waiter Fred Morgan, who came in 1972 and has also been serving at the counter ever since. Thanks, too, for the wonderful memories from Frank D'Alessio, the paper vendor who befriended Harry Rosen in 1949 and has been servicing Junior's needs since opening day in 1950.

As to the Story of Brooklyn

The story of Brooklyn is told here, decade by decade, with an attempt to tell it from the Rosen family's point of view—from the downtown corner of Flatbush Avenue Extension and DeKalb Avenue. If these walls could talk? Well, they do. They talk us through the internal evolution of the Enduro Sandwich Shop to the Enduro Restaurant and Cafe to Junior's Most Fabulous Restaurant Caterers and Bakers. They also talk us through the external changes—the rise and fall of a downtown theater district—from vaudeville to lavish stage shows and movies to rock 'n' roll extravaganzas to nothing at all. They describe the slow change of a once high-fashion downtown Fulton Street shopping area to the lively but raffish Fulton Mall to the rise of MetroTech. They take us through a major world war and more than one World Series in which the Brooklyn Dodgers fought for the championship. Any bits of Brooklyn history that originated downtown or affected downtown we tell here because they undoubtedly affected Junior's.

For exact details of Brooklyn history during the decades when the Rosens were serving pastrami, malts, and cheesecake, there were many places to turn for help. I've listed many of them in the bibliography; books, papers, and articles which guided me to the history of Brooklyn from 1930 to the present.

I want to extend thanks to those who gave me oral histories. Tom and Margaret Murray of Gerristen Beach, who grew up in Park Slope and Red Hook during the same years that the Enduro and Junior's came of age, welcomed me into their home, and gave me details about the real-life experience of downtown Brooklyn. Thanks, too, to Marianne Quinones, Anne Curry, and Sherry Berke, whose accounts of life downtown in the 1950s and 1960s were very helpful.

To John Manbeck, the Brooklyn historian and director of the Kingsborough Historical Society, thanks for welcoming me into your home, giving me an interview based in your own memories, and pointing me in many focused directions for further research. Thanks, too, for giving us access to the Kingsborough Historical Society Collection.

Special thanks to Ken Cobb at the City of New York Municipal Archives, who helped me retrieve a photo of the Enduro restaurant (circa 1940) and then was so helpful in finding other vintage photos of Brooklyn. Michelle Hackwelder, the head librarian at the Brooklyn Historical Society, gave us extra-kind attention while she was under pressure to move the library for a yearlong renovation. Thanks to Judy Walsh and Joy Holland at the Brooklyn Public Library Brooklyn Collection, who helped with details of Brooklyn history and gave me so much time to review photographs from the *Brooklyn Daily Eagle* collection. And to all those who took time to tell us their memories of Junior's, some of whose quotes appear in the book, thank you.

—JUDITH BLAHNIK

The Story Before Our Story

SEVERAL YEARS BEFORE Harry Rosen, the creator of

Junior's, was born, his parents, Barnett and Sarah Rosen,

immigrated to New York from Ukraine.

The year was 1895. Barnett had been a

farmer and a conscript soldier in Ukraine.

Barnett and Sarah moved into a

tenement building on Cherry Street on the

My father, Harry Rosen, was born into a poor family in 1904, but was dressed as aristocracy for his first photo. He was dapper his entire life.
Courtesy of the Rosen family

Lower East Side of Manhattan. They were very poor. Barnett built the beds for each of their six children as they came along and worked twelve hours a day in the slaughterhouse—Wilson & Company at First Avenue and Thirty-eighth Street. Later on he became a coat presser in a loft factory on Greene Street. He was a charter member of the International Ladies' Garment Workers' Union, founded in 1900. Their six children, Esther, Edna, Hershel (Harry), Mike, Bob, and Bill, were all born early in the century. Harry Rosen, who would become the founding force behind Junior's of Brooklyn, was born in 1904.

Sarah Rosen was ten years younger than her husband. She was illiterate but energetic, resourceful, wise, skillful, and always active with good deeds. To help bring in income, she ran a small newsstand. She was probably the single source that inspired her sons to success. She fiercely protected the time they spent in school, insisting that they learn to read and write. At age fifty-one, while struggling to gather for her family bits of ice that had fallen from an ice wagon, she was pinned under the heavy wheel. The injury was so bad her right arm was amputated. Still she continued to work.

Sarah taught her children how to seize the opportunity and make the best of

what they had. Her oldest boys, Harry and Mike, at ages fourteen and sixteen worked after school at Marchioni's Ice-Cream Parlor on Grand Street. For two years Sarah saved their earnings. She gave them only fifty cents a week to spend recklessly. When she had $1,500, she bought them a partnership in a luncheonette on Duane Street and Broadway. So at ages sixteen and eighteen, Harry and Mike Rosen were running their own luncheonette. When their older partner wanted to retire, they bought him out. They soon started to expand, setting up businesses one by one in the city. They called their unique shops the Enduro Sandwich Shops. Enduro was the name of a stainless steel

Here are the Rosen brothers, about 1921. From left—Harry and Mike, who were partners in the Enduro luncheonettes and restaurant, and Bob and Bill. Courtesy of the Rosen family

The Story Before Our Story

manufacturer who supplied equipment to luncheonettes and Harry loved the name.

By 1928, when the Junior's story begins, Harry and Mike Rosen were already very successful. Barnett and Sarah Rosen were able to enjoy some of that success with their sons. Barnett died in Brooklyn in 1937 at the age of seventy-seven. Sarah Rosen died at Christmastime in 1949 at the age of seventy-nine.

We don't know what they were celebrating, but this picture speaks of success and family. My father, Harry Rosen, has his arm around my grandmother, Sarah. My Uncle Mike is next to Harry. At the right is my grandfather Barnett Rosen, my aunt Edna, and my uncle Bill. Courtesy of the Rosen family

1930s – In Brooklyn, the Art of Survival!

THE 1920S WERE roaring to a peak. It was 1928, and

from the Cotton Club in Harlem to Luna Park in Coney

Island, New York was the ragtime

and jazz, movie and theater,

dance and art capital of the world.

This was a boom town that invented

and reinvented modern culture, not

The Brooklyn Bridge in 1904 was twenty-one years old and still the tallest structure on either side of the river. The Fulton ferryboats continued service until 1924. Courtesy of the Municipal Archives Department of Records and Information Services, City of New York

as a by-product of civic activity, but as if the city had lungs and lively art was oxygen. If it was exciting, it was here.

Prohibition was in its eighth year, but no matter. Playboy mayor Jimmy Walker was at the helm and speakeasies were filled with flappers and imbibers of all ages. Business was lucrative for bootleggers and crime bosses. Business was also good for my father then. He and my uncle Mike owned several Enduro Sandwich Shops in Manhattan, one in the prestigious Daily Mirror building. Radio was humming into its golden era with big band sounds broadcast live from the Savoy and Roseland Ballrooms at night, and fifteen-minute episodic dramas, sponsored by soap companies, broadcast daily.

In 1928, Brooklyn was marking its thirtieth year as part of New York City. Back in 1898, after about two hundred years as the fourth-largest independent city in the country, Brooklyn had been politically dragged, kicking and screaming, into the official confines of New York City, thereby becoming a mere borough. In 1928, old Brooklynites were still miffed about it.

So, What's the Deal with Brooklyn?

Industry, invention, education, and art were thriving in Brooklyn in 1928. Since more immigrants had settled here than in any other borough, Brooklyn benefited from their strong shoulders, their dreams and desires, their talents and know-how. The place was teeming with struggle and productivity.

There was an active waterfront, which employed tens of thousands of longshoremen and truckers. Brooklyn was a major port, taking care of at least 25 percent of United States foreign trade. There were glassworks and manufacturers of fine porcelain here. The ironworks in Greenpoint had made hundreds and thousands of stoves, railings, gates, lampposts. It had even made the iron for the U.S.S. *Monitor*. And the famous pencil maker Eberhard Faber was turning out millions of the yellow #2s we would carry to school and work for the next seventy years. Domino Sugar had their plant here. Drakes Cakes was one of many confectioneries with its main bakery in Brooklyn. There were hat and coat, boots and shoes, furniture and clock manufacturing—the most famous clock factory was the Ansonia in Park Slope, now a condominium.

Brooklyn was home of Yuban Coffees, Boar's Head Meats, and Fox's U-Bet Chocolate Flavor Syrup in Brownsville (Junior's won't make an egg cream without it). Charles Pfizer had his pharmaceuticals plant in Williamsburg, where it still stands today. And John Mack, owner and founder of Mack Truck Manufacturing, had his place on Third Avenue and Twenty-second Street. In Wallabout Bay, just off the East River, was the 127-year-old Brooklyn Navy Yard, which was just about to launch (in 1929) the first peacekeeping vessel, the U.S.S *Pensacola*.

Down on the Boardwalk

Coney Island's Luna Park with its handcarved (by German immigrant craftsmen) carousel, and Steeplechase Park, which dubbed itself *The Funny Place*, were swinging, gliding, banging, bouncing, rolling, strolling, and feeding about a million visitors a day in the summer of 1928. The Cyclone Racer, the most thrilling roller-coaster ride of its day, had just opened in 1927 next to a Coney landmark, Feltman's Ocean

The boardwalk at Coney Island from the Steeplechase Pier in 1930. That's Child's Restaurant with the flags waving and, in the distance, the Half Moon Hotel. Photo by Irving Underbill from the Brooklyn Public Library Brooklyn Collection. Courtesy of the Kingsborough Historical Society

Steeplechase was a pavilion of laughter and zany fun. This shows the entrance on Surf Avenue about 1925. The famous Parachute Jump wouldn't mark the horizon until 1941.

Photo by Irving Underhill from the Brooklyn Public Library Brooklyn Collection, courtesy of the Kingsborough Historical Society

Pavilion. Charles Feltman, who is touted for inventing the hot dog on a roll in his restaurant in East New York, ran a different class of place in Coney. There were several fancy dining rooms at Feltman's, each serving seashore dinners or house specials—not a hot dog on the menu. And each dining room had its own orchestra.

The hot dog trade became the empire of Brooklyn resident Nathan Handwerker, who set up a stand—Original Nathan's Famous Frankfurters—in Coney Island on Stillwell and Surf in 1916. Nathan sold a hot dog for a nickel—half the price of his competition. That and the unique flavor of his hot dogs made him—even today—the hot dog king. He has outlasted Feltman's, Steeplechase, and Luna Park. Only the bright lights of Nathan's, the clackity-clack of the Cyclone Racer, and the calliope of the carousel remain of the 1928 Coney Island empire.

Brooklyn at Night

Theater and movie culture was thriving in Brooklyn. Ever since 1800, when vaudeville gave rise to hundreds of fine ornate theaters, Brooklynites had paid a dime or

more to see top headliners of the day. And they created a few, too. Brooklyn-born Mae West was seven years old when she sang her first song on the stage of the Royal Theater on Fulton Street. It was 1903. Vaudeville had been the source of entertainment and sometimes education prior to radio. All of Brooklyn was used to stepping out for the night.

When movies at two-for-a-nickel began luring the vaudeville audiences away, many vaudeville theaters countered by offering both a stage variety show, which often included a ballet or concert, followed by a silent movie accompanied by an organ. One of the finest vaudeville/movie theaters ever was built right in downtown Brooklyn, a stone's throw from where Junior's stands today. Everybody knew of the vaudeville impresario E. F. Albee, and when he built his new theater, which took up nearly a square block on Fulton at DeKalb Avenue, it was big news.

The place was a state-of-the-art magnificent tribute to the high esteem Albee had for both the audience and the traveling performers. Much of the block-long theater was living accommodations for performers—apartments, recreation rooms, daycare facilities, a laundry. And for the audience, there was a lavish use of imported marble and fine rugs, from the vaulted lobby to the plush interiors. The Albee stage headlined Smith and Dale, Mae West, Joe Yule, Jack Benny, Burns and Allen, Buddy Rogers, and many more before it became strictly a movie theater later on.

On Ninth Street near Eighth Avenue, the Prospect was a popular neighborhood vaudeville house from the late nineteenth century into the 1930s when it became a movie theater. A supermarket occupies the building today.
Courtesy of the Municipal Archives Department of Records and Information Services, City of New York

The Albee Theater, photographed from the Fulton El at the junction of DeKalb Avenue and Fulton Street, dwarfed the grand Dime Savings Bank on the right. About fifty yards to the right of the bank was the Enduro Restaurant. Courtesy of the Brooklyn Historical Society

When the Albee opened in 1925, Bill Robinson, who lived for a time and died in Brooklyn, was the headliner. People were talking about it for years. Mr. Bojangles himself, who popularized the saying "Everything is copasetic," was called then, as he is now, *the* greatest tap dancer of all time. He's the same man who would later choreograph and perform the show-stopping number on the stairs with Shirley Tem-

Welcome to Junior's!

ple in *The Little Colonel* in 1935. Robinson was the first African American anywhere to be the featured headliner in the white-controlled vaudeville world (perhaps foreshadowing another Robinson who in Brooklyn would be the first African American in white baseball). Brooklyn-born Eddie Cantor, according to old *Brooklyn Daily Eagle* clippings, was in the audience when Mr. Bojangles opened the Albee. So were Ed Wynn and Al Jolson.

The Downtown Theater District

Three years after the Albee opened downtown, the spectacular Brooklyn Paramount opened in November 1928. It took up the entire northeast corner of DeKalb and Flatbush Avenue Extension. Its huge Paramount sign mounted on the roof was a lighted spectacle that changed a nondescript corner into a downtown theater district. The Paramount was the first theater anywhere to be built especially for the new talking pictures—it was wired for sound. And its huge proscenium (think of Radio City Music Hall) was designed for large production numbers. It was more palatial than any theater anywhere in Brooklyn, rivaling the much touted, cathedral-like Loew's in Flatbush.

Brooklynites swarmed downtown, four thousand of them on opening day, for the chance to sit within the palatial walls and see the magnificent stage show and the premier of *Manhattan Cocktail*. The glitzy interior was appointed with three million dollars worth of sculptures, paintings, and antiques. Its grand (some would say grandiose) lobby was a copy of the famous Hall of Mirrors in Versailles. The pipes of a huge Wurlitzer organ must have sent chills through those who came that day. Some of the top talents of the time played the Brooklyn Paramount and crowds would turn out for them. On one occasion in the early thirties, so many people started lining up to buy tickets to see George Jessel that Mayor La Guardia made an appearance just to keep the crowds calm.

Not to be outdone by Paramount, William Fox opened his extravagant Fox Theater at the same time, one block away at Nevins and Fulton. It competed for the consumer's ticket with a vast, opulent space, winding marble staircases, and imported crystal chandeliers. The Fox also boasted the largest pipe organ in the world, which was true until Radio City Music Hall built one a few years later. The playbill for opening day listed: the Grand Orchestra led by Charles Previn, plus a

1930s—In Brooklyn, the Art of Survival!

fifty-voice chorale, plus Ruby Keeler, plus thirty dancing girls all preceding the premier showing of Dolores del Rio and Charles Farrell in *The Red Dance*. These new theaters and the beautiful Loew's Theater on Fulton escorted the modern movie culture into downtown with style and ostentatious splendor. They made movie-going a classy thing to do and they added new character to the downtown theater scene, which had long included legitimate houses such as the Majestic, the Strand, the Brooklyn Academy of Music, and several opera, burlesque, and vaudeville houses. By Christmas 1928, Brooklyn could boast its own theater district.

All We Need Now Is a Good Sandwich

In 1928 my father stood with his bride-to-be, Ruth Jacobson, on the corner of DeKalb and Flatbush Avenue Extension in downtown Brooklyn. "Right here is where we will open the next Enduro Sandwich Shop."

My mother didn't know my father all that well—they had been courting less than a year. But she knew the Enduro by reputation. My father and uncle owned several successful shops in the midst of Manhattan's busiest thoroughfares. Now here she was, a twenty-year-old girl from the Bronx standing on a corner in Brooklyn no less, which as far as she knew was infamous for gangsters, bootleg breweries, waterfront dives, and a negligible downtown. She didn't see things the way my father did.

Neither the impressive Paramount Theater towering over her, its huge marquee setting the corner ablaze with light, nor the rumble of the packed Fulton Street El a block away, nor the trolley stop at DeKalb and Flatbush, busy with Brooklynites boarding and unboarding, nor streams of pedestrians, nor the delivery trucks causing traffic jams, had any effect on my mother's opinion.

"Harry, what are you thinking?" she said. "This place is a morgue." She could see a sign for a bowling alley which pointed down a flight of stairs, not the mark of powerful urban enterprise, and in the window above 386 Flatbush Avenue Extension, the address my father had his eye on, was an ad for learning secretarial skills.

"The Enduro can't survive here," she said. "You'll never sell enough sandwiches to pay the rent."

Downtown Brooklyn as my father saw it in 1930 held great business opportunities. The area was packed day and night. This is looking down Fulton Street, which remained covered by the "black spider," or the elevated train tracks until the early forties. Courtesy of the Brooklyn Historical Society

My father looked at her and smiled the smile she would come to recognize as his love of challenge and his confidence in a sure bet. "If I listen to you, my darling," he said, "we'll be wearing cigar boxes for shoes."

In February 1929, the Enduro Sandwich Shop opened in a storefront rented from Dime Savings, the sole owner of the building. A luncheonette-style place, the Enduro had a small kitchen, a counter, and a few tables. It was designed to serve

1930s—In Brooklyn, the Art of Survival!

the hurried downtowner with a comfortable place to sit down and good sandwiches and soups.

Business was OK, even though the Enduro was competing with several other sandwich stands and luncheonettes in the area. It did well by offering Brooklynites what they might get in a neighborhood deli but weren't getting downtown at the time—overstuffed sandwiches, especially Jewish standards: corned beef, roast beef, rolled beef, tongue, or brisket on rye; egg salad or whitefish salad on thick Challah or club, a crispy Italian bread. There were soups, too—matzoh ball, as well as chicken and rice and the ever-popular tomato. My father was always looking for something to make eating out (even in a sandwich shop) more pleasurable and rewarding.

Then, in September 1929, Harry and Ruth got married. While they were on their honeymoon at Niagara Falls, the stock market took its fatal dive on Black Monday in late October. So did lots of investors who had money tied to suddenly failed businesses. My father came home from his honeymoon to tremendous losses—a couple hundred thousand dollars—equal to a major fortune today. He and my uncle Mike eventually sold most of the Enduro Shops in Manhattan and put all of their energies into the Brooklyn Enduro. No one but he knew at the time that he had great hopes and dreams for this little sandwich shop.

Everybody's Depression

By 1932 the Depression had full momentum. Relief rolls were up—nearly a hundred thousand were out of work—and the city proposed a 2 percent sales tax to aid in relief efforts. The eight square miles of Brooklyn continued to grow in population as new immigrants flooded in looking for work. It passed Manhattan as most populated borough with 2.8 million residents. And just as everywhere, there was as much productivity and a scrambling sense of make-do as there was despair, poverty, and organized crime. Brooklyn-born Al Capone had grown up on Garfield Place and had worked as a bouncer in Coney Island. He and Albert Anastasia were big names among a throng of hoodlums who made easy money during Prohibition and the Depression.

Brooklyn's Backbone: The Neighborhood

Neighborhoods were geographically, architecturally, and ethnically distinct but they were bound together by one common experience in the 1930s—economic struggle. There were the tall apartment buildings lining the streets of Bensonhurst, the tenements of Williamsburg, the Victorian brownstone bays of Park Slope and Fort Greene, the brick two-stories of Bay Ridge, the modest single homes in Flatbush, and the large homes of the rich in Clinton Hill and along Albemarle Road off Coney Island Avenue.

Wherever your neighborhood was, it was yours. It nourished you. And you stood up for it as the best place in Brooklyn. A boy couldn't get past the third grade without at least one fight defending his neighborhood. And even with the occasional ethnic flare-ups among kids—the Greeks would fight the blacks, the Irish would gang up on the Jews, the Italians against the Lebanese—for the most part, crime was nonexistent. Doors were unlocked, hearts were open.

In too many neighborhoods during these years, young men—recent, able-bodied high school graduates—looked out of place as they hung out with nothing to do, without promise of jobs. They might pass the time playing touch football in the street. There were store windows with for-rent signs up for so long they had faded.

This is Ninth Street just west of Eighth Avenue in Park Slope. The baby in the buggy was just about one year old when this picture was taken in 1931. So was Marvin Rosen. Courtesy of the Municipal Archives Department of Records and Information Services, City of New York

Apartment buildings had permanent vacancy signs because in order to make ends meet, grown children had moved back home, bringing their own children with them.

The streets, stoops, fire escapes were teeming with people. Kids perfected the art of stoopball or stickball in the streets. No one insulated themselves. Life in joy and sorrow was lived on the stoops and windowsills.

Welcome to Junior's!

In Bedford-Stuyvesant, rent parties became an unhappy custom. All too frequently, a family's belongings sitting out on the street signaled eviction. Neighbors would throw a party for the family in need. Neighborhood musicians—jazz drummers (the great jazz drummer Max Roach was a boy in Bed-Stuy), horn and bass players—would come to play for free. Neighbors would bring food and a nickel or a dime.

Bells, Songs, and the Pushcart Trade

If you never left your neighborhood, the world eventually would come to you. And you could hear it coming before you saw it. A man with a pushcart came by regularly to sharpen knives and sell pots, ringing a bell to announce his arrival. Another pushed a cart with roasting chestnuts and baked sweet potatoes. He didn't ring. You could smell him coming. He would tear open a hot sweet potato, lump butter inside, plop it on a piece of newspaper, and hand it to you for a nickel. Another man with a huge pack on his back, the old-clothes man, would walk the neighborhood early in the morning singing out loud, "Old clothes, old clothes, I cash, I cash."

If you lived in or near Coney Island in 1933, you might have bought Gold's Horseradish from a pushcart. Tillie Gold, who lived on McDonald Avenue, survived the Depression by grinding horseradish every day and spooning the seasoned mixture into a bottle with a simple label. Her husband sold it from a pushcart. Gold's Horseradish, now on Long Island, is the largest purveyor of bottled horseradish in the world and, of course, of the horseradish we use today.

The iceman would make his rounds. If you heard his bell and called to him from your window, he'd grab hold of a huge block of ice from his truck, using iron tongs. Then he'd hoist it on his back and make his way, sometimes six flights up to your icebox. The coal man would pull up with a delivery. There was the milkman and the bread man. The fruit-and-vegetable man pushed a large cart or he might have an open truck showing off the produce. You could yell down from your window to him to ask how much for fresh peppers or green beans. In the summertime a bakery man would ring the bell attached to a spiffy little white truck and sell fresh pies—blueberry, cherry, lemon meringue.

For a kid, the best street food was what you made yourself. "Let's go roast a Mickey," someone might call to you. This meant you'd take a potato from home, find

1930s—In Brooklyn, the Art of Survival!

By 1925, automobiles had replaced the horse in the downtown area, but horse-drawn delivery wagons and vendor carts were common in residential neighborhoods throughout the 1930s. This produce man visits a street of row houses down near the Navy Yard. Photo by A. Clyde, courtesy of the Brooklyn Historical Society

Neighborhood stores sold foods from home countries as well as foods to send home. This store's sign says "We send coffee to Italy in 2-kilo and 5-kilo packages." Courtesy of the Municipal Archives Department of Records and Information Services, City of New York

some scrap wood or coal and an open space—either a vacant lot or wide sidewalk—and build a fire. Into the fire, or under hot coals, went the potato—and in the time it took you to keep the fire going, there was a burnt-on-the-outside, delicious-on-the-inside meal for you and your pals.

Venture from your door, and within a few blocks you could find a grocery, butcher, fruit-and-vegetable shop, barber, baker, beauty parlor, ice cream parlor, furniture store, and saloon. On any given day, there would be a baby carriage or two parked outside the butcher, baker, or grocer. No one ever worried about leaving the

1930s—In Brooklyn, the Art of Survival!

baby outside—the carriages were big, the babies were safe, of course. There was always a candy store; we call them newsstands today. But in those days you could buy penny candies, one of several different newspapers, cigars, cigarettes, magazines. Sometimes there was a counter where you could get an egg cream, or, if you brought your own pitcher, you could fill it with home brew. You could always leave messages for others at the candy store, and later in the thirties, most candy stores had a telephone, which much of the neighborhood depended on.

Light at the End of the Tunnel

In 1932, Mayor Jimmy Walker resigned when auditors threatened to look at his books. The new mayor, Fiorello La Guardia, looked promising—down to earth, fiery, and no airs about him. And in 1932, F.D.R., who had promised a New Deal for all of us, including a repeal of Prohibition, was elected by a landslide, sending Republican Herbert Hoover into the role of elder statesman. With the end of Prohibition came a new lease on life for the once great brewing business in Brooklyn. German immigrants, who from 1870 had owned and operated forty-some breweries and beer gardens here, had tried to hang on through Prohibition making a nonalcoholic brew. Near beer is what they called it. But most did not survive.

After the repeal however, some breweries returned to Brooklyn, and by the mid-thirties Rheingold, Schaefer, and Piel's of Brooklyn brought this borough back to the status of the largest beer-producing city in the United States. It would stay that way long into the fifties.

The Enduro Sandwich Becomes the Enduro Steak

The repeal of Prohibition spurred my father to imagine a more full-scale restaurant, not just a sandwich shop, one with casual dining and a bar. Once the shop next door was vacated, my father expanded the space and the menu. As part of the new Enduro, he created a unique bar, one that surrounded an elevated bandstand. The

cafe
€nduro
RESTAURANT
OPPOSITE BROOKLYN PARAMOUNT THEATRE

This corner of DeKalb and Flatbush Avenue Extension around 1939–1940 was home to a bowling alley (the entrance marked by the American flag), Boro Hall Secretarial Academy above, Smitty's Luncheonette, and the Enduro Restaurant. From 1934 to 1949 the Enduro was the place to dine before going to the Paramount or Albee theaters. Courtesy of the Municipal Archives Department of Records and Information Services, City of New York

Enduro Sandwich Shop became the Enduro Restaurant and Cafe, complete with cocktails and live entertainment.

My father considered himself *the* connoisseur and entertainer and he believed that if he offered cocktails with music and a fine menu featuring prime sirloin steaks, chops, side dishes, and desserts, this new place would thrive.

The new Enduro did very well. Its location and its lively character made it a must for anyone coming downtown for theater and dinner. In 1939, the year of the World's Fair, my father hosted a weeklong celebration that culminated in a party to celebrate ten years in downtown Brooklyn. The party menu featured Champagne cocktails, canapés l'Enduro, sliced prime sirloin, and petits fours for dessert. There was much to celebrate. He and my uncle had built a sandwich business into a first-

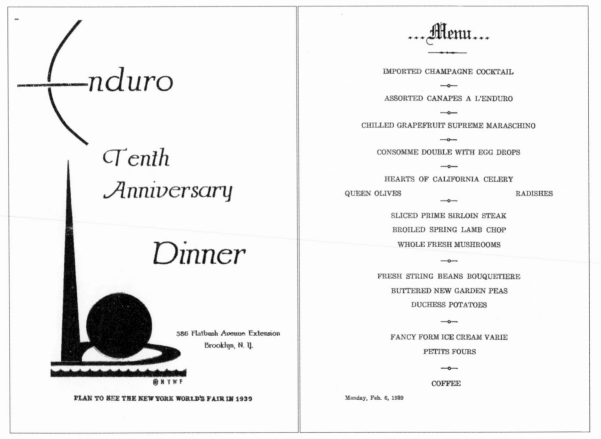

It took ten years to grow from a luncheonette to a full-service restaurant. My father celebrated with a banquet at the Enduro. Courtesy of the Rosen family

class restaurant in the prestigious and fashionable downtown area—during the Depression no less. Not only that, but the thirties had been good in two other ways. He and my mother had brought two healthy sons into the world. Marvin was born in 1930. Walter came along in 1934.

Is Anybody Here from Brooklyn?

Brooklyn had thousands of soon-to-be-famous faces in the thirties. Mickey Rooney was already ten years old in 1930, and when he wasn't at home in Brooklyn, he was traveling with his Brooklyn-born dad, actor Joe Yule, on the theater/vaudeville circuit. Wide-eyed Eddie Cantor was a singing waiter at Feltman's in Coney Island. The "great schnozzola" Jimmy Durante accompanied him on piano. Mel Brooks was fending off the bullies of Brownsville with wisecracks. The actor Vincent (*Moonstruck*) Gardenia was seven years old, playing the Majestic Theater with his father's Italian theater troupe.

George and Ira Gershwin, who had grown up in East New York and Coney Island, were already Broadway legends. *Girl Crazy* was their latest hit in 1930. They had actually ventured to the Brooklyn Paramount earlier that year to hear a sensational new voice they had been told about. Thus was Ethel Merman discovered for the Broadway cast of *Girl Crazy*.

Henry Miller left Brooklyn in 1930 to live in Paris, but always identified himself as a Brooklyn boy. Julius LaRosa was born here in 1930. So was Jackie Mason. The poet Marianne Moore moved here in 1931 and set up house on Cumberland Street in Fort Greene. Comedian Jerry Stiller was two years old. Eli Wallach was a boy living amid Jewish and Italian families in Red Hook. His dad's candy store on Union Street was an occasional contact point for messages from or for mob notables such as Al Capone.

In 1932 Beverly (Belle) Sills at age three sang her first aria in Tompkins Park at the Miss Beautiful Baby of Brooklyn contest. Yes, she won. Joseph Heller was growing up in Coney Island. It would be a few years before he'd write *Catch-22*. Phil Silvers was almost a teenager by the mid-thirties and on his way out of Brownsville to Broadway. Playwright Arthur Miller lived on Avenue M at the time and graduated from high school in 1932.

A railroad dining car made a fine neighborhood luncheonette in the 1930s. Still does. This one stood in an area of Williamsburg/Greenpoint that would be forever changed by the Brooklyn-Queens Expressway later in the 1940s. Courtesy of the Municipal Archives Department of Records and Information Services, City of New York

Jack Gilford, who had grown up in Williamsburg, was already playing clubs by 1930. Jackie Gleason was living the life in Brooklyn which would prepare him for his role as Ralph Cramden in *The Honeymooners*. Dom DeLuise was born in Bensonhurst in 1933. Mary Tyler Moore was born in Flatbush in 1937. Joan Rivers was just a kid living on fashionable Eastern Parkway. And Betty Comden, the great lyricist who would team up with Adolph Green on such hits as *Singing in the Rain* and *A Wonderful Town*, was at Erasmus Hall High School. Lena Horne was a fifteen-year-old on Chauncey Street. And that great choreographer Michael Kidd (*Seven Brides for Seven Brothers*) was the son of a barber, going to school in New Utrecht.

Steve Lawrence was born in Brownsville in 1935. He would discover Edie while working the Sid Caesar show in 1955. The great fiction writer Isaac Bashevis Singer immigrated and settled in Brooklyn in 1933. The next year Carl Sagan was

Welcome to Junior's!

born in Brooklyn; so was Peter Nero. And the year after that, Woody Allen. Elliot Gould came into the world in Bensonhurst in 1938. Paul Sorvino came one year later, same neighborhood. The great Penn State football coach Joe Paterno, born and raised in Flatbush, was ten years old in 1936. Another winning coach, Vince Lombardi, grew up in Sheepshead Bay, and Pete Hamill, the journalist, spent his youth in Park Slope.

Ya Bum, Ya!

Casey Stengel was managing the Dodgers in 1935 and he led the team out of a slump to a big defeat of the Giants—one that ruined the Giants' chance for a pennant. But then the team spent the rest of the 1930s struggling before loyal but dwindling crowds. It was during this long slump that a particular fan could be heard shouting and moaning from the stands, "Ya bum, ya!" The sportswriter Sid Mercer featured

Charlie Ebbets Field, home to the Brooklyn Dodgers, was built in 1913 at a cost of $50,800. Extensive renovations were done in 1938 to add night lighting and restore the ornate brick, glass, steel, and marble grandeur of the park. It was called the jewel in Crown Heights.
Courtesy of the Brooklyn Historical Society

the guy in his column, I guess finding him more interesting than the players. He called the guy "the Spirit of Brooklyn," and sports headlines began to refer to the team and Brooklyn itself as "the Bums."

By 1939, as the World's Fair opened in Queens and as the Enduro was celebrating ten years in downtown Brooklyn, the Dodgers slipped deeper into a slump and into debt. Ebbets Field was run-down and it seemed that the Depression was getting the best of the team. But as history would show us, the Dodgers, like much of Brooklyn, were merely in a darkness before a dawn. As the next decade unfolded, so did the golden era of the Dodgers. And even though my father might not have considered the Enduro in struggle or darkness, events were about to bring on a golden age for the Enduro as well, one which my father could have never imagined.

1930s—Pushcarts & Soda Shoppes

IN THE THIRTIES, you didn't have to walk far for food—it came right to you. Especially in Brooklyn.

There were pushcarts everywhere. The iceman brought big blocks of ice (they were always heavy and huge). The milkman came with bottles of fresh milk; the vegetable man often had green beans and snaps (peas) that had just been picked that morning.

From another pushcart, you could treat yourself to a baked sweet potato, oozing with butter, for just a nickel. From that same cart on another day, you could buy some hot roasted chestnuts, or you could sink your teeth into a slice of freshly baked cherry pie from still another cart.

Better yet, you and your beau could meet at the Enduro Sandwich Shop for a cup of soup, homemade chicken salad sandwich on Challah, or a hot Reuben. And you never forgot to order one of their Skyscraper Chocolate Ice Cream Sodas.

It always came with two sipping straws so you could share.

Welcome to Junior's!

Wine from Water

HARRY ROSEN WAS **known for using everything around him to make** delicious food. *Everything* **includes water. Here, an uncooked chicken turns water and a few vegetables into a chicken stock. It's used to make Matzoh Ball Soup. Or if you would rather, use the same strained stock, some of the cooked chicken, and some thin egg noodles to turn it into chicken noodle soup.**

MAKES 3 QUARTS STOCK

15 cups water

5 pounds chicken parts, on bone, white and dark meat

3 large carrots, scrubbed and sliced, 1 inch thick

2 large shallots, peeled and sliced, ¼ inch thick

1 extra-large yellow onion, peeled and cut into 8 wedges

1 large parsnip, peeled and sliced 1 inch thick

1 large turnip, peeled and cut into 1-inch cubes

1 tablespoon salt

3 tablespoons chicken stock seasoned base or
     6 chicken bouillon cubes

1 teaspoon ground white pepper

Few drops yellow food coloring (optional)

> ### The Junior's Way—
> When simmering a stock, never never cover the pot. Let the soup simmer slowly in the open pot for several hours (three, for this recipe). As the stock simmers away, some of the liquid evaporates, leaving less soup in the pot, but one that's richer, more delicious, and more intense in flavor.

1. Bring the water and chicken to a boil in a large stockpot over high heat. Skim off any foam that collects.

2. Stir in all of the remaining ingredients and bring the mixture back to a boil. Reduce the heat to medium-low and simmer, without covering the pot, for 3 hours.

3. Strain the stock through a large sieve into a heatproof bowl. Discard the chicken meat, bones, and vegetables. Use the stock in Matzoh Ball Soup (page 26) or use to make your favorite chicken noodle soup.

4. To store: Let the stock cool. Pour into covered containers and refrigerate or freeze. Use refrigerated stock within 3 days and frozen stock within 3 months.

1930s—In Brooklyn, the Art of Survival!

Matzoh Ball Soup

*E*ATING MATZOH, that is, eating unleavened bread made from flour and water, is a Jewish tradition during the spring holiday of Passover. Matzoh balls are small round dumplings made from matzoh meal. At Junior's, they're cooked and served in their homemade Wine from Water chicken stock. This soup's always on the menu!

MAKES 2 QUARTS SOUP

FOR THE MATZOH BALLS

4 extra-large eggs

¼ cup vegetable oil

¼ cup boiling chicken stock or water

1 cup matzoh meal

1 teaspoon salt

¼ teaspoon ground white pepper

FOR THE SOUP

8 cups Wine from Water chicken stock (page 25)

2 bay leaves

> *The Junior's Way—*
> Always cook the matzoh balls in boiling stock just until they're cooked through—no longer. Too much cooking can make the matzoh balls spongy.

1. Whisk the eggs in a medium-sized bowl until frothy, about 2 minutes. Add the oil and ¼ cup chicken stock and whisk again until combined. Add the matzoh meal, salt, and pepper and whisk until smooth, about 2 minutes more. Cover and refrigerate the batter for 20 minutes.

2. Meanwhile, fill a stockpot half full with water and bring to a boil over high heat.

3. Using a spoon and your hands, shape the matzoh mixture into balls (using about 1 heaping tablespoon for each ball) and drop them into the boiling water (you will have about 16 matzoh balls). Lower the heat to medium-low, cover the pot, and simmer just until the matzoh balls are cooked through, about 20 minutes.

Welcome to Junior's!

4. Meanwhile, bring the chicken stock and bay leaves to a boil over high heat. Remove bay leaves.

5. To serve, ladle 2 matzoh balls into each soup bowl and ladle over the hot chicken stock.

Split Pea Soup

NOTHING'S FANCY ABOUT this pot of soup—just good ol' home cookin'. What's even better: It's the type of good cooking that seems to cook itself. In fact, this is one pot of soup that really doesn't need much pot-watching. The slower and longer the soup simmers, the better it tastes.

MAKES 2 QUARTS SOUP

TO SOAK PEAS

2 cups (1 pound) dried green split peas

6 cups water

FOR THE SOUP

½ cup (1 stick) unsalted butter, preferably clarified (page 314)

1 cup finely chopped peeled carrots

1 cup finely chopped celery

1 cup finely chopped onions

¼ cup chicken stock seasoned base or 8 chicken bouillon
   cubes

½ teaspoon ground white pepper

6 cups boiling water

2 cups cooked ham, cut into bite-size strips (optional)

FOR THE CROUTONS

8 slices white bread

6 tablespoons (¾ stick) unsalted butter, preferably clarified (page 314)

1 tablespoon vegetable oil

The Junior's Way—
Don't skip the soaking step in this recipe—it's very important. If you have time, soak the peas overnight in cold water. If you're in a hurry, cook the peas in boiling water for two minutes, then let them soak in the hot water for an hour.

continued

1930s—In Brooklyn, the Art of Survival!

1. Rinse the peas, then soak them overnight in a large stockpot in the 6 cups of *cold* water, then rinse and drain. Or if you don't have the time for soaking overnight, cover the peas with 6 cups of *boiling* water, bring to a full boil over high heat, and boil for 2 minutes. Cover the pot and let the peas stand in the hot water for 1 hour, then rinse and drain. You now have 4 cups of soaked, plump peas, and they're ready to use in the soup.

2. For the soup, melt the butter in a large stockpot over medium-high heat. Add the carrots, celery, onions, chicken stock base, and pepper. Sauté the vegetables until golden and tender, about 7 minutes. Stir in the soaked peas, then pour in the 6 cups boiling water. Bring the soup to a full boil.

3. Reduce the heat to medium-low and simmer the soup, without covering the pot, until the peas are tender and the soup has thickened, about 1 hour. After 45 minutes of cooking, add the ham, if you wish. Stir the soup occasionally to prevent any possible sticking, adding a little more water if needed.

4. Meanwhile, make the croutons: Cut off the crusts from the bread with a serrated knife. Cut the slices of bread into 1-inch cubes. Heat the butter and oil in a large skillet over medium-high heat. Add the bread cubes and cook, turning frequently, until golden. Remove the croutons with a slotted spoon to paper towels to drain.

5. To serve: Ladle the soup into bowls and sprinkle with a few croutons.

Welcome to Junior's!

White Meat Tuna Fish Salad

WHAT CAN BE special about tuna fish salad? A lot—provided it's made the Junior's Way. The chef begins with only white albacore tuna fish that's packed in spring water, not oil. Then he uses only whole mayonnaise, as the lighter lower-in-fat variety can get watery and separate as the salad stands. But the real secret is the complex blend of flavors—tartness from fresh lemon, hotness from white pepper, and zest from Dijon mustard.

MAKES 5 CUPS SALAD

FOR THE SALAD

4 6-ounce cans white albacore tuna packed in spring water

1 cup finely chopped celery

FOR THE DRESSING

¾ cup *Hellmann's* Real Mayonnaise (not the light variety)

2 teaspoons fresh lemon juice

1 teaspoon Dijon mustard

¾ teaspoon ground white pepper

½ teaspoon garlic powder

⅛ teaspoon salt

The Junior's Way—
Use your fingers, not a knife, to finely shred the tuna. This gently flakes the tuna instead of crushing it.

1. Place the tuna in a colander to drain well. Transfer the tuna to a medium-size bowl and break it up with your fingers into flakes. Stir in the celery.

2. Mix all of the ingredients for the dressing in a small bowl. Spoon the dressing on top of the tuna-celery mixture. Gently stir in the dressing until all of the salad ingredients are well coated. Use in sandwiches or serve as a salad on crisp lettuce leaves. Tightly cover and refrigerate any leftovers.

1930s—In Brooklyn, the Art of Survival!

White Meat Chicken Salad à la Junior's

*J*UNIOR'S CHICKEN SALAD has chunks of real white meat chicken that's juicy and tender—not the finely chopped or ground-up kind. The chicken is sprinkled with fresh lemon juice to keep its white color.

And the dressing is not just mayonnaise—it has sour cream that makes it extra-smooth and creamy. Even the flavors that Junior's uses are different—fresh dill, a hint of garlic, and a spicy bite from Dijon mustard.

MAKES 6 CUPS SALAD

FOR THE SALAD

Celery leaves (optional)

1 teaspoon salt

1/8 teaspoon ground white pepper

2 pounds boneless skinless chicken breasts (about
        2 large whole breasts or 4 large halves)

1 tablespoon fresh lemon juice

1 cup diced celery

1 tablespoon snipped fresh dill

The Junior's Way— Simmer the chicken breasts in seasoned water, adding a few celery leaves for extra flavor.

FOR THE MUSTARD CREAM DRESSING

3/4 cup Hellmann's Real Mayonnaise (not the light variety)

1/3 cup sour cream

1 tablespoon Dijon mustard

1 teaspoon salt

1/4 teaspoon ground white pepper

1/4 teaspoon garlic powder

1. To cook the chicken, fill a large saucepan half full with water. Add a few celery leaves, if you wish, plus the salt and white pepper, and bring to a boil over

high heat. Slide in the chicken breasts, reduce the heat to medium-low, and simmer until the chicken turns opaque and the juices are no longer pink, about 8 minutes. Transfer the chicken to a colander with a slotted spoon, and rinse with cold water. Pat the chicken dry with paper towels and cut into ¾-inch chunks (you need 5 cups).

2. Place the chicken in a medium-sized bowl and sprinkle with the lemon juice and toss well. Add the celery and dill and toss again.

3. Mix all of the ingredients for the dressing in a small bowl. Spoon the dressing over the chicken mixture and stir until all of the chicken and celery are well coated. This salad's great for making sandwiches on thick slices of white or Challah Bread (page 32), or simply serve as a salad on curly lettuce leaves. Refrigerate any leftovers.

1930s—In Brooklyn, the Art of Survival!

Challah Bread

CHALLAH IS A light, airy, and very special loaf of bread, so special that it's traditionally baked only for the Jewish Sabbath, or for ceremonial holidays, such as Rosh Hashanah and Yom Kippur.

But every day is special at Junior's, so any day you can enjoy Challah. Often it's baked in a long 18-inch loaf, then cut into thick slices for sandwiches.

Other times it's braided into a fancy loaf for adding to bread baskets, twisted into delicious little rolls on Fridays (you'll often get two of these when you order a bowl of soup), even baked into long thin baguettes.

But however Junior's shapes it, you're in for a treat—a golden loaf with a shiny glossy top, showered with sesame seeds on the outside and a light yellow grain on the inside that's rich with eggs and has just a hint of sweetness.

MAKES ONE 18-INCH LOAF, BRAIDED OR PLAIN

FOR THE DOUGH

2 ¼-ounce packages active dry yeast

⅓ cup plus 1 tablespoon sugar

½ cup lukewarm water (105° to 115°F)

5 extra-large egg yolks

3 extra-large eggs

3 tablespoons vegetable oil

1 tablespoon salt

3¼ cups all-purpose flour

FOR THE GLAZE

1 extra-large egg

¼ teaspoon vegetable oil

2 tablespoons sesame seeds

The Junior's Way—
To braid, lay three ropes of dough side-by-side. Begin at the center and braid out to one end. Turn over the dough, then start at the center again and braid out toward the opposite end. When beating the egg for the glaze, add a little oil . . . this breaks up the stringy pieces of egg white, making it easier to brush on the bread.

1. Dissolve both packages of the yeast and the tablespoon of sugar in the water in a small bowl. Let the mixture stand until it's foamy and double its size.

2. Meanwhile, while the yeast is rising, fit a mixer with the paddle blade. Beat the egg yolks and whole eggs in a large bowl with the mixer on high until light yellow. Add the ⅓ cup of sugar, the oil, and salt and beat until blended. Reduce the speed to low and beat in the yeast mixture, then the flour.

3. Attach the dough hook (if your mixer has one) and knead on low for 5 minutes. Or knead the dough on a well-floured board by hand for 5 minutes. Place the dough in a generously buttered large bowl, turning the dough over once to coat it well with the butter. Cover the bowl with a towel and let the dough rise at room temperature until it's double its size (this will probably take about 1 hour).

4. Preheat the oven to 375°F and butter a baking sheet. Punch the dough down gently with your fist, then turn it out onto a lightly floured surface.

5. To make a plain loaf, pat and shape the dough into an oblong loaf, 16 inches long and about 3 inches high. *For a braided loaf*, cut the dough into 3 equal pieces. Shape each piece into a rope, about 16 inches long and 1½ inches in diameter. Lay the 3 ropes side-by-side. Starting at the center, braid the ropes out to one end, tucking the ends under. To make a prettier and more authentic braid, now turn the dough over (braided part and unbraided ropes). Then start at the center again and braid out to the opposite end, tucking the opposite ends under too. Transfer the loaf to the baking sheet.

6. Make the glaze by whisking the egg and oil in a small bowl. Brush the top and sides of the loaf with the glaze, then sprinkle generously with the sesame seeds. Cover with a clean towel and let the loaf rise 30 minutes more or until double its size.

7. Bake the Challah for 20 minutes or until golden and firm to the touch. Let the bread cool for 5 minutes on the baking sheet, then slide it onto a rack to cool at least 10 minutes more before slicing. Challah is great for eating as is or for slicing and toasting or grilling for Junior's sandwiches, especially Chicken on a Bun (page 316). It's also delicious when lightly spread with butter, toasted, and topped with strawberry jam.

1930s—In Brooklyn, the Art of Survival!

Reuben Sandwich

WHO REALLY INVENTED the Reuben? That's a good question. It depends upon which story you wish to believe. Any good Nebraskan claims that Reuben Kulakofsky, owner of Omaha's Central Market in the 1920s, created it for his poker buddies, who played frequently at the Blackstone Hotel.

They would regularly break for a midnight lunch. Reuben's sandwich creation was a favorite. One of his buddies, Charles Schimmel, liked the sandwich so much that he put it on the hotel menu and featured it as the *Reuben*.

But New Yorkers often claim the sandwich for their own. Arnold Reuben owned a deli (nothing fancy, but it did have a sandwich counter) called Reuben's Restaurant, located on East Fifty-eighth Street in New York City. It was a favorite eatery for show-business celebrities such as Jackie Gleason, Ginger Rogers, and ZsaZsa Gabor.

Legend has it that Reuben created this sandwich in 1914 for an actress named Annette Seelos, presumably before moving to the Big Apple. However, instead of naming his legendary creation after Annette, he gave the dish his own name—The Reuben Special.

MAKES 1 SANDWICH

2 tablespoons unsalted butter

2 slices rye bread

6 ounces lean corned beef, sliced very thin (about 10 slices)

½ cup drained fresh sauerkraut

4 slices Swiss cheese (4 ounces)

FOR THE GO-ALONG (OPTIONAL)

Red Potato Salad (page 321)

Welcome to Junior's!

1. Melt the butter on a hot grill or in a large skillet. Grill both slices of bread on one side.

2. At the same time, grill the corned beef in one stack and the sauerkraut in another. Cook until both are heated through.

3. Turn over one slice of the bread on the grill. Stack on the corned beef, top with the sauerkraut, then the cheese, and the second slice of bread, grilled side down.

4. Continue grilling the Reuben until it's hot and melted, turning the sandwich over once. This usually takes 5 to 7 minutes. Serve immediately, hot off the grill, with potato salad on the side, if you like.

The Junior's Way—

Use fresh sauerkraut, not the kind that comes in a can. Look for it already sliced in see-through plastic bags in the deli or meat counter at your supermarket. Or if you're lucky enough to live near a Jewish market, they might dish it out fresh for you at the deli counter. Slice the Reuben the Junior's Way—vertically into two pieces, one piece twice the width of the other. Slice the larger piece on the diagonal into two equal triangles, to make three smaller over-stuffed sandwiches. Stack them attractively on a plate and scoop out a generous helping of potato salad to serve alongside.

1930s—In Brooklyn, the Art of Survival!

Lemon Meringue Pie

*E*ARLY IN THE morning, you can always see this pie at Junior's—proudly displayed inside the glass window of the bakery. If it's early enough and the pies haven't sold out yet, you will even see a few in the bakery case.

They all look the same, yet each one is really different. Each pie is crowned with the highest meringue I've ever seen, swirled up to a towering peak in the center.

Junior's master baker personally twirls each one around on his pastry turntable and peaks each meringue by hand, in about twenty places with his fingers.

MAKES ONE 9-INCH DEEP-DISH PIE

1 recipe Thin Sponge Cake Layer, the one for the cheesecake (page 223)

½ recipe Pie Pastry, enough for a single-crust pie (page 40)

FOR THE LEMON FILLING

2⅓ cups sugar

⅔ cup cornstarch

½ teaspoon salt

2 cups cold water

5 extra-large egg yolks (whites reserved)

2 teaspoons grated lemon rind

*⅓ to ½ cup fresh lemon juice (depending on how
       tart you like your lemon pie)*

3 tablespoons unsalted butter

1 teaspoon pure vanilla extract

¼ teaspoon lemon extract

FOR THE MERINGUE

5 extra-large egg whites

½ teaspoon cream of tartar

1 cup sugar

The Junior's Way—

To keep the meringue standing up straight in fancy peaks, cover the filling with a thin layer of sponge cake, then spoon on the meringue. If the egg whites start to weep, the cake soaks up any liquid. This bit of sponge cake adds a delicious taste surprise to the pie, too.

Welcome to Junior's!

1. Prepare the Thin Sponge Cake Layer and set it aside to cool.

2. Preheat the oven to 400°F and butter a 9-inch deep-dish pie plate. Mix and chill the pastry. Roll it out ⅛ inch thick on a lightly floured surface and trim to a 15-inch circle. Transfer the pastry to the pie plate, leaving a 1½-inch overhang. Fold under the edge to stand up 1 inch high and flute. Prick it all over with the tines of a fork. Place the unbaked shell in the freezer for 15 minutes.

3. Completely bake the shell before filling it: Place a piece of foil in the center and weigh it down with pie weights, uncooked beans, or rice. Blind-bake the crust just until it sets, about 10 minutes. Carefully remove the foil and pie weights and continue baking the pie shell until golden, about 7 minutes more. Transfer the crust from the oven to a cooling rack. Reduce the oven temperature to 375°F.

4. While the crust is baking, make the filling: Mix the 2⅓ cups of sugar, the cornstarch, and salt together in a large saucepan. Gradually pour in the water, whisking as you go (no lumps of cornstarch should appear). Cook the custard over medium heat until the mixture thickens (do not overcook or the custard could separate). Remove the custard from the heat.

5. Meanwhile, using an electric mixer set on high, beat the egg yolks until thick and light yellow, about 5 minutes. Pour a little of the hot thickened cornstarch mixture into the egg yolks, then return all of this egg mixture to the saucepan. Whisk over low heat just until the mixture is hot and the custard around the edge of the pan starts to cook (watch carefully, as too much heat at this stage can overcook the eggs and break and separate the custard). Remove the filling from the heat and whisk in the lemon rind and juice, the butter, vanilla, and lemon extract. Pour the filling into the baked shell (you will have 4 cups of filling). Lay the thin sponge cake layer on top of the hot filling and press it down slightly, covering the filling completely.

6. To make the meringue: Place the egg whites and cream of tartar in a clean bowl and beat the egg whites with clean beaters on high until frothy. Gradually add the 1 cup of sugar and continue beating until stiff peaks form, about 10 minutes in all. Gently spoon the meringue on top of the pie, mounding it in the center. Make sure the meringue is sealed around the edges (this prevents the meringue from breaking and weeping). Make high peaks in the meringue with your fingers in about 20 places, turning the pie round and round as you go. Bake the pie until the meringue is golden, about 15 minutes, and cool on a wire rack for at least 2 hours before cutting. Store any leftover pie in the refrigerator.

Cherry Pie

ANY RESTAURANT WORTH its raves usually has a fabulous cherry pie—and Junior's is no exception! Fresh cherries are usually available only about three weeks each summer, so Junior's makes its cherry pie with fresh-frozen cherries the rest of the year. They add a little vanilla and almond extracts to sparkle up the flavor.

Whatever the reasons for the great taste, it's hard to stop after eating just one piece.

MAKES ONE 9-INCH DEEP-DISH PIE

1 recipe Pie Pastry, enough for a double-crust pie
(page 40)

2 cups sugar

3 tablespoons quick-cooking tapioca

2 tablespoons cornstarch

¼ teaspoon salt

6 cups tart drained sour cherries (fresh or fresh-frozen,
thawed and drained) or canned pitted cherries
packed in juice (about 4 pounds)

1 tablespoon fresh lemon juice

2 teaspoons pure vanilla extract

½ teaspoon almond extract

2 drops red food coloring (optional)

2 tablespoons unsalted butter, cut into small pieces

1 large egg yolk

¼ teaspoon vegetable oil

The Junior's Way—

When baking this cherry pie, always use the tart-sour Montmorency cherries (the light reddish-golden ones), not the dark sweet Bing cherries. Look for fresh or fresh-frozen cherries. If you can't find them, buy canned cherries packed in water, not the ones in the canned pie filling. They make a much more homemade-tasting pie. Before putting the top crust on the pie, cut a small hole in the center of the top crust as they do at Junior's. This not only lets the steam escape but lets everyone know, at a glance, what type of pie filling is inside.

1. Butter a 9-inch deep-dish pie plate. Roll out half of the pastry ⅛ inch thick on a lightly floured surface, and trim to a 15-inch circle. Transfer the pastry to the pie plate, leaving a 1½-inch overhang. Place the shell and the rest of the pastry in the refrigerator while you make the filling.

2. Mix the sugar, tapioca, cornstarch, and salt together in a medium-sized bowl and set aside.

3. Place the cherries in a colander, rinse them with cold water, and drain them well. Mix the cherries, lemon juice, vanilla extract, almond extract, and food coloring, if you wish, together in a large bowl. Sprinkle the sugar mixture over the cherries and toss until all of the cherries are well coated.

4. Place a rack in the center of the oven and preheat the oven to 425°F. Spoon the cherry filling into the pie shell, mounding it high in the center. Dot with the butter.

5. Roll out the remaining pastry ⅛ inch thick, trim it to a 13-inch circle, and cut a small circle in the center of the pastry to let the steam escape. Transfer the pastry to the top of the pie. Moisten the edges of the pastry with a little ice water, fold the edges under, and pinch them tightly to seal. Shape the edge of the pastry to stand up 1 inch high, then flute.

6. Whisk the egg yolk with the oil and brush on the top of the pie. Bake the pie for 10 minutes at 425°F. Reduce the oven temperature to 350°F and continue baking the pie until the crust is golden and the filling is bubbly, about 45 minutes. If the top crust browns before the pie is done, lay a piece of foil loosely over the top of the pie for the rest of the baking time. Cool the pie on a wire rack for at least 2 hours before serving.

1930s—In Brooklyn, the Art of Survival!

Pie Pastry

*E*VERY JUNIOR'S PIE begins with a perfectly shaped piecrust. Bakers mix up enough pastry at a time to make about two hundred and fifty crusts. They put a ball of dough into each pie plate, then use an automatic piecrust pressing machine to shape it into a perfect crust.

But you don't need one of these machines to make a great crust with this recipe. This pastry rolls out easily, without sticking to the pastry board, pie after pie.

MAKES ENOUGH PASTRY FOR A DOUBLE-CRUST PIE OR 2 SINGLE CRUSTS (8 OR 9 INCHES—REGULAR PIE PLATE OR DEEP-DISH)

1¾ cups all-purpose flour

¾ cup cake flour

3 tablespoons sugar

1 teaspoon salt

6 tablespoons vegetable shortening

¼ cup (½ stick) unsalted butter

½ cup ice water

¼ teaspoon lemon extract

The Junior's Way—Chill the pastry at least an hour before rolling out the dough. If you're making a single-crust pie, shape the remaining pastry into a six-inch disk, then freeze it and use within a month. This recipe makes one of those pie pastries that thaws and rolls out perfectly.

1. Mix both of the flours with the sugar and salt in a large bowl.

2. Fit your electric mixer with a paddle blade (if your mixer has one). Using the lowest speed of the mixer, work in the shortening and butter until coarse crumbs form, 2 to 3 minutes.

3. Add the ice water and lemon extract and mix just until a dough forms, about 1 or 2 minutes more, adding another tablespoon of ice water if needed. Do not overmix or the pastry may become tough.

4. Turn out the dough onto a lightly floured surface and knead for 1 minute; then divide it into two equal pieces. Pat each piece of dough into a 6-inch disk and wrap tightly in plastic wrap. Chill the pastry for at least 1 hour before shaping it into 2 single crusts or 1 double crust. Bake as the pie recipe directs.

1940s—When Brooklyn Was . . . Everything

*I*N THE 1940s, Brooklyn was the world. At least that's

what we thought. Nearly 2.5 million people from all over the world

—Italians, Irish, African Americans, Jews, Poles, Russians,

Arabs, Greeks, Chinese, Japanese, Scandinavians, Swedes,

Germans, Puerto Ricans, West Indians, and Cubans lived here.

I hope I didn't leave anyone out. There was no place anywhere in

the United States or the world with such a diverse conglomeration

of world cultures, customs, traditions, foods, values, and religions.

All through the 1940s, trolley transport was the most convenient way to get around Brooklyn. This car, the driver in the middle window, is at the intersection of Atlantic and Flatbush avenues. The Long Island Railroad Terminal and Williamsburgh Savings Bank are in the background. Courtesy of the Kingsborough Historical Society

We were all mixed together in some twenty-five different sections of Brooklyn which comprised dozens of small neighborhoods. The thrilling thing was that all of Brooklyn belonged to everybody—from Nathan's Famous hot dog stand in Coney Island to the posh Roof Top Restaurant of Hotel Bossert in Brooklyn Heights; from Abe Stark's Men's Clothiers on Pitkin Avenue in Brownsville to Frederick Loeser's department store on Fulton Street; from a corner grocery in Flatbush to the huge Wallabout

Welcome to Junior's!

Market by the Navy Yard; from Lundy's seafood in Sheepshead Bay to the tender steaks and chops at the Enduro across from the Brooklyn Paramount. It was all yours, mine, anybody's for a nickel, the cost of a trolley ride.

Hey, How Do I Get to Brooklyn?

There wasn't an abundance of family automobiles, especially during the war. Instead, three thousand fine-looking streetcars running on twenty-eight lines over five hundred miles of track carried you to and through the richly diverse neighborhoods of Brooklyn. The trolley-rail system, although it would soon be replaced by automobiles and gasoline-powered buses, was among the finest and most up-to-date rail-car system in the United States. Since 1890, thousands of electric trolleys, which replaced the horse-drawn trolleys, traversed the length and width of Brooklyn. In those early days, Brooklynites were an endangered species, in peril of electrocution by falling wires or just being clobbered by the new, fast version of the old horse-drawn cars. Those who quickly jumped out of harm's way earned the nickname "trolley dodgers."

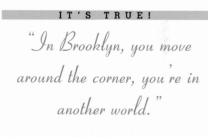

IT'S TRUE!

"In Brooklyn, you move around the corner, you're in another world."

—Henny Youngman

The streetcar was tireless and even elegant in a way, clanging and rolling to stops such as Ebbets Field, Prospect Park and the Zoo, the Brooklyn Museum and Botanic Garden, hundreds of libraries and concert halls, theaters, stores, the Children's Museum, and the three bridges that connected us to Manhattan. The DeKalb Avenue trolley also stopped in front of the Enduro. Passen-

No relation. Just a fine early 1940s example of an "everything good for the table" market on Myrtle Avenue, not far from downtown. Courtesy of the Municipal Archives Department of Records and Information Services, City of New York

From inside a neighborhood market-deli in 1940. Courtesy of the Municipal Archives Department of Records and Information Services, City of New York

gers could gaze into our "window kitchen" where steaks and chops sizzled over charcoal fires.

The trolley journey was a multiethnic adventure. The car rolled and swayed through neighborhoods such as Bay Ridge, where tall blond Scandinavians walked alongside short dark Italians, and where a Jewish delicatessen was bordered on one

Welcome to Junior's!

Little Coney Island in Williamsburg in 1940—a neighborhood sandwich stand that thrived. Courtesy of the Municipal Archives Department of Records and Information Services, City of New York

side by a Syrian bakery that emanated sweet, warm aromas and displayed large flat breads in the window. On the other side was a Chinese laundry and next to that an Italian fruit-and-vegetable shop with oranges, apples, melons, tomatoes, bunches of carrots and celery neatly displayed in open crates in the window. The car passed houses in Brownsville or Coney Island where a Jewish housewife might be dropping off some gefilte fish for her Irish neighbor who had shared corned beef and cabbage with her last Thursday. It passed a Catholic church with a bazaar going on outside on the streets, then a synagogue with families filing in for temple services. If you didn't know Brooklyn was *the world*, one trolley ride would show you.

1940s—When Brooklyn Was . . . Everything

In 1940 President Franklin D. Roosevelt, or "Presivelt," was real popular in Brooklyn. So was the gifted Mayor Fiorello "the Little Flower" La Guardia, who had presided, in 1940, over the closing of the Fulton Street elevated train downtown, the "black spider," we called it. Once it was gone in 1941, downtown was a brighter, roomier place. The mayor would also capture the hearts of all New York City in 1945. During the newspaper strike that year, he read the funnies over the radio to the kids of New York.

A BROOKLYN ADDRESS

"At one time, a stretch of years in the early forties, a single [boarding] house on Middagh Street boasted a roll call of residents that read: W. H. Auden, Richard Wright, Carson McCullers, Paul and Jane Bowles, the British composer Benjamin Britten, impresario and stage designer Oliver Smith, and authoress of murderous entertainments Miss Gypsy Rose Lee, and a Chimpanzee accompanied by 'Trainer."

—Truman Capote

The Dodgers were popular in 1940, too. After struggling during most of the 1930s in the cellar, "the Bums," as they were nicknamed by sportswriters, were making a comeback. New owners had renovated Ebbets Field in 1938, installing outdoor lighting for the first time, which made Ebbets Field on game nights a huge glowing monument in Crown Heights. And Leo "the Lip" Durocher had taken over as manager. With the Dodgers' new headquarters downtown on nearby Montague Street, Durocher was a colorful, sometimes rowdy, presence at his favorite nightspots and restaurants, such as the Roof Top at the Hotel Bossert in Brooklyn Heights. Dodger bars and hangouts, including the Dodger Café across the street from the Enduro on DeKalb, were thriving then.

Some now-famous Americans were making their way up in those days. Neil Sedaka was born in 1939 in Brighton Beach. Come the 1950s, he'd team up with his first girlfriend Carole King (Klein in those days) for pizza and slow-dancing to the sounds of "Earth Angel" on the jukebox. Martin Landau was twelve years old in Flatbush. During the war he'd be a Civil Defense bicycle messenger as wailing air raid drills sent us in off the streets. Broadcaster Larry King was also a kid during the forties, honing his talk-show art with friends on the stoops of Bensonhurst. He and Sandy Koufax, who would sign with the Dodgers in the fifties, graduated a year apart from Lafayette High School.

Lou Gossett, Jr., was born at Coney Island Hospital and grew up in Coney Island. Buddy Hackett was a kid in Borough Park. He would spend the late forties perfecting his comedy in the thirty or forty nightclubs in Brooklyn—from Brighton Beach to Brownsville. And Bensonhurst's Vic Damone was taking singing lessons. He'd become Brooklyn's swooner/crooner of the year in '49. Ben Vereen was a kid in Bedford-Stuyvesant on Chauncey Street. And in 1941, Marvin Rosen was eleven years old and just beginning to come to work with his dad at the Enduro Restaurant and Cafe on Saturdays. Walter would join in 1944 as soon as he turned ten.

What Was What

In 1940, downtown Brooklyn was a place with a character all its own. People came here for work and business, for the fast-paced excitement, the bright theater lights, the smells, and sounds. There were legitimate theaters, first-run movies with stage shows, fine restaurants, and all the important government buildings that were clustered at the bend of Fulton Street in a kind of Victorian architecture village. The domed courthouse, which stood where Brooklyn Law School now stands, was the most ornate.

And people came for the first-class department stores on Fulton Street—A&S, Frederick Loeser's, A. I. Namm & Son, and Martin's, among others, that before the turn of the century had offered floor above floor filled with the beautiful merchandise you couldn't get in your neighborhood.

Shoppers looked forward to the upscale service in the large downtown stores. A woman in Flatbush, for example,

GOT A NICKEL?

In 1940, one nickel could buy you a hot dog or root beer, a knish or a hot sweet potato from a vendor, a chocolate malted, a plate of hot macaroni and cheese at the Horn & Hardart. Almost any ride at Coney Island (dubbed the Nickel Empire) cost five cents. So did a ride on the trolley, subway, or bus. Newspapers were four cents and a creamy delicious charlotte russe was three cents.

might take the streetcar downtown one morning just for a breather while the kids were at school. In those days, shopping could be a pleasure; department stores pampered their customers. The saleslady in Namm's might show the woman a dozen pairs of gloves and help her try them on without pressuring and without pushing for a sale. The same woman might go to the famous Garden Room Restaurant at A&S for lunch or she might meet a friend here at the Enduro, order her favorite, the Welsh Rarebit, and be home before the kids came home from school.

If you were a kid in the 1940s, downtown was a thrilling place. You could jump the Flatbush or DeKalb Avenue trolley after school or on Saturdays and head for a first-run movie at the Fox or for Loeser's department store, which every kid knew had the finest toy department anywhere. For sheer volume and variety, however, A&S seemed to have it over the other stores.

At Christmastime, all the stores would compete for the most dazzling window displays. Like Manhattan families with their tradition of taking in the Saks Fifth Avenue and Lord & Taylor

Looking up Flatbush at Fulton Street with DeKalb Avenue behind us, this shows the Fox Theater, the Williamsburgh Savings Bank, and two trolley cars up near Atlantic Avenue. *The Jolson Story,* playing at the Fox, opened in 1946. Photo by the *Brooklyn Daily Eagle.* Courtesy of the Brooklyn Public Library—Brooklyn Collection

1940s—When Brooklyn Was . . . Everything

Downtown Fulton Street at Albee Square, only one long block from Junior's, a postcard, about 1941. Courtesy of the Brooklyn Historical Society

Christmas windows, Brooklyn families would bundle up and stroll on Fulton Street on the nights before Christmas just for the delight of seeing our downtown windows.

Food for the Masses

For the hurried workers and downtown shoppers there were stand-up snack bars, such as Delicious Drinks on Fulton and Flatbush. Some even came with penny arcades attached. There was Chock Full O' Nuts with its reputation for nutted cheese sandwiches, rich brownies, good coffee, fast service, and cleanliness. Nedick's was great for frankfurters with sauerkraut and famous for their orange sodas. Then there was the famous Fulton Street Horn & Hardart Automat, where a few nickels could dispense a hot dish of spaghetti and meatballs or macaroni and cheese or any of the variety of casseroles, soups, and sandwiches on display in ingenious glass compartments.

Downtown provided well for the casual and elegant diner, too. Some of the

Welcome to Junior's!

finest restaurants and nightspots in Brooklyn were here—Joe's on Court Street, the Chinese Royal American, the Roof Top at the Hotel Bossert in the Heights, which also featured dining and dancing to the band sounds of Freddy Martin. Gage & Tollner on Fulton Street was a landmark restaurant in the forties and still is. There was also Schrafft's, the Brass Rail, the Hotel St. George, the Hotel Margaret, and, of course, the Enduro Restaurant and Cafe across from the Paramount.

Downtown might not have been Times Square, but on New Year's Eve it was exciting to see the bright lights of the theaters, to hear the music and cheer flow out from these nightspots, and the incredible noise as tugboats, freighters, fireboats, and Navy vessels in the East River sounded their horns at midnight.

One block up from the Enduro, on the corner of Fulton and Flatbush Avenue, Delicious Drinks did a whale of a business with the stand-up crowd.
Courtesy of the Brooklyn Historical Society

ENDURO
RESTAURANT and CA
386 Flatbush Ave. Extensi
OPPOSITE BROOKLYN PARAMOUNT THEATR

My father had this postcard rendered for the reopening of the Enduro after expansion in 1943. Courtesy of the Brooklyn Historical Society

Meet Me at the Enduro

The Enduro Restaurant was well situated in a triangle formed by the huge Brooklyn Paramount, the prestigious Albee Theater, and the palatial Fox Theater. At 386 Flatbush Avenue Extension, it was the entryway to a thriving downtown, where energy and excitement were palpable day and night.

By 1942, after the closing of Smitty's Luncheonette, which had dominated the corner of DeKalb and Flatbush for years, my father took the space and extended the

This is a good view of the Paramount, from opposite the Enduro Restaurant on DeKalb Avenue. *The Lone Wolf Meets a Lady* and *The Ghost Breakers* with Bob Hope and Paulette Goddard were on the first-run double bill.
Courtesy of the Municipal Archives Department of Records and Information Services, City of New York

Enduro Restaurant to the corner. On reopening day in early 1943, the corner of DeKalb and Flatbush had been transformed. A sleek Art Deco facade stretched about forty feet down DeKalb, around the corner, and about another forty feet down Flatbush Extension, much as the Junior's front today. It was a black Carrara tile

1940s—When Brooklyn Was . . . Everything

facade above the windows with the silver lettering like liquid steel: *Enduro Restaurant and Cafe.* A vertical Enduro marquee, also like Junior's today, marked the corner entrance. Inside were comfortable booths and tables and much more room for a bar and bandstand. It was a congenial place, always crowded, with a sit-down relaxed atmosphere where you could enjoy appetizers, steaks, chops, and entrées from a complete lunch and dinner menu. Or you could just come in and enjoy the impressive bar featuring live music every night! Many a young man brought his first date here for a fine steak dinner, then to the Albee for a movie. My father prided himself on the quality of our steaks—tender cuts, charcoal-broiled in our "window kitchen," which was visible from inside as well as outside.

The Enduro catered to businesspeople, shoppers, workers from the nearby Brooklyn Navy Yard, the downtown workers during the day, and mostly theater crowds at night. Whatever happened at the Paramount across the street, however, affected us both day and night. In 1942, for example, the Dodgers formed an off-season semi-pro basketball team, which, for some reason, had quite a following. Because Brooklyn did not have a huge indoor stadium, they played their league games on the massive Paramount stage. On game days, the Enduro was packed with sports fans.

When the Paramount premiered *It Happened in Brooklyn*, the blocks stretching either side of Flatbush Avenue Extension and DeKalb swarmed with thousands of fans. Frank Sinatra, Jimmy Durante, and Peter Lawford, who starred in the picture, had trolleyed over the Brooklyn Bridge for the opening day. I don't think we saw crowds like that again until later in the 1950s when the rock 'n' roll idols played the Paramount.

"Day of Infamy" and the Brooklyn Navy Yard

First came the front-page photographs in early 1941—the Nazis were ransacking Holland, desecrating the serene beauty of the place. Conversations at the Enduro and the look on my father's face revealed a tension out of the ordinary. Then in December, after Japan's sneak bombing of Pearl Harbor, we all listened to President Roosevelt's call to action—his "day of infamy" radio speech. In the forties, Brooklynites, immigrants or their descendants, had fierce loyalty to this new country which for many of them consisted of Brooklyn. So there was a readiness to leap to this country's defense.

Brooklyn itself had been strategically involved in military efforts since the opening of the Brooklyn Navy Yard in 1801. The Navy Yard, a waterfront industry very close to downtown Brooklyn, had built and launched a huge number of fighting ships, including in 1915 the biggest of them all, the U.S.S. *Arizona*.

After Japanese planes bombed our Pacific naval base at Pearl Harbor on December 7, 1941, the *Arizona* lay submerged, with American sailors dead inside her hull at the bottom of Pearl Harbor. Those who died numbered 3,700 and, needless to say, for most people from Brooklyn, the Japanese might just as well have bombed us.

When the president asked defense plants to work round the clock, Brooklyn Navy Yard workers responded with a huge rally on Christmas Eve, 1941, and a commitment to speed up production on the U.S.S. *Iowa*. They worked continuous shifts and launched the new battleship in August 1942, seven months ahead of the promised date. New York and national papers dubbed the shipbuilders the Brooklyn "Can-Do" Yard.

PROUD SHIP

" . . . the super dreadnought 'Arizona,' mightiest war craft ever wrought by hand of man, was successfully launched at 1:11 o'clock this afternoon at the Navy Yard, while 50,000 persons roared a mighty cheer. A whistle blew a signal. Miss Esther Ross, one of Arizona's fairest daughters, sent a wicker bottle crashing against the huge steel hull, and with a white feather of champagne mixed with water on her steel plates, the biggest warship of them all slipped smoothly down the greased ways into Wallabout Basin."

—The Brooklyn Daily Eagle, June 1915

Between 1941 and 1945, the Yard hired thousands of women and men, until the numbers peaked at about seventy thousand. It expanded from forty acres to three hundred acres of waterfront with three hundred buildings. Tireless workers kept the place going twenty-four hours a day, seven days a week. Even Orthodox Jewish workers labored through the holy days of Rosh Hashanah and Yom Kippur on the advice of their rabbis. During the course of the war, crews managed to repair five thousand battleships, build four aircraft carriers—the *Bennington, Bonhomme Richard, Kearsarge*, and the *Franklin Delano Roosevelt*—and three battleships—the

For quick meals down by the Navy Yard, there were dozens of luncheonettes during the war. This is the lunch counter at the YMCA. Courtesy of the Brooklyn Historical Society

Carolina in 1940, the *Iowa* in 1942, and the *Missouri* in 1944. It didn't go unnoticed by anyone from Brooklyn that the final peace treaty to end the war was signed aboard the *Missouri*—a fitting end after the loss of the *Arizona* at the start of the war.

Entertaining the Troops

The Brooklyn Navy Yard was so close to the downtown area that its workers and servicemen had always been important to business at the Enduro. During the 1940s, with so many ships in for repair, hundreds and thousands of servicemen shopped, ate, drank, visited relatives, and took in a show right here in downtown Brooklyn. Because the Enduro offered a supper-club atmosphere, a nightspot where you pressed and dressed for dinner, different from the waterfront saloons near the Yard, where a sailor could drink until he rolled back on ship, the Enduro was always packed. As the war years went on, more and more servicemen who had been to Europe and had tasted fine cuisine came looking for a place like the Enduro. Our menu featured roasted meats, fresh fish, and especially tender steaks and chops, which were charcoal-broiled to order at the one-of-a-kind Enduro "window kitchen" broiler. Here, vertical piles of red-hot embers, piles as tall as a man, seared and cooked the meat to perfection. There was no turning the steaks on a grid as they do today. The steaks fit in individual racks which were suspended from a rod between the pillars of searing hot coals. With twelve vertical grills set up the whole length of the window, the columns of red coals and the searing steaks were a real eye-catcher, a visual spectacle for passers-by and customers. Those grills were also tactical nightmares, so much so that my father depended heavily on the one man who seemed to be able to keep all the grills going as well as to handle individual orders to perfection. My father affection-

During the war, women went to work at the Navy Yard and Bush Terminal. Here, best friends pose in front of Arma Corporation at Bush Terminal. Courtesy of the Brooklyn Historical Society

ately called him George the Greek. We called him Mr. Kanakaris.

During those years it seemed as if we never closed. There was no breakfast served, but lunch began at 11:00 A.M. and the place often didn't close until 4:00 A.M. We were fourteen and ten years old in those days, and if we wanted to see my father at all, we came in to help out on Saturdays and Sundays. Marvin was a food checker.

1940s—When Brooklyn Was . . . Everything

Walter helped sell fresh roasted chickens from the rotisserie to the take-out trade—a novel (and profitable) idea in the 1940s.

We loved helping out at the Enduro. It was exciting for us. The restaurant was filled all day and into the night. There weren't only ships docking, there were troops who came to Brooklyn just to disembark—marines, infantrymen, and sailors from all over the United States. The place was teeming with groups of sailors huddled together, couples and singles sitting at the grand oval bar listening to the live continuous music. My father hired bands such as the Four Toppers (who later became Steve Gibson and the Red Caps), the Angie Bond Trio, and Guy Granada.

In 1945 at Coney Island, the Parachute Jump at Steeplechase was a major attraction. Photo by Wide World Photos, courtesy of the Kingsborough Historical Society

Smells of grilled and roasted meats wafted from the broiler "window kitchen." Waiters and waitresses carried huge trays of steaming plates to packed booths and tables. The restaurant was filled with food, conversation, colorful people, and music. We were young boys who didn't yet know a lot about life, war, and death. But we knew the Enduro was exciting.

Downtown theaters were busy too. The Loew's (pronounced Loey's) Metropolitan on Fulton Street sponsored all kinds of contests and giveaways prior to or between features. One popular drawing awarded a serviceman in the audience a free weekend at the Waldorf-Astoria. There were beauty contests emceed by a host before show times, puppy giveaway drawings, even pony giveaways, and the presentation of awards for the best essays submitted by high school students the week before. The Fox started its famous Monday night amateur hour in 1941, an idea that caught on and flourished in smaller Brooklyn theaters such as the Prospect in Park Slope.

Brooklyn's Own Effort

The papers, especially the *Daily Eagle*, were full of stories about Brooklyn's war effort. The Pfizer pharmaceutical plant in Williamsburg had converted one of its main structures to make the new wonder drug penicillin. Because of Pfizer, penicillin was carried by the medics on D-Day, 1944.

Brooklynites were rationing, too, just like the rest of the country. There were shortages of meat, fresh produce, and dairy products, but instituting meatless Tuesdays and encouraging neighborhoods to plant victory gardens helped put food on the table. The Botanic Garden up on Eastern Parkway converted much of its space into victory gardens. Men over fifty and kids formed teams that competed to grow the largest lettuce, longest carrots, the most beans. In backyards from Greenpoint to South Brooklyn to Canarsie, people grew corn, cabbages, and string beans. Some cultivated tomatoes on fire escapes and rooftops.

Fort Greene Park right down the street was also the site of a famous victory garden grown by the kids of the neighborhood. The garden effort was such a successful galvanizer of the neighborhood energy that it continued on into the 1950s. Kids got involved with saving everything from newspapers and tin cans to bacon fat. Up at Ebbets Field a kid could get into the game for free on Fat Day, if he brought a can of saved fat.

1940s—When Brooklyn Was . . . Everything

Advertising a Brooklyn dynasty, Drake's Cakes' billboard boosted morale during the war. Courtesy of the Brooklyn Historical Society

Every week there were air-raid drills—screaming sirens that sent everyone inside where they sat with the lights out unless they had blackout curtains. The bright lights of the Paramount, the Fox, and the Albee were dimmed throughout the entire war.

Car headlights had to be fitted with black eyelids, and if you couldn't afford the lids, you could paint the top halves of your headlights black. At night high-powered beams would search the sky for aircraft. And in strategic areas all around Brooklyn, particularly on rooftops at the Navy Yard and along the waterfront in Red Hook near Todd Ship Yards, antiaircraft artillery was poised for defense. Weekly convoys of jeeps, tanks, trucks, and motorcycles would rumble down secretly designated streets to the navy vessels waiting to ship them overseas. It didn't take some kids long to figure out the rotation pattern of which street would have the convoy during which particular week. It was a thrill for kids to be there and cheer the show of power.

HEADLINES

Nearly five hundred thousand troops were shipped off to war from the port of Brooklyn during World War II.

Welcome to Junior's!

Turning Point

When Roosevelt died in June of 1945, the news hit Brooklyn hard. Women were crying on the streets. People were dazed. The talk coming from the clientele in the Enduro was despairing. "Now the war will never end. What do we know about this Truman guy, anyway?" Brooklyn had already sent so many of its own men and women into the war. Some papers reported that Brooklyn had sent nearly 330,000 to war, more than thirty-three states combined. "If it took Roosevelt almost ten years to pull us through the Depression," people were saying, "how can this Harry Truman possibly get us out of the war?"

Truman surprised the entire world by ordering the first and last (so far) nuclear bomb drops on Japan. The bombs' power effectively ended the war, but we wouldn't know the extent of their devastation for years. All we knew in September 1945 was that the war was over and everybody was partying in the streets. One after another, ships docked with servicemen coming home. In neighborhoods from Brighton Breach and Dyker Heights to Crown Heights, East New York, and Fort Greene, block parties started that didn't stop for a year. Christmas lights were strung across streets from building to building. There were flags and bunting, singing and dancing. People hung up signs in their windows welcoming their sons, brothers, and husbands home. There were also signs of remembrance and respect for the seven thousand Brooklynites who didn't make it back.

Every weekend for nearly a year—fall, spring, and summer—neighbors set up tables of hot food in front of their buildings—casseroles, meat loaf, spaghetti and meatballs, stuffed cabbages, cakes, and pies. The parties went on all night. Downtown here all the restaurants and bars were packed. The Enduro was overflowing for three months straight.

You Ain't Seen Nothing Yet

There was nothing but optimism after the war. The years had been good for all businesses. Brooklyn had always been a hub of manufacturing, but the war years had brought increased demand and increased output. By 1947 even the Dodgers were doing better at the gate. Riding the winds of optimism, Branch Rickey, principal owner of the Dodgers, had hired Jackie Robinson, the first African American to play in the heretofore all-white baseball leagues. Not only had the world changed with the war, but now baseball was about to change forever.

When Jackie Robinson made his debut with the formerly all-white Dodgers at Ebbets Field in April 1947, the eyes of all America and, we felt, the whole world, were on Brooklyn. With his first at-bat, Robinson ended an eighty-year-old ban against black players in major league baseball. Half the fans in the ballpark that day were black. And Jackie Robinson's rookie year broke attendance records at Ebbets Field. Nearly two million crammed into the park before season's end.

Those 1947 Dodgers

They had been in the cellar, coming in last or near last place, for most of the 1930s and 1940s. But the Dodgers' fan base stayed strong. In fact, sometimes the fans were more notable than the players. Brooklyn-born Hilda Chester was well known for her cowbell, her bellowing from the outfield bleachers, and her sign HILDA IS HERE. Another fan, a man who thought Cookie Lavagetto was the best player of all time, would send up balloons with Cookie's name on them. At home you'd hear Red Barber call the game on the radio, but down in the seats next to the dugout you'd hear a retired public address announcer cup his hands and shout things like, "Ladies and gentlemen, a little boy has been found lost." Or, "Attention please. Would all the people in the front row, next to the railing, kindly remove their clothes."

There were no rules of decorum at Dodgers games. The Sym-Phony band, an irreverent bunch of guys from Greenpoint with a couple of drums, a clarinet, trombone, and cymbals, would roam the stands. When the three umpires (as we had in those days instead of four) came onto the field, they played "Three Blind Mice." They had a song or sound effect for everything—from an opposing pitcher being taken out to one of our guys striking out.

When fans left after the game, they took the shortest route out of the stadium—sometimes that meant right across the outfield grass to the exit in the fence. The fence around the outfield was plastered with billboards from local merchants. The Brass Rail Restaurant, one of the Enduro's competitors, was up there along with

Welcome to Junior's!

Gem Razor Blades, Van Heusen Shirts, and under the scoreboard, the famous "Hit Sign, Win Suit" sign. Abe Stark, who was a men's clothier in Brownsville, sponsored the sign. If any player at bat was able to hit the sign, Abe would give the guy a suit. I don't think he gave away too many suits but the sign made him famous. Stark was also a good friend of my father's and he often enjoyed steak here at the Enduro. He became Brooklyn borough president later on in the 1950s and danced at Walter's wedding in 1959.

Ebbets Field was the smallest park in the league, which made every fan feel close to the action. By 1947 its capacity was 33,000, but nearly 38,000 packed in to watch the Dodgers clinch the pennant that year. In September of 1947, with the help of the new rookie Jackie Robinson and others like Duke Snider, the Dodgers took their first pennant since 1941. They beat the Cardinals. For years, a 1947 pennant hung behind the bar at the Dodger Café across the street.

A long, noisy motorcade of dealer-loaned convertibles streamed from Grand Army Plaza all the way down Flatbush to Fulton Street and up to Borough Hall steps. There were flags and bunting and cheering crowds. Borough President John Cashmore presented the players with wristwatches and pledged Brooklyn's support as the Dodgers faced their nemesis, the Yankees, for the championship.

The Dodgers lost the championship to the Yankees that year, but with a league title and at least a crack at the World Series, they had come to stand for the "can-do" attitude of Brooklyn in the 1940s, the same attitude that had helped to win a war and guarantee a future. They stood for hardworking, pro-union people of Brooklyn who looked ahead and said, You ain't seen nothing yet! Wait till next year! Wait till next year!

1940s—When Brooklyn Was . . . Everything

1940s—Stand-Up Snack Bars & Steak Houses

A FEW NICKELS in your pocket in the forties meant good eating! They could bring you a fast stand-up lunch at a snack bar of a frankfurter with sauerkraut and all the trimmings, or a quick sit-down meal at the local luncheonette of an overstuffed cream cheese sandwich on date-nut bread and a fudgy brownie for dessert.

In the evening, the feasting was doubly good. A few dollars at the Enduro Steak House bought all-you-could-eat, plus lively entertainment at the same time. There was always great fare to choose from—a crock of onion soup dripping with melted cheese to start, then charcoal-broiled steak with onions and peppers on-the-side, or a huge helping of goulash over buttery egg noodles, or a thick slice of beef brisket smothered with delicious gravy.

And you couldn't leave without delving into their famous strawberry shortcake swimming in fresh strawberry sauce; a slice of buttery pound cake, still warm from the oven; an overstuffed piece of homemade apple pie with a shovel of vanilla ice cream draped over the side.

Jumbo Shrimp Cocktail

ALMOST SYNONYMOUS WITH a steak dinner at Junior's is the traditional appetizer of shrimp cocktail. But you don't have to be dining in the evening and you don't even have to be ordering steak to splurge on jumbo shrimps, each one pink and succulent and topped with spicy red cocktail sauce. If you're in a hurry, you can even buy shrimps already shelled, deveined, and boiled. Just be sure they're the special jumbo ones.

MAKES 4 COCKTAIL SERVINGS
MAKES 1 CUP SAUCE (THIS RECIPE DOUBLES EASILY)

1 pound jumbo shrimps

2 teaspoons salt

1 extra-large lemon

FOR THE COCKTAIL SAUCE

½ cup ketchup

½ cup bottled cocktail sauce

2 tablespoons horseradish

¼ teaspoon hot pepper sauce

The Junior's Way—
Cocktail sauce should be zippy—hot, but not too hot. Shaking in just the right amount of hot pepper sauce is the secret.

1. Several hours before you're planning to serve, cook the shrimps: Fill a large saucepan half-full with water. Add the salt, squeeze in the juice from the lemon, then toss the lemon rind into the pot. Bring to a boil over high heat. Slide in the unpeeled shrimps, and boil just until they turn opaque, about 5 minutes. Transfer the shrimps to a colander with a slotted spoon and rinse with cold water. Peel and devein the shrimps, leaving their tails on. Refrigerate the shrimps until they are cold.

2. To make the cocktail sauce, stir together all of the ingredients for the sauce in a small bowl and blend well. Taste and add a little more hot sauce if it's not hot enough for your taste.

3. Arrange the cold boiled jumbo shrimps in stemmed cocktail dishes. Spoon plenty of cocktail sauce over the shrimps.

Crock of Baked Fresh Onion Soup Gratinee

*B*AKED ONION SOUP is always on the menu at Junior's—look for it under soups, menu item Number 151 to be exact. It's the deep rich oniony kind with lots of sautéed onions and plenty of mozzarella melted on top—in fact, there's usually so much cheese that it's often bubbling over the sides.

"Slowly cooking the onions in butter is one secret . . . simmering them with a spoonful of sugar is another . . . lacing the finished soup with a splash of dry sherry right before it's removed from the simmering pot is a third," explains the chef. Finally, each crock of soup is covered with cheese and baked in a very hot oven until melted and golden brown.

MAKES 1 ½ QUARTS SOUP

4 pounds onions, Bermuda or Spanish (about 4 extra-large onions)

½ cup (1 stick) unsalted butter, preferably clarified (page 314)

2 tablespoons onion powder

1 tablespoon salt

1 tablespoon sugar

½ teaspoon ground white pepper

3 tablespoons all-purpose flour

4 cups canned beef broth

Few drops Gravy Master (optional)

2 tablespoons dry sherry

8 slices mozzarella cheese (8 ounces)

The Junior's Way—
Cook the onions very slowly in the butter and seasonings so they have time to develop a soft buttery texture.

FOR THE CROUTONS

3 tablespoons unsalted butter, preferably clarified (page 314)

1 tablespoon vegetable oil

4 slices French bread, about ¾ inch thick

1. Peel the onions and cut them crosswise into thin slices, ⅛ to ¼ inch thick, then separate the slices into rings.

2. Melt the butter in a large stockpot over medium-low heat. Add the onions and sprinkle in the onion powder, salt, sugar, and pepper. Cook and stir the onions until they are soft, translucent, and tender, about 20 minutes. Stir in the flour and cook 3 minutes more.

3. Pour in the beef broth, plus a few drops of Gravy Master, if you wish. Increase the heat to medium-high and bring the soup to a full boil. Return the heat to medium-low, and simmer, without covering the pot, until the stock is full of flavor and slightly thickened, about 30 minutes. Stir occasionally. Remove from the heat and stir in the sherry.

4. While the soup is simmering, fry the croutons: Heat the butter and oil in a large skillet over medium-high heat until the butter is melted and hot. Add the French bread slices and pan-fry until crispy and golden on both sides, turning each slice only once, about 6 to 7 minutes in all. Transfer the croutons to a plate and keep warm.

5. A few minutes before the soup has finished cooking, preheat the broiler. Set out 4 ovenproof soup crocks (each large enough to hold 1½ cups of soup) and place in a large shallow baking pan.

6. Ladle the soup into the crocks, top each with a crouton, and cover each with 2 slices of cheese. Broil, about 6 inches from the heat, until the cheese bubbles and melts, about 4 minutes (watch closely). Serve immediately.

New England Clam Chowder

$\mathcal{M}$OST FOLKS IN New England—and especially Brooklyn—expect the "white kind" when they order clam chowder. And if they're at Junior's, they know they'll be served a large bowl of chowder that's made very rich from heavy thick cream and minced fresh chowder clams, lots of them. The "Regulars" know they can always get this chowder freshly made, always on Fridays.

MAKES 2 QUARTS CHOWDER

½ cup (1 stick) unsalted butter

2 cups finely chopped celery

2 cups finely chopped onions

2 tablespoons minced garlic

⅓ cup all-purpose flour

2 cups clam broth

4 large boiling potatoes, peeled and cut into 1-inch cubes (4 cups)

2 teaspoons dried thyme

1 teaspoon salt

½ teaspoon ground white pepper

2 bay leaves

4 cups heavy cream (1 quart)

1 quart minced fresh chowder clams, in their own juices (4 cups)

The Junior's Way—
Use the heavy whipping cream when making this chowder. Light cream or half-and-half will not make as rich a chowder as they serve at Junior's. Once the cream has been added, be sure to simmer, never boil, the soup. Too high a heat can cause this chowder to curdle and separate.

1. Melt the butter in a large stockpot over medium-high heat. Add the celery, onions, and garlic and sauté until the vegetables are golden and tender, about 7 minutes. Stir in the flour until the vegetables are coated.

2. Stir in the clam broth, the boiling potatoes, thyme, salt, white pepper, and bay leaves. Bring the soup to a full boil.

Welcome to Junior's!

3. Reduce the heat to medium-low, add the cream, and simmer the chowder, without covering it, until the potatoes are tender and the soup has thickened slightly, about 20 minutes. Stir the chowder occasionally to prevent any possible sticking.

4. Stir in the fresh clams and their juice. Return the heat to medium-high and cook the chowder 10 minutes more or until the clams turn opaque and are cooked through (do not overcook at this stage, as the fresh clams can become tough). Remove the chowder from the heat. Discard the bay leaves. Serve steaming hot.

Mashed Potatoes

*N*OTHING TASTES MORE down-home and comforting than homemade mashed potatoes. As you might expect, these are fluffy, creamy, and buttery. Junior's whips them until they're smooth. But if you want to leave a few lumps so everyone knows they're mashed from real potatoes, that's OK!

MAKES 6 CUPS

3 pounds all-purpose boiling potatoes, peeled

2 teaspoons salt

½ cup (1 stick) unsalted butter, cut into small pieces

¼ to ½ teaspoon ground white pepper

¾ cup milk

Extra pats of butter (optional)

The Junior's Way—

When mashing potatoes, use good all-purpose boiling potatoes, not russet baking potatoes. Since boiling potatoes are much more moist and lower in starch than russets, they are ideal for mashing.

1. Place the potatoes in a large saucepan and cover with cold water. Add 1 teaspoon of the salt. Cook the potatoes in the open pan over high heat until tender, about 15 to 20 minutes. Drain them and transfer to a large bowl.

2. Fit an electric mixer with the paddle, if your mixer has one. Add the butter to the potatoes, the remaining teaspoon of salt, and the pepper to the potatoes, then beat them on low or until they begin to break up.

3. With the mixer still running, slowly add the milk. Increase the speed to medium-high, and continue beating until the potatoes are smooth and fluffy. Serve immediately with extra pats of butter if you wish.

1940s—When Brooklyn Was . . . Everything

Charbroiled Steak Smothered with Peppers and Onions

EVER SINCE THE days of the Enduro steak house, the Rosens have been famous for serving some of the finest steaks in Brooklyn. They begin with only *prime* beef—aged and marbled long enough to give the best flavor, the tenderest steak around. If you like, Junior's gladly tops off charbroiled steaks and steak sandwiches with smothered peppers and onions. Brown the onions fast and smother them slowly, with just a little sprinkling of sugar, to bring out their best flavors.

MAKES 4 SERVINGS OF STEAK
MAKES 4 CUPS SMOTHERED PEPPERS AND ONIONS

4 individual steaks (prime rib, sirloin, or porter-house/T-bone), 16 to 23 ounces each, 1½ to 2 inches thick

1 pound green bell peppers

1 pound Spanish onions

½ cup (1 stick) unsalted butter

2 tablespoons cooking oil

1 teaspoon sugar

The Junior's Way—When grilling steaks, keep in all of their natural juices by charbroiling them without any seasoning. Wait until after cooking to sprinkle on salt and pepper, if you wish. For the tenderest, juiciest charbroiled steaks, choose ones that are at least 1½ inches thick and are aged and marbled with plenty of those tiny white flecks of fat.

1. To charbroil the steaks, preheat the grill until it's hot (the coals will turn ash-white when it's time to put on the steaks). Grill the steaks, turning each one only once, until they are cooked to your liking (this takes about 15 minutes total for a medium steak that's 1½ inches thick and grilling about 4 inches from the hot coals).

2. While the steaks are grilling, make the smothered peppers and onions: Cut the peppers into halves, trim off the stems, remove the seeds, and place each half cut-side-down on a chopping block. Using a sharp paring knife, cut each half lengthwise into thin strips, about ¼ inch wide. You will have about 3 cups of pepper strips.

Welcome to Junior's!

3. Peel the onions and cut them into halves and place each half cut-side-down on a chopping block. Cut each half lengthwise into thin strips, about ¼ inch wide. You will have about 3 cups of onion strips.

4. Heat the butter and oil in a large skillet over medium-high heat (use an iron skillet if you have one) until the butter melts. Add the peppers, onions, and sugar and cook the vegetables quickly, turning them constantly with a spatula and mixing them as you go, until the vegetables wilt and start to brown. Reduce the heat to low, cover the skillet, and smother the vegetables until they are browned and tender, about 8 minutes. Top each charbroiled steak with a generous helping of peppers and onions. These are also the perfect go-along for charbroiled chopped steak.

Prime Ribs of Beef with Fresh Mushroom Sauce

WE BUY THE best ingredients we can find—only the best. Nothing else comes into Junior's kitchens. That's the Rosen way. Always has been, always will be."

Another policy—nothing is wasted at Junior's. This gravy, called a sauce on the menu, is an example. The fat on top of the pan drippings from the daily-roasted roast beef is used to make the roux, a fat and flour mixture that's whisked together into a paste in a hot skillet. It becomes the thickener for gravies, sauces, and soups. For this recipe, the rest of the drippings are strained into the sauce, then sautéed mushrooms are stirred in.

MAKES 6 TO 8 SERVINGS
MAKES 3 CUPS SAUCY MUSHROOM GRAVY
(THIS RECIPE DOUBLES EASILY)

FOR THE PRIME RIBS OF BEEF

1 standing rib prime beef roast, 2 to 3 ribs
 (5 to 6 pounds)

Coarse kosher salt

Fresh herbs, such as sprigs of thyme and rosemary
 (optional)

FOR THE MUSHROOMS

8 ounces white mushrooms (3 cups)

3 tablespoons unsalted butter, preferably clarified
 (page 314)

1 tablespoon minced garlic

FOR THE SAUCY MUSHROOM GRAVY

¼ cup fat skimmed off the top of pan drippings from
 cooking a roast beef or meat loaf or ¼ cup
 (½ stick) unsalted butter

The Junior's Way—

Only prime beef is served at Junior's. For home, get the best grade of beef you can afford. When roasting a rib roast, baste it frequently with the pan drippings. After roasting, strain off the drippings to make the gravy (this is important). It makes a smooth even-flavored saucy gravy, while still benefiting from the intense flavor of the drippings. If you have four cups of pan drippings, this gravy recipe doubles easily.

⅓ cup all-purpose flour

¼ teaspoon ground white pepper

2 cups strained pan drippings from cooking meat as below or 2 cups beef broth

2 tablespoons dry sherry

1. Preheat the oven to 325°F. Sprinkle the rib roast with the salt, then stand it up on its rib bones, fat-side-up, in an open roasting pan. Sprinkle with fresh herbs, if you wish. If you have a meat thermometer, insert it in the thickest part of the meat in the center of the roast (make sure the thermometer is not touching a bone).

2. Roast the meat until the temperature reaches 140°F for rare; 160°F for medium; 170°F for well done. *Tip*—Remove the roast from the oven when the thermometer reads 5 to 10 degrees below the desired temperature. Even after it comes out of the oven, the roast continues to cook (the heat from the outside of the roast travels into the center, cooking it a few minutes more). Let the roast stand for at least 15 minutes before slicing to allow the fibers of the meat to firm up and hold on to its juices.

3. During the last half-hour of roasting, wash the mushrooms and pat them dry with paper towels. Trim off about ¼ inch of the stems. Using a sharp paring knife, slice the mushrooms vertically, ¼ inch thick.

4. Melt the 3 tablespoons of butter over medium-high heat in a large skillet (use an iron skillet if you have one). Add the mushrooms and the garlic and sauté until the mushrooms are golden and brown, about 8 minutes. Transfer the mushrooms to a bowl.

5. To make the saucy gravy: Heat the fat from the drippings or melt the butter in a large skillet over medium heat. Whisk in the flour and pepper until smooth. Slowly add the strained pan drippings and continue whisking until the gravy thickens, about 3 minutes.

6. Stir in the sautéed mushrooms and heat until bubbly. Stir in the sherry. Serve hot with slices of the prime rib roast. This gravy tastes just as great when made from the pan drippings from the Fresh Brisket of Beef (page 82) or the Baked Meat Loaf (page 142).

Hungarian Beef Goulash
with Egg Noodles

*I*N HUNGARIAN, *GULYÁS*, pronounced **GOO**-lahsh, refers to a meat-and-vegetable stew that's flavored with Hungarian paprika and often served over hot buttered egg noodles. Junior's variety is no exception. But as you might expect, this recipe has its own finishing touch. Right before serving, a good variety of dry sherry is stirred into the sauce. It's a wonderful addition—and turns the dish into one that's special enough to serve at a dinner party.

MAKES 6 SERVINGS

FOR THE GOULASH

3 pounds boneless beef chuck roast

1 tablespoon salt

1 teaspoon ground white pepper

2 tablespoons vegetable oil

2 large yellow onions, chopped (2 cups)

1 tablespoon minced garlic

3 to 3½ cups water

1 6-ounce can tomato paste (¾ cup)

1 rich brown seasoning packet (3.9 grams) or beef bouillon cube

1 tablespoon paprika

1 bay leaf

Paprika (optional)

FOR THE NOODLES

12 ounces uncooked egg noodles (about 9 cups cooked)

2 tablespoons unsalted butter

The Junior's Way—
Choose a well-marbled piece of beef chuck roast off the bone. Its extra richness that comes from the extra fat marbled throughout keeps the meat moist and flavorful during the slow simmering in the stew pot. The slow moist cooking tenderizes the meat and flavors the dish at the same time.

Welcome to Junior's!

FOR THE SLURRY

2 tablespoons all-purpose flour

½ cup water

3 tablespoons dry sherry

1. Ask your butcher to cut the meat into 1½-inch chunks. Mix the salt and pepper together and rub into the meat.

2. Heat the oil in a 5-quart stew pot or Dutch oven over medium-high heat. Add the meat and cook and stir it until the meat cubes are brown on all sides. Using a slotted spoon, transfer the meat to a large bowl (reserve the pan drippings).

3. Add the onions and garlic to the drippings in the pot and sauté until the onions are crisp-tender, about 5 minutes. Transfer the vegetables to the bowl with the meat, using a slotted spoon (reserve the pan drippings).

4. Stir the 3 cups of water, the tomato paste, the beef seasoning packet or bouillon cube, the paprika, and the bay leaf into the drippings in the pot. Add the browned meat, vegetables, and any juices that have accumulated.

5. Bring the mixture to a boil. Reduce the heat to low, partially cover, and simmer until the meat is tender, about 1 to 1½ hours. Stir the stew occasionally and add a little more water (up to ½ cup) if needed to keep the meat and vegetables covered with liquid.

6. While the meat is simmering, cook the noodles according to the manufacturer's directions. Toss the noodles with the butter and keep warm.

7. To serve: Thicken the goulash by making a slurry. Dissolve the flour in the ½ cup of water in a small bowl. Stir about 1 cup of the hot gravy into the slurry, then return this mixture to the pot. Stir constantly until the liquid comes to a boil and thickens. Remove the bay leaf and stir in the sherry. Ladle the goulash over the hot buttered noodles and dust with additional paprika, if you wish.

Fresh Brisket of Beef with Delicious Gravy

EVERY MORNING, ONE of the oversized ovens in the Junior's downstairs kitchen is busy roasting a giant-sized brisket of beef. And for good reason: This is one of Junior's blue-ribbon specialties. It's just one more taste of that home-style cooking that Junior's is famous for—served up in style with its own gravy, made straight from the pan drippings (what else?).

The best part of this dish: It roasts in the oven for three hours, asking for very little attention from you. But the flavors are so delicious that it tastes like you've worked all day.

MAKES 6 TO 8 GENEROUS SERVINGS
MAKES 4 CUPS DELICIOUS GRAVY

1 fresh brisket of beef, first cut (about 5 pounds)

2 tablespoons salt

1 teaspoon ground white pepper

2 cups chopped carrots

6 large garlic cloves, minced

FOR THE DELICIOUS GRAVY

3 tablespoons fat skimmed from the drippings or

    3 tablespoons unsalted butter

6 cups strained pan drippings (save the vegetables, if you wish)

3 large garlic cloves, minced

3 tablespoons all-purpose flour

The Junior's Way—

Most brisket recipes ask you to boil the meat in a pot of water. Junior's does it differently: The chef roasts the brisket in an open pan. He starts the roasting with enough water in the pan to come about two-thirds up the sides of the beef. As the drippings begin simmering, he bastes the meat with the drippings several times during cooking. The brisket comes out very tender, but with a roasted flavor. "Always slice the meat on the diagonal—it's guaranteed to be tender and juicy."

1. Preheat the oven to 350°F. Rub the brisket with the salt and pepper and place it, fat-side-up, in a roasting pan. Pour in enough water to come about two-thirds up the sides of the brisket. Sprinkle the carrots and garlic into the water around the roast.

2. Roast the brisket, without covering it, until it is browned and tender, about 3 hours, spooning the pan drippings frequently over the meat. If necessary, add a little extra water during the cooking to keep the liquid at least halfway up the sides of the brisket. Transfer the brisket to a serving platter.

3. To make the delicious gravy: Skim off any fat from the drippings into a large skillet. You need 3 tablespoons of fat; if necessary, just add a little butter to equal this amount. Strain the drippings into a large heatproof measuring cup, reserving the vegetables for the gravy, if you wish.

4. Heat the fat in the skillet over medium-high heat. Add the garlic and cook until it begins to soften. Whisk in the flour and cook, stirring constantly, until the flour mixture bubbles all over, about 2 minutes. Gradually pour in the strained drippings and continue cooking and whisking until the gravy thickens. Remove the gravy from the heat and stir in the reserved vegetables, if you wish.

5. To serve: Slice the brisket on the diagonal, about ½ inch thick. Serve it up hot with a generous helping of gravy ladled over the top. This goes great with Mashed Potatoes (page 75).

Smothered Onions

ORDER STEAKBURGER B at Junior's and you'll get a 10-ounce charbroiled burger topped with onions—either these smothered onions or a slice of raw red onion. Order the onions smothered—you'll be glad you did.

The secret is in the cooking. The chef first browns the onions on a very hot griddle.

From then on, the cooking is nice and easy. He covers the onions, letting them smother in their own juices, until they glisten and turn a golden brown. Then he scoops out a generous helping for the top of each burger.

MAKES 2 CUPS

1 pound Spanish onions

½ cup (1 stick) unsalted butter

1 teaspoon sugar

The Junior's Way—
Sprinkle the onions with a little sugar to cut the strong "bite" and smooth out the flavors.

1. Peel the onions and cut each of the onions in half. Place each half cut-side-down on a chopping block. Using a sharp paring knife, cut each half lengthwise into thin strips about ¼ inch wide. You will have about 3 cups of onion strips.

2. Melt the butter in a large skillet (use an iron skillet if you have one) over medium-high heat or on a hot griddle as they do at Junior's.

3. Add the onions and sugar and cook them quickly, tossing and turning them constantly with a spatula until the onions start to brown. Reduce the heat to low, and slowly smother the onions in their own juices in the open skillet until they glisten, turn a golden brown, and become tender, about 8 minutes. Great with hamburgers or steaks.

$\mathcal{J}$Roasted Spring Chicken

THIS ROASTED CHICKEN is what comfort food is all about. It comes out of the oven with a rosy crisp skin, still juicy on the inside. The flavors are simple—a hint of rosemary, garlic, and lemon, with dry sherry pulling it all together.

At Junior's, you get a whole half of chicken in a single serving, plus a heaping helping of Spanish Rice on the side.

MAKES 6 SERVINGS

1 recipe cooked Spanish Rice (2 quarts) (page 86)

1 roasting chicken (about 5 pounds), giblets removed

FOR THE BASTING SAUCE

¼ cup dry sherry

3 tablespoons fresh lemon juice

2 to 3 tablespoons minced garlic (depending on the amount of garlic you like)

1 tablespoon salt

1 tablespoon paprika

1 teaspoon dried rosemary leaves

½ teaspoon ground white pepper

The Junior's Way—
At Junior's the chef usually roasts the chickens unstuffed and bakes the Spanish Rice separately in a large pan. But if you wish, you can prepare and bake the rice ahead of time. Then use some to stuff the bird before roasting it. Keep the rest of the rice warm for lining the serving platter with, then arrange the whole bird on top.

1. Preheat the oven to 400°F. Set out a roasting pan.

2. Prepare and bake the Spanish Rice as the recipe directs.

3. While the rice is baking, rinse the chicken and pat it dry with paper towels. Remove the giblets (these may be saved for making a giblet gravy later, if you wish). Mix all of the ingredients for the basting sauce in a small bowl. Generously brush the inside cavities and the outside of the chicken with the sauce. If you want to stuff the bird, use about half-a-recipe of the baked Spanish Rice. Loosely pack the rice stuffing into both cavities, being careful not to stuff it too tight, as the rice will expand more during roasting. Truss the chicken, place it on the bottom of the roasting pan, and brush it again with the sherry sauce.

continued

4. Roast the chicken at 400°F for 30 minutes, then reduce the oven temperature to 350°F. Continue roasting the chicken until the juices run clear (this means the chicken is done) or until a thermometer inserted into the thickest part of the chicken thigh registers 175°F (the temperature will rise to 180°F upon standing). You will need a total of about 2 hours to roast an unstuffed chicken; 2½ hours for a stuffed bird. Baste the bird frequently with the sherry sauce throughout the entire roasting, using all of the sauce.

5. Let the chicken stand for 15 minutes before slicing and serving with the Spanish Rice. Refrigerate any leftovers.

Spanish Rice

*I*T HAPPENED ONE morning when I was talking to the chef. He walked back to the oven, right in the middle of a sentence, and began stirring a mixture in this huge baking pan. Not soup, though it had quite a lot of liquid at this stage . . . not a stuffing . . . definitely not a casserole. I could see rice and bits of onion, peppers, and tomatoes, but this dish was nowhere on my list. No one had mentioned anything that looked like this, but did it ever look wonderful and delicious!

"It's Spanish Rice . . . I make it every day . . . everyone seems to like it. We serve it with roasted chicken, and even by itself as a side dish, if the customer asks." Trust me, once you make this one, folks will ask for it, again and again.

MAKES 2 QUARTS RICE

2 tablespoons (¼ stick) unsalted butter, preferably clarified
    (page 314)

3 tablespoons minced fresh garlic

8 ounces fresh mushrooms, trimmed and sliced vertically
    (3 cups)

Salt and ground black pepper, to taste

4 tablespoons olive oil

1½ cups uncooked long-grain white rice

1 extra-large yellow onion, chopped (1½ cups)

1 large green bell pepper, seeded and chopped (1 cup)

4 ribs celery with leaves, chopped (1 cup)

1 28-ounce can peeled tomatoes in juice, undrained

3 cups boiling water

Paprika

The Junior's Way—

This is one of those rice dishes that miraculously doesn't lump and stick together. The secret is first browning the rice in the skillet in hot oil. Be sure to cook it until it's brown and toasty. This not only firms up the starch in the rice and keeps the grains from sticking together but also adds extra flavor to the dish.

1. Preheat the oven to 350°F and butter a 13 × 9 × 3-inch baking dish. Melt the butter in a large skillet over medium-high heat. Add 1 tablespoon of the garlic and sauté until tender, about 2 minutes. Stir in the mushrooms, and sprinkle them with salt and pepper to taste. Sauté the mushrooms until golden, about 5 minutes, stirring constantly. Transfer to the baking dish.

2. Heat 2 tablespoons of the oil in a large skillet over medium-high heat. Add the uncooked rice and sauté until golden brown and toasty. Transfer the rice to the baking dish containing the mushrooms.

3. Add the remaining 2 tablespoons of oil to the same skillet and stir in the onion, bell pepper, celery, and the remaining 2 tablespoons garlic. Sauté until the vegetables are crisp-tender, about 5 minutes, then stir them into the rice mixture.

4. Pour the juice from the canned tomatoes over the rice; cut up the tomatoes and add them to the dish. Stir all of the ingredients together and mix them well. Pour in the boiling water and stir again.

5. Bake the rice, without covering it, until tender, about 30 to 40 minutes, stirring and tossing it frequently. Sprinkle with paprika and serve hot with Roasted Spring Chicken (page 85), freshly baked ham, or simply "as is" for a side dish.

Yellow Rice

IT'S NOWHERE ON Junior's menu. But order stuffed filet of sole and it comes out on a bed of this heavenly golden rice.

Order chicken and it's also likely to be perched on top of a great big helping. The "Regulars" know this Yellow Rice is always made every day and ask for it on-the-side time and again.

MAKES 6 CUPS RICE

3 tablespoons vegetable oil

2 cups uncooked long-grain white rice

2 cups chopped green onions

¼ cup (½ stick) unsalted butter

3 tablespoons chicken stock seasoned base or
6 chicken bouillon cubes

4 cups boiling water

1 teaspoon salt (optional)

½ teaspoon ground white pepper

Few drops yellow food coloring

Paprika

The Junior's Way—
Ever wonder how some rice dishes cook up full of flavor and spice? In this recipe, the secret is in the chicken stock base. It infuses flavor into the rice while it bakes in the oven. Look for this flavored stock base in a jar in the spice rack at your supermarket.

1. Preheat the oven to 350°F and butter a 13 × 9 × 3-inch baking dish.

2. Heat 2 tablespoons oil in a large skillet over medium-high heat. Add the uncooked rice and sauté until golden brown and toasty, then transfer to the baking dish.

3. Add the remaining tablespoon of oil to the same skillet and stir in the green onions. Sauté the onions until they are crisp-tender, about 5 minutes, then stir them into the rice mixture.

4. Place the butter and chicken stock base in a saucepan, pour in the boiling water, and stir until the butter has melted and the stock base has completely dissolved. Sprinkle in the salt, if you wish, plus the pepper and a few drops of yellow food coloring. Stir until thoroughly mixed, then pour over the rice mixture and stir again.

5. Bake the rice, without covering it, until tender, 30 to 40 minutes, stirring frequently. Sprinkle with paprika and serve the rice hot with baked chicken, or use as a stuffing for filet of sole.

Russian Dressing

SINCE THE EARLY 1900s, this dressing has been synonymous with the popular American salad of a wedge of iceberg lettuce, often topped with a slice of rosy ripe tomato. An ample serving of dressing is draped over the salad. The dressing got its name from earlier recipes, which always included Russian caviar in their ingredient lists.

MAKES ABOUT 1 ¼ CUPS

¾ cup Hellmann's Real Mayonnaise (not the light variety)
¼ cup ketchup
¼ cup bottled chili sauce
3 tablespoons sweet pickle relish

1. Mix all of the ingredients together in a small bowl. Store in the refrigerator.

2. Use as a spread on ham or roast beef sandwiches or as a dressing for Chef's Salad and other salads made with fresh greens.

The Junior's Way—
Behind the deli counter where all of the sandwiches and salads are freshly made to order, this dressing is always available. Junior's never makes a Chef's Salad without it.

*F*ORGET THE DIET for today and order a slice of apple pie at Junior's. When it arrives, you'll immediately know you're in for a treat, even before taking the first bite. As you might expect, every slice of apple pie is oversized and overstuffed, completely filling up the plate.

But the best part is that this apple pie doesn't "stand up straight." Instead, apples and cinnamony juices are gently peeking out from under the crust and even falling out along the sides, coaxing you to take a bite. Once you do, you'll want to bake up one yourself.

Go ahead, serve it slightly warm and à la mode, with a generous scoop of vanilla ice cream, just like they do at Junior's.

MAKES ONE OVERSTUFFED 9-INCH PIE

1 recipe Pie Pastry, enough for a double-crust pie
     (page 40)

FOR THE APPLE FILLING

1 cup granulated sugar

1 cup packed light brown sugar

2 to 3 tablespoons all-purpose flour (depending on the
     juiciness of the apples)

2 tablespoons cornstarch

¾ teaspoon ground cinnamon

¼ teaspoon salt

3 pounds tart-sweet red apples, such as Rome Beauty,
     Jonathan, McIntosh, or Cortland

3 tablespoons fresh lemon juice

2 tablespoons unsalted butter, cut into small pieces

The Junior's Way—
Flute the crust about 1 inch higher than the edge of the pie plate. Then spoon in the filling, mounding as many apples as high as possible in the center. Cover with the top crust, then glue the edges together well with a little water. The apples cook down as they bake, and the crust takes on its own homemade look—irregular, a little bumpy, and glistening with a golden shine.

1 large egg yolk

½ teaspoon vegetable oil

2 tablespoons granulated sugar (optional)

1. Butter a 9-inch deep-dish pie plate. Mix the pastry, shape into two 6-inch disks, wrap in plastic wrap, and refrigerate. Roll out one of the pastry disks ⅛ inch thick on a lightly floured surface, and trim to a 15-inch circle with a pastry wheel or sharp knife. Transfer the pastry to the pie plate, leaving a 1½-inch overhang. Place the shell in the freezer for 15 minutes while you make the filling. (Keep the other pastry disk in the refrigerator.)

2. Mix the granulated and brown sugars, the flour, cornstarch, cinnamon, and salt together in a medium-sized bowl, then set aside.

3. Peel, core, and slice the apples ¼ inch thick into a large bowl (you need 8 cups of apples). Drizzle the apples with the lemon juice and stir to mix. Sprinkle the cinnamon-sugar mixture over the apples and toss until all of the apple slices are well coated.

4. Place a rack in the center of the oven and preheat the oven to 425°F. Spoon the apple filling into the pie shell, mounding it as high in the center as possible. Dot with the butter.

5. Roll out the remaining pastry disk ⅛ inch thick and trim to a 13-inch circle. Cut out a 1-inch circle in the center of the top crust to let the steam out (it also quickly tells the customers at Junior's which type of pie they're buying). Transfer this pastry circle to the top of the pie. Moisten the edges of the pastry with a little ice water, fold the edges under, and pinch them to seal. Shape the edge of the pastry to stand up at least 1 inch high, then flute.

6. To glaze the pie: Whisk the egg yolk with the oil and brush on the top of the pie. Sprinkle the pie with the 2 tablespoons granulated sugar for an extra glistening touch, if you wish.

7. Bake the pie for 10 minutes at 425°F. Then reduce the oven temperature to 350°F and continue baking until the crust is golden, the apples are tender, and the filling is bubbly, about 50 minutes to 1 hour. If the top crust browns before the pie is done, lay a piece of foil loosely over the top of the pie for the rest of the baking time. Cool the pie on a wire rack for at least 2 hours before serving.

Pound Cake

EVERY BAKER WORTH his cakes seems to have a favorite pound cake recipe. And the bakers at Junior's are no exception.

Any day of the week you can get a slice of this old-time favorite—so fresh that you know it just recently came out of the oven. One slice I was served recently was still warm and can only be described as heavenly ecstasy. Unlike many other pound cakes I have eaten, Junior's trademark cake has a very fine, tender, and oh-so-buttery texture that melts away in your mouth the minute you take a bite. The secret is in the making—the batter is beaten for thirty-five minutes!

MAKES TWO 1-POUND LOAVES
(9 × 5 × 3 INCHES OR 8½ × 4½ × 2¾ INCHES)

3¾ cups cake flour

1 teaspoon baking powder

1 teaspoon salt

¼ teaspoon ground nutmeg

1 cup (2 sticks) unsalted butter, at room temperature

1 cup shortening

2 cups sugar

9 extra-large eggs

2 tablespoons pure vanilla extract

¾ cup milk

The Junior's Way—
If you want to bake a cake with the same fine, delicate texture that Junior's is famous for, start with all of the ingredients at room temperature—including the butter, shortening, eggs, and milk. And don't skimp on the beating time. The bakers beat the batter for thirty-five minutes. However, with a little less beating if you're in a hurry, you'll still get a delicious cake that your friends will rave about.

1. Place a rack in the middle of the oven and preheat the oven to 325°F. Butter 2 loaf pans (9 × 5 × 3-inch or 8½ × 4½ × 2¾-inch), then line the bottoms with parchment or wax paper. Sift the cake flour, baking powder, salt, and nutmeg together into a medium-size bowl and set aside.

2. Cream the butter and shortening in a large bowl with an electric mixer on high until light yellow, about 5 minutes. Then, while the mixer is still running, add the sugar, about ½ cup at a time, beating 1 to 2 minutes after each addition. Now,

add the eggs, one at a time, beating 3 minutes after adding each one. Beat the batter until it is light-yellow, airy, and starts crawling up the sides of the bowl, a total of about 35 minutes in all. Beat in the vanilla.

3. Sift about one-fourth of the flour mixture over the batter and stir it in by hand, then stir in one-third of the milk. Repeat by adding one-quarter more flour, one-third more milk, another one-fourth of the flour, then the rest of the milk. Finally, stir in the rest of the flour. Stir after each addition until the ingredients are well incorporated.

4. Gently spoon half of the batter into each loaf pan. Set the 2 pans side-by-side in the oven, making sure they are not touching each other. Bake the cakes until the tops are golden and the center of each cake springs back when you touch it lightly and a toothpick inserted in the center comes out with moist crumbs (not batter) clinging to it, about 1 hour. Let the cakes cool on a wire rack for 30 minutes before removing them from the pans.

1940s—When Brooklyn Was . . . Everything

Sponge Cake

*M*IX UP THIS sponge cake and you have the start of several of Junior's cakes—such as their famous Fresh Strawberry Shortcake and their towering Lemon Coconut Layer Cake. Or simply serve it warm with just a light sprinkling of powdered sugar, as I like to do.

Take a taste and you'll notice something very special about this sponge cake: It's airy and light, golden and buttery, and never fails to impress (just like it pleases the customers day after day at Junior's).

Best of all, this sponge cake is moist when it comes out of the oven, and stays moist, until that last heavenly bite.

MAKES ONE 9- OR 10-INCH SPRINGFORM CAKE OR TWO 9-INCH CAKE LAYERS

1⅓ cups sifted cake flour

1 tablespoon baking powder

½ teaspoon salt

9 extra-large eggs, separated

1 cup sugar

1 tablespoon pure vanilla extract

¼ teaspoon lemon extract

½ cup (1 stick) unsalted butter, melted and cooled

½ teaspoon cream of tartar

The Junior's Way—
Don't skimp on the beating time—it's the secret to a light and airy cake. Beat the egg yolks for 10 minutes, until thick light-yellow ribbons form.

1. Preheat the oven to 350°F and butter a 9-inch or 10-inch springform pan or two 9-inch layer cake pans, then line with parchment or wax paper. Sift the cake flour, baking powder, and salt together in a medium-sized bowl and set aside.

2. Beat the egg yolks in a large bowl with an electric mixer on high for 5 minutes. Then, with the mixer still running, gradually add ¾ cup of the sugar and continue beating until thick, light-yellow ribbons form in the bowl, about 5 minutes more, scraping the bowl 2 or 3 times. Beat in the vanilla and lemon extracts.

3. Sift the flour mixture over the batter and stir it in by hand until no more white flecks appear. Then blend in the butter (the batter may look a little separated at first, but just keep stirring until the butter is no longer floating on top).

4. In a clean bowl, using clean dry beaters, beat the egg whites and cream of tartar together on high until frothy. Gradually add the remaining ¼ cup sugar and continue beating until stiff peaks form (the whites should stand up in stiff peaks, but not be dry). Stir about 1 cup of the whites into the batter, then gently fold in the remaining whites (don't worry if a few white specks remain).

5. Either spoon all of the batter into the springform pan or divide it evenly between the two layer cake pans. Bake the cake just until the center springs back when lightly touched, about 40 minutes for the springform pan and only 25 minutes for the layer cake pans. Let the cake cool on a wire rack for 15 minutes before removing from the pan. Then stand the cake top-side-up on the rack to cool. This cake freezes great.

Junior's Famous Fresh Strawberry Shortcake

ALMOST TWO MILLION fresh strawberries—that's what it takes every year to supply Junior's bake shop. And many of those berries end up in strawberry shortcakes. Every day, every week, every month, hundreds of berries are gently sliced, moist buttery sponge cakes seem to always be coming out of the oven, and one of the giant-sized mixers seems to forever be whipping up more cream for these shortcakes. And for good reason—second to the cheesecakes, these short-cakes are Junior's most popular dessert.

All shortcakes have four layers of moist buttery sponge cake, varying in size from small 5-inch shortcakes, to larger 8-inch ones, even bigger 12-inch restaurant sizes, and giant 16-inch party sizes. Each shortcake has plenty of whipped-cream fill-ing and sliced berries stuffed between the layers, then filled and swirled with more mountains of whipped cream on the sides and top, and finally decorated with more ripe berries. The finishing touch: generous scoops of Fresh Strawberry Sauce.

MAKES ONE 9-INCH CAKE ABOUT 7 INCHES HIGH

1 recipe Sponge Cake (page 94)
6 cups large ripe strawberries (3 pints)

FOR THE WHIPPED CREAM FROSTING

1 tablespoon plain unflavored powdered gelatin
3 tablespoons cold water
2 pints very cold heavy whipping cream (4 cups)
1 cup confectioners' sugar
2 tablespoons pure vanilla extract

FOR THE STRAWBERRY SAUCE

1 recipe Fresh Strawberry Sauce (page 98)

The Junior's Way—Take a tip from the Junior's bakery: Bake the cake layers either the day before assembling this cake or at least four hours before. Let the cake cool completely before slicing and filling the layers. Here's another tip from the bakers: Whip fresh whip-ping cream for the frosting, but then stabilize it to make it stiffer and much easier to ice and decorate the cake. To stabilize the cream, whip in a little plain gelatin that's been dis-solved in cold water.

Welcome to Junior's!

1. The day before or the morning of the day you plan to serve this cake, pre-heat the oven to 350°F. Butter two 9-inch layer cake pans and line the bottoms with wax paper. Make and bake the sponge cake batter and divide it evenly between the two pans. Bake each cake layer just until the center springs back when lightly touched, about 25 minutes. Let the cakes cool on a wire rack for 15 minutes, then remove the cakes from the pan, and cool them completely, at least 4 hours or overnight. (To keep overnight, wrap in plastic wrap and refrigerate.) When it's time to frost the cake, cut each cake layer horizontally into two equal layers, giving four even layers.

2. Wash, sort through, and hull the strawberries. Pat them dry with paper towels. Set aside 9 of the most beautiful berries for decorating. Slice the remaining berries ¼ inch thick and set aside.

3. To stabilize the whipped cream frosting, sprinkle the gelatin in the bottom of a small saucepan and stir in the cold water until the gelatin thickens. Stir over medium heat until the gelatin thoroughly dissolves and the mixture turns clear. Remove the pan from the heat and keep warm.

4. Beat the cream in a chilled bowl, with an electric mixer on high, until the cream begins to thicken. While the mixer is still running, gradually add the sugar and continue beating until semi-stiff fluffy peaks form (be careful not to overbeat). Beat in the vanilla, then the dissolved warm gelatin, all at once. Refrigerate the whipped cream frosting until ready to use.

5. To assemble the shortcake: Place one of the four cake layers on a cake plate. Spread with about 1½ cups of the whipped cream, then spread over one-third of the sliced berries. Repeat two more times, then place the remaining cake layer on top. Refrigerate the cake and the remaining cream until chilled and set, about 1 hour.

6. Frost the sides and decorate the top of the cake with the rest of the whipped cream. For Junior's finishing touch, use a pastry bag fitted with a large fluted tip to pipe several rosettes of whipped cream on top of the cake. Place a whole berry, with its pointed end up, in the center of each rosette. Refrigerate the cake until time to serve. Cut in slices and serve with generous scoops of Fresh Strawberry Sauce. Store any leftover cake in the refrigerator.

Fresh Strawberry Sauce

*T*HERE ARE ALWAYS fresh strawberries in Junior's bakery, no matter what time of day you visit. Someone seems to always be sorting through the berries, choosing the perfectly shaped ones to decorate the cheesecakes and pies.

The rest of these great-tasting berries are sliced up for this sauce. Whenever the waiter serves Junior's signature Fresh Strawberry Shortcake, this fresh strawberry sauce is generously ladled over the top. It appears again over strawberry sundaes.

The strawberries are always plump and juicy and the sauce slightly sweet and just thick enough to drip perfectly over anything you choose to serve it with.

MAKES 1 QUART SAUCE

3 quarts fresh ripe strawberries

1¼ cups cold water

1½ cups sugar

3 tablespoons cornstarch

Few drops red food coloring (optional)

1 teaspoon pure vanilla extract

The Junior's Way—
Pick the biggest, ripest strawberries you can find. Slice the berries ½ inch thick, no thinner. This size keeps them plump and juicy in the sauce.

1. Wash, sort through, hull, and slice the berries ½ inch thick.

2. Bring 1 cup of the water and the sugar to a boil in a medium-sized saucepan over high heat. Boil for 5 minutes.

3. Mix the cornstarch and the remaining ¼ cup water together in a cup until the cornstarch thoroughly dissolves. Slowly whisk this mixture into the boiling syrup. Return to a full boil and boil for 2 minutes.

4. Remove the syrup from the heat and whisk in the food coloring if you wish. Stir in the vanilla and gently fold in the strawberries. Store in the refrigerator for up to 3 days or in the freezer for up to 1 month. This is *the* sauce for Junior's Famous Fresh Strawberry Shortcake (page 96) and Mountain High Fresh Fruit Strawberry Sundae (page 44). Some other day, try it over a slice of Pound Cake (page 92).

Welcome to Junior's!

Rice Pudding

WHEN IT COMES to rice pudding, *this is it*—the best! It's creamy, rich, delicate, and sweet, with just a hint of vanilla. All of this, without being heavy. If you're dining at Junior's, the pudding comes to you almost swimming in a pool of Fresh Strawberry Sauce. If you buy a bowl of puddin' to take home, some thoughtful person always tucks in a container of this signature sauce to pour over the top.

MAKES 2 QUARTS PUDDING

2 cups water

½ teaspoon salt

1 cup uncooked regular white rice, medium-grain
    (not parboiled)

4 cups heavy cream (2 pints)

5 extra-large eggs

1 cup sugar

1 tablespoon pure vanilla extract

1 recipe Fresh Strawberry Sauce (page 98)

> ### The Junior's Way—
> Use plain regular white rice, not the parboiled variety, then cook it first until all of the water is absorbed. The rice is ready to use in the pudding when it looks moist and fluffy.

1. Bring the water and salt to a boil in a large saucepan over high heat. Stir in the rice and return to a boil. Cover the pot, reduce the heat to low, and cook until all of the water is absorbed, about 20 minutes. Check the pot occasionally and stir to prevent the rice from sticking.

2. Slowly stir 3½ cups of the cream into the rice and stir gently over low heat until the cream is incorporated (make sure it does not boil). Remove the pan from the heat.

3. Whip the eggs and sugar with an electric mixer on high until light yellow and thick. Beat a little hot cream into the eggs, then stir this egg mixture into the rice until it's blended throughout.

continued

1940s—When Brooklyn Was . . . Everything

4. Return the pudding to the heat and stir it gently until it has thickened. It's very important not to let the mixture boil at this stage, as excess heat can curdle the eggs.

5. Remove the pudding from the heat and immediately stir in the remaining ½ cup of cream and the vanilla. Transfer the pudding to a heatproof bowl and let it cool at room temperature for 30 minutes. Lay a piece of plastic wrap directly on the surface (this prevents a skin from forming on top) and refrigerate the pudding until it's cold. Store any leftovers in the refrigerator.

6. While the pudding chills, make the Fresh Strawberry Sauce. To serve, ladle generous portions of the pudding into large dessert bowls and spoon over lots of the sauce.

Welcome to Junior's!

CHAPTER THREE

1950s – Up from Brooklyn's Turbulent Change . . . Junior's

TO TALK ABOUT Brooklyn in the 1950s you have to divide the subject into three categories: 1) changes; 2) big changes; and 3) upheaval. What we might have called familiar life in Brooklyn either left, died, or was razed during the 1950s. One rocky transition after another affected everybody and everything, including our family and the Enduro.

Changes started after World War II. In 1947, there was a marked difference in business coming into downtown Brooklyn.

The thousands of servicemen who had spent money in stores and restaurants had gone home. Then Mayor La Guardia, who had been an emotional leader through the Depression and the war years, died of cancer. The new mayor, Robert Wagner, wasn't the hands-on, one-of-us type we were used to. In 1947, too, the famous nickel ride for subway, train, and trolley doubled. In 1953, it'd go up again to fifteen cents.

Come Away with Me, Lucille . . .

The backbone of Brooklyn, its people and neighborhoods, felt the strain of changes first. Because of a big push from American tire manufacturers and Detroit auto factories to get consumers into automobiles and to get gasoline-powered buses into the city neighborhoods, our trolleys began to vanish. Starting in 1947 and continuing through 1956, Brooklyn's trolleys were one by one dumped into basins like the Canarsie Sand Pit. Gasoline and electric buses replaced them. It was an emotional thing—the slow death of the trolley car. Brooklynites had identified with them. The streetcar was the great equalizer among a hundred different ethnic neighborhoods. An accessible trolley ride had seemed to guarantee freedom and equality for all.

> ## LETTING GO
>
> "You thought things would never change. You'd hang out on the corner, go to the movies with your friends, grow up, get married, go over to your parents' for dinner. You thought Brooklyn would always be Brooklyn."
>
> —Stewie Stone, comedian

I remember the last run of the Brooklyn Bridge trolley. It was in March of 1950 and it was documented by a story in the *Brooklyn Daily Eagle*. Several Borough Hall officials pressed their smiling faces against the windows of the last trolley car ever to roll off the bridge. A lone Boy Scout played taps on a bugle.

Although we hated losing the trolleys, we *loved* buying cars. Most Brooklynites never had need for a car and did just fine without one, but now suddenly they *had* to have one of those sporty Chevrolets, or Buick convertibles, or plush Cadillacs. Every young guy yearned for his own. Dealerships sprang up on Coney Island Avenue and Flatbush Avenue Extension with showrooms displaying the dazzling

Car dealerships sprang up like weeds in the fifties because of the hot trend to have your own wheels. Brooklynites bought so many cars in the 1950s that by the early 1960s when this was taken, posing with a new car was a grand photo opportunity for Miss Brooklyn, Janet Parker. Courtesy of the Brooklyn Historical Society

chrome two-toned and white-walled ships of the future. It seemed to be a necessary trade-off—the trolley for the American Dream.

Another American Dream—owning your own house and yard—took hold of Brooklyn's working and middle classes, too. The desire was to drive your new car to the new suburbs which were springing up on Long Island farmland. And there,

Delicatessens are still an easy find throughout Brooklyn! Courtesy of the Brooklyn Historical Society

Welcome to Junior's!

where developers were attracting veterans with low-interest mortgages, you'd live in the home of your dreams.

By 1955, the first wave of old-generation Brooklynites, about 135,000, had gone to the new suburbs, leaving behind housing for 100,000 African Americans, Middle Easterners, West Indians, and Puerto Ricans who came to Brooklyn in pursuit of their dreams. The new immigrants were soon disappointed, however, as the banks, practicing discrimination in those days, tried to control the property values by refusing loans in some neighborhoods. Without money to renovate, many neighborhoods of low-income home owners and new low-income immigrants quickly deteriorated.

Peacetime Ends the Enduro

By 1949, business at the Enduro had been failing for a few years, ever since the heavy influx of servicemen clientele had dropped after the war. The civilian public didn't patronize the steakhouse and bar as they had before the war, and the business was going into debt. Eventually, my father's unsuccessful attempts to gamble the Enduro out of debt (the only flaw in the fabric of a capable man) left the Enduro broke. The family was scraping by.

My uncle Mike wanted to cut losses and call it quits, which he eventually did. It was my mother who encouraged my father to find a way to stay in business on the prime corner of Flatbush Avenue Extension and DeKalb. Where twenty years earlier she saw no future, she now challenged my father to invent something new.

The Enduro closed in 1949, but my father was full of ideas for salvaging the business, paying off debts and building something new. After all, downtown Brooklyn still had thousands of people who needed to eat. He imagined a restaurant for the future—a family-style place, serving breakfast, lunch, and dinner with a small bakery, soda fountain, and both counter and table service. The menu would offer omelettes and soups, deli sandwiches and fountain desserts at first, and if business grew, so would the bill of fare to include full-course home-style dinners. He had seen such places on his vacations in Florida—airy bright comfortable restaurants that catered to large crowds at all hours of the day.

He didn't have a significant nickel to pull this off. Still, my father convinced our landlord, the Dime Savings Bank next door, to rent him reduced square footage. He kept the corner location and the landlord walled off what had been the famous oval bar and bandstand. That space became a TV store for the next decade.

The Shape of the Future

The new family-style place would have to have a bright and cheerful look. The muted nightclub colors and the glitzy mirrored columns of the Enduro weren't appropriate. But my father had no money for construction materials, let alone money to hire an architect/designer as one would do today. Instead, his friend Julie Palumbo, a contractor, offered to supply materials and work on speculation. He agreed to take no payment at all until the new restaurant was up and running. In those days friends took such risks on a handshake. My father never forgot Julie.

Over the course of the next few months, they gutted the old Enduro and put up a restaurant that was completely modern for its day. It had sleek clean lines, light wood counters, modern-looking hanging lamp fixtures, bright orange Naugahyde booths and chairs. Nowadays, we call it the 1950s look, but this design was making history in downtown Brooklyn. In all, it took a year to pull everything together.

In the meantime, my father lined up Eigel Peterson, a Danish-born baker, to work full time turning out specialties for the new restaurant. Peterson, as time would tell, played a pivotal role in the success of the new place. Another man who'd play a big role was Frank D'Alessio, a young guy then, just out of the army and working for a paper goods company. Frank saw the restaurant under reconstruction in 1949 and went inside to meet my father. He had some great ideas—like printed paper place mats, a new idea in those days, and paper coasters, also an innovation.

Frank was the kind of guy my father really took to. If we needed something new, Frank would design it and have it manufactured—from take-out containers and

Opening Day of Junior's Restaurant was Election Day, 1950—a hot Indian summer day. We can't identify the men in the picture, but it does look as if they are checking finances after an evening of bowling. Courtesy of the Rosen family

bags to napkins with logos. If we ran out of something in the middle of the night, Frank was here in no time with more. He's still providing the same energetic service almost fifty years later.

My father called the restaurant *Junior's* in honor of us, even though neither one of us is technically a Harry Rosen, Jr. A vertical neon marquee, in style with the Paramount's across the street, replaced the old Art Deco Enduro sign at the corner

By 1958, Junior's had become an unmistakable landmark with its bright orange awnings and neon lettering. Courtesy of the Brooklyn Historical Society

entrance. On Election Day, 1950, Junior's opened with red, white, and blue bunting billowing outside. Sweet bakery aromas drew people inside, where a full fountain service featured the mile-high malteds we're now famous for and sundaes drenched with syrup and whipped cream. People sat on stools at the counter or in booths or at tables and ordered our thick broiled hamburgers, overstuffed sandwiches such as corned beef on seeded rye, fresh brisket on Challah, creamy egg salad, tuna salad, cream cheese and jelly, or any number of Junior's specialties. At last, Junior's was up and running.

Have You Seen What They're Doing Downtown?

Today, many Brooklyn neighborhoods look almost exactly as they did fifty years ago. But in a few short years in the 1950s, our neighborhood, downtown Brooklyn, changed dramatically. While Junior's was putting down roots, much of downtown was being torn up. The beautiful Victorian buildings which gave Brooklyn a style and elegance—such as the Courthouse with its baroque facade and distinctive dome, the Hall of Records, the Arbuckle and the Jefferson buildings, all fell to the wrecker's ball. Another landmark gem slated for demolition and rebuilding in 1955 was the *Brooklyn Daily Eagle* building. Shortly before destruction, however, the eminent 114-year-old newspaper stopped its presses and closed permanently, leaving us all stunned and bewildered.

Fulton Street, the heart of the area, used to wind its way down past Brooklyn Heights to the old Fulton Ferry landing, which Walt Whitman wrote so eloquently about in "Crossing Brooklyn Ferry." By the end of the 1950s, Fulton Street stopped just this side of Brooklyn Heights, severing the Heights' connection with downtown. A huge, shall we say, less impressive court building would eventually stretch along Adams Street, creating a fortresslike barrier between Brooklyn Heights and downtown.

Frankly, we were beginning to think that Robert Moses, the Commissioner of Land Management for New York City, just didn't like Brooklyn very much. Moses was the impetus behind much of the so-called rebuilding of Brooklyn, which displaced neighborhoods in favor of highways and tore down elegant buildings in favor of his idea of a modern civic center.

Landmark department stores also chose the 1950s to depart downtown. The long-established Frederick Loeser's and A. I. Namm's, a first-class store which had moved to Brooklyn from Manhattan in 1893, closed permanently in 1957. Martin's and Oppenheim Collins soon followed. A&S stayed through the eighties. The store itself is now Macy's. The only store still here today from that era is Modell's Sporting Goods.

With the demolition of the trolley system, the razing of landmark buildings, the rerouting of streets and the departure of merchants, there was rubble, dust, and anxiety everywhere.

When This Old World Starts Getting Me Down . . .

Up from the rubble, racket, and tensions of the early 1950s came the wild and spirited sounds of rock 'n' roll, soul, and doo-wop. The new music came up fast. It seemed that one day in 1954 we were all listening to Patti Page, Perry Como, and Eddie Fisher; then the next day, the new soul sounds of Little Anthony and the Imperials, the Penguins, or the fierce rock 'n' roll of Elvis, Bill Haley and the Comets, and Bo Diddley.

And Brooklyn didn't merely consume the new music; the whole borough seemed to create it. There were doo-wop singing gangs of kids from Midwood and Coney Island to Bed-Stuy. They would gather on benches and picnic tables in the parks, in front of candy stores, in apartment building lobbies and on subway platforms, anywhere just to sing a cappella. On a weekend they might sing all day and into the night. Maybe six would start and be joined by another six, sometimes building to thirty kids until neighbors complained and they would move to another corner.

During school vacations in the late 1950s, the Paramount and the Fox theaters downtown became Mecca to thousands and thousands of young music fans. Two famous music promoters, Alan Freed, a disc jockey at radio station WINS, and Murray the "K" produced shows for the Paramount and the Fox, which featured newcomers and the biggest names in rock 'n' roll and soul. Beginning in 1955, these shows actually saved the lives of these theaters, since television by that time had effectively stolen much of the movie business.

"We weren't poor, we just didn't have anything."

—Barbra Streisand

There were three to five shows every day and each one was three hours long. Every performance was packed with nearly four thousand kids, most of whom had shown up at six A.M. to buy tickets. During the shows the kids got to express themselves—sing along, dance in the aisles, cheer. Girls would throw love notes at performers. Even Eddie Fisher, when he sang "Oh My Papa" here at the Paramount, got mash notes hurled up on the stage. Sometimes one audience would refuse to leave, and when the next audience couldn't get in, there would be bedlam in the streets.

Legendary artists appeared on the Paramount and Fox stages during the golden age of rock 'n' soul—1955 through about 1963. LaVern Baker sang "Tweedly Dee" at the first Paramount show in 1955. The Penguins and the Moonglows were headliners that day too. The Platters, Chuck Berry, Buddy Holly, Fats Domino, the Solitaires, Frankie Lymon and the Teenagers would also pack the house in the next few years. Jerry Lee Lewis literally set his piano on fire during a performance of "Great Balls of Fire" at the Paramount in 1957. Some say that the stunt truly ignited his career. Bo Diddley, Little Richard, Jan and Dean, the Chiffons, the Drifters, and Little Stevie Wonder would make their Brooklyn debuts down the street at the Fox.

Who Was Who

Soon-to-be music legends were making their way up in Brooklyn in the 1950s. Barbra (Barbara then) Streisand, who had grown up in Williamsburg, graduated from Erasmus Hall High School in 1959. Three years later, she'd perform her showstopping Miss Marmelstein role in *I Can Get It for You Wholesale* at the Shubert Theatre. She worked opposite fellow Brooklynite Elliot Gould in that show.

Neil Diamond graduated from Erasmus Hall the year after Streisand. Harry Chapin was growing up in Brooklyn Heights. Neil Sedaka and Carole King were Lincoln High grads that decade. Richie Havens, yet to write his first hits, was still a boy in Bed-Stuy.

Tony Danza was born in East New York in the early 1950s. Harvey Keitel graduated from Lincoln in the late fifties. The great dancer and actor Gregory Hines was just a kid in the 1950s, too, and he would go on to attend Brooklyn College. The brilliant and playful mind behind Toys "Я" Us, Norman Richen, was just a little boy, more excited about living on the same block as Dodgers Walt Alston, Pee Wee Reese, and Duke Snider than anything else.

Soviet spy Emil R. Goldfus was maybe the most infamous Brooklynite of the decade. He had moved to Brooklyn Heights in 1953, was living as an artist on Hicks Street, and renting a studio in a building with other artists on Fulton Street. He had some famous neighbors at the time. Norman Mailer had a studio in the same building. So did Jules Feiffer and Ralph Ginzburg, who was then an editor at *Look* magazine. Goldfus had endeared himself to his neighbors with an easygoing nature, some mellow guitar-playing, a penchant for cookies, and his earnest attempts at painting.

When Goldfus was captured by federal agents in a store on Fulton Street in August of 1957, Brooklynites were once again shaken out of a world we thought was secure. Not only was the Cold War a political threat, it was sneaking around our streets and backyards. Goldfus was really Colonel Rudolf Ivanovich Abel of the KGB, the highest ranking espionage agent ever caught in the United States. He was tried here in Brooklyn and sentenced to life in prison. Only those who were paying close attention in 1962 noticed that it was American-held prisoner Emil Goldfus, a.k.a. Rudolf Abel, who was exchanged on a bridge in Germany for the Russian-held prisoner United States U-2 pilot Francis Gary Powers. Powers's spy plane had been shot down in Soviet airspace in May of 1960 and he had been a prisoner there until the exchange of Goldfus.

The infamous George Metesky, the "Mad Bomber," who had eluded capture

At Walter and Sandy's wedding in 1959, she had to climb a ladder to cut the cake!
Courtesy of the Rosen family

1950s—Up from Brooklyn's Turbulent Change . . . Junior's

"Somebody said, if you want to see a 'real' game of baseball, go over to Ebbets Field, so here I am."

—Douglas MacArthur, May 1951

for decades, set off an explosive here at the Paramount during the Christmas season of 1956. He was caught, too, later in 1957.

General Douglas MacArthur was very popular in Brooklyn during the 1950s, more so than President Eisenhower. Although he had been fired by Harry Truman, New York welcomed him home with a hero's ticker-tape parade up Broadway in April 1951. Then he settled into a life as an avid Dodger fan. He slept at the Waldorf-Astoria but he lived, it seemed, at Ebbets Field. With box seats as a gift from Dodger owner Walter O'Malley, MacArthur rarely missed a game.

Bums No More

And how 'bout those Dodgers! They won the pennant again in 1949, 1952, and 1953 but then lost all three attempts to steal the World Series crown from the hated Yankees. "Wait till next year" was wearing thin as a threat; it had about as much punch

as a nursery rhyme. In 1955, the Dodgers won the pennant again and with it came another chance to take the World Series title away from the Yankees.

The Yankees took the first two games. The Dodgers took games three, four, and five, and the Yankees won game six. For the last and deciding game seven, Dodger pitcher Johnny Podres took the mound in Yankee Stadium. Brooklyn was leading 2–0 in the sixth inning. Incredibly, Podres was throwing a shutout. The only breathless moment came when Yankee Yogi Berra threatened with a huge fly to

Jackie Robinson and Pee Wee Reese on the road to the pennant and series. Courtesy of the Brooklyn Historical Society

left field with two men on and two out. Dodger Sandy Amoros raced the ball down and caught it with a desperate lunge, retiring the side. Podres finished with a shutout, and the Dodgers, finally after seventy-five years and countless attempts, were world champions.

While the players (we were told) joined hands and said a prayer of thanks in the locker room, all of Brooklyn erupted into one street party after another. Improvised motorcades of horn honking and cheering streamed up and down Flatbush, Broadway, Ocean Parkway, Coney Island Avenue. People danced and sang in the streets. The tugboats and freighters on the East River sounded their horns. The front page of the *Daily News* said it all: "Who's a Bum!"

But then in 1957, the Dodgers left Brooklyn, too. They played their last game at Ebbets Field and headed for Los Angeles. Why? How could this happen? Dodger owner Walter O'Malley said the ballpark was falling apart and there was no room for parking. This was true—Ebbets Field was very old and in need of renovation, and it was ensconced in Crown Heights and hemmed in by residential life. Who would ever have thought in 1913, as Charles Ebbet built his stadium, that one day the American automobile population would boom and parking spaces would become a national worry. O'Malley, however, turned down a spacious site by the Brooklyn Battery Tunnel which the

The press had called the Brooklyn Dodgers "the Bums" since the mid-1930s when the team could not get out of the cellar. When the Dodgers took their first World Series in 1955, the press helped them shake the label! Courtesy of the Brooklyn Historical Society

BIG LEAGUER

"I was thrilled to get number 4, the number of my favorite baseball player of all time . . . and he wasn't a Dodger, he was a Yankee—Lou Gehrig. Getting to wear Gehrig's number and play for the Brooklyn Dodgers was as much as a 20-year-old . . . just up from the Texas league could ever dare ask for."

—Duke Snider

city offered him. He also turned down a site in Queens, saying that he'd go to Los Angeles before he'd see the Dodgers play in Queens. We understood that kind of stubbornness. Jackie Robinson, after being traded to the Giants in '56, chose retirement over playing for another New York team.

Fans, organized by the sporting goods mogul Henry Modell, turned out by the thousands for demonstrations during the year prior to the move. They stormed Borough Hall and the Dodger headquarters, but nothing deterred O'Malley from his decision. After

This is one of the last photos taken of the Ebbets Field scoreboard in 1957. Abe Stark's "Hit Sign Win Suit" sign was up to the very end. Courtesy of the Brooklyn Historical Society

the last game at Ebbets Field in 1957, the organist played "Auld Lang Syne" before a meager crowd of 6,700. And it was over.

This might have been the hardest blow. Brooklyn didn't merely lose a baseball team. The Dodgers had been the fighters and scrappers who represented millions of people who had struggled to make good in a new country. And the battle had paid off. The Dodgers were the homegrown symbol of how to win—when you get knocked down, you get up again—the eternal secret to success.

When we lost baseball, we lost the one single culture that every hardworking immigrant from who-knows-where had created and shared with one another. It had been a culture of trial, hope, and exhilaration ever since the team first banded together in 1883. They were the Brooklyn Baseball Club then and Charles Ebbet was only the guy who printed tickets and scorecards.

On that last day at Ebbets Field, an entire way of life was eradicated. O'Malley would receive hate mail for decades. In the window of the Dodger Café across the street from Junior's that day, one fan taped up a sign listing three names—O'Malley, Hitler, Stalin—in that order.

In 1960, Ebbets Field was demolished. Most of the brick and rubble was used as landfill for new real estate ventures, but we have a small piece of brick from the famous ballpark. It's beautifully mounted on a color rendering of Ebbets Field which hangs next to Walter's desk here at Junior's. This small memento is a big reminder of the days when Brooklyn housed a stadium where ordinary bums became heroes.

"Sprinkle a Little Sugar . . ."

Meanwhile, Junior's was becoming a safe and reassuring place amid the turbulent changes that were shaking the confidence of Brooklynites. Business was good. The early style of Junior's was one that offered excellent food, impeccable service, and the best desserts anywhere. It was shaped by my father's stubborn perfectionism and his devotion to the customer's happiness. In fact, the one thing my father could not tolerate was mediocrity of any kind. He was constantly on the lookout for ways to make Junior's more attractive. "Sprinkle a little sugar on the table," he'd say to us, "and the ants will come." If something wasn't working on the menu, he'd get rid of it. Eggs, for example! We had lots of egg dishes at first and they weren't selling. My father took the menu one day and tore it up and made a new one. When the next menu didn't work out, he tore that one up too. One after another, he'd tear up menus until he had the one that the public wanted. Egg specialties on the menu were soon replaced by hamburgers, which eventually made the business take off—big time!

Eigel Peterson, our baker, worked full time just to develop special breads, cakes, and pies that would set Junior's apart. And my father worked alongside Peterson, bringing him sweet cakes and unusual breads from other cafés or restaurants. Peterson would then not only re-create the flavors and textures for Junior's menu but add something special to make them better. My father did the same thing alongside the cooks in the kitchen, developing main dishes with character and flavor that would become unique to Junior's.

My father hired the wait staff himself, and he'd fire them, too, if they didn't live up to his standards. Our best waiters were and are the ones who give the customer what he wants before he knows he wants it. My father also knew that food had to look great on the plate, that the eyes eat first, and that customers would come back if the eyes as well as the stomach had been satisfied. Of course, the only way to do things was his way. A pastrami sandwich had to be placed "just so" on the plate; if it was on the way to the table and wasn't right, he'd intercept it and take it and the waiter back to the kitchen.

My father was a tough, no-nonsense boss, but waiters and waitresses liked working for him because everything ran smoothly with him in charge. He never asked more of them than he gave of himself. A waiter worked six days a week. My father worked seven. He was up at five every day, impeccably dressed and ready to leave for work at five-thirty. By the time we were both twenty years old, we were coming in every day, too. (We both started college but came into the business before graduating.) If we weren't ready to leave home with him at five-thirty, we had to take the subway. Once, Walter came home from a date at five A.M. He was slipping his pants off to go to bed when my father looked in on him.

Welcome to Junior's!

"So, you're ready early," my dad said, obviously impressed. Walter put his pants back on and went into work with him. Didn't say another word.

At Junior's, we did everything, helped out everywhere. My father met with his assistant at six and did all the ordering and purchasing for the day. Then, he'd make up the menu for the day. When it came to running a restaurant, there was no one better than my father. He let nothing go to waste, ever! Yesterday's leftovers were today's soups and casseroles. After setting the menu for the day, he'd work the front of the house greeting and seating people. We'd work the back. He'd call out to us, table for two, table for three, and we would seat the people. Customers loved my father's big extroverted way with them, and of course he was always remarkably well dressed. Sometimes a "Regular" might compliment him, "Nice suit you're wearing, Harry." Then he'd open the jacket and see a Saks Fifth Avenue label. There was no way my father could afford a suit from Saks in those days. We were struggling on a shoestring through most of the 1950s. My father bought his suits at Howard Clothiers, or H. L. Ward, as we used to call the store. Then he'd get his tailor in the neighborhood to sew in the Saks Fifth Avenue labels. That was my father. He knew it was important to appear confident. Even through our worst financial struggles, he always had a smile of confidence.

All You Want, As You Want It

By 1958, Junior's had evolved from serving simple breakfasts, soups, sandwich and fountain menus to a full-course restaurant. Patrons were coming back with regularity for a freshly made home-cooked meal.

For $2.50, a complete three-course dinner included: choice of an appetizer such as crabmeat cocktail, chopped chicken liver, and pickled lox in cream sauce or a soup such as matzoh ball, borscht with sour cream, and chicken gumbo.

For the entrée, your choice of one of twenty: roast turkey and chicken liver dressing with candied sweet potatoes and sautéed corn; roast loin of pork with red wine cabbage and fluffy mashed potatoes; fresh sea scallops; broiled halibut steak; Long Island flounder; fried oysters; prime beef goulash; charcoal-grilled steak; veal cutlet; or crispy southern fried chicken.

There were Jewish specialties too: boiled chicken in a pot with homemade noodles; matzoh balls in broth with fresh vegetables; and a prime boiled beef flanken in a pot.

For about three dollars, you could go all out and have the sizzling platter: charcoal-broiled prime filet mignon with French fried onion rings, carrots and peas, and hot baked Idaho potato.

Dessert was always included in the price of the meal. It wasn't until the late fifties that Peterson and my father developed what would become Junior's famous cheesecake, but my father's favorite strawberry cream cheese pie was frequently on the menu. It's the same recipe we serve today. Apple strudel and cheese strudel from the fifties menu and the chocolate fudge layer cake are still offered today, as is another favorite of my father's: fresh strawberry short-cake (four layers!) with fresh strawberry sauce.

While the rest of downtown Brooklyn was suffering massive changes during the fifties, Junior's was distinguishing itself as a dependable place. We were Brooklynites, unlike the Dodgers, unlike the well-loved trolleys, unlike the great A. I. Namm's and Frederick Loeser's department stores, unlike all of those evaporating Brooklyn traditions. Junior's was taking hold as a new Brooklyn tradition. And Junior's was staying!

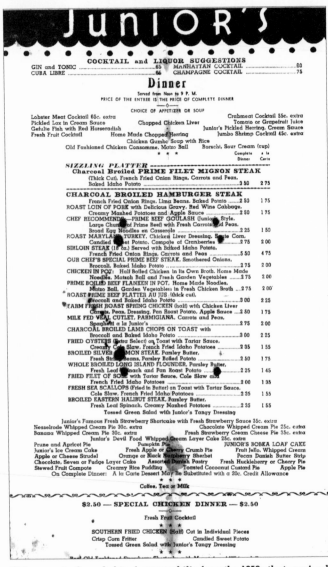

This menu is the only bit of memorabilia from the 1950s that survived the fire. It's Junior's Sunday Dinner Menu from October 28, 1956.
Courtesy of the Rosen family

Welcome to Junior's!

1950s–Loading the Table

FROM THE DAY Junior's opened its doors on Election Day 1950, the tables were always loaded with food. Even when a customer first sat down early in the morning, a basket of warm breads arrived—filled with just-baked yellow cornbread squares, fresh blueberry muffins, soft Vienna rolls, and of course Junior's famous Rugelach. Nothing was ever said; the basket just kept being filled up with more breads hot-out-of-the-oven, as fast as one could eat them. But the "Regulars" at Junior's didn't eat too many, for they knew that thick French toast, light 'n' golden pancakes, or an overstuffed omelette would soon be coming.

The rest of the day was no exception—and still isn't. The tables were loaded once again, but this time with bowls of beets, cole slaw, onions, peppers, and pickles. And again, they just seemed to magically appear. The rest of the meal was also overloaded, with favorites such as meat loaf, home fries, and mac and cheese.

What was served for dessert in the fifties? One of Junior's oversized towering sundaes, smothered with hot fudge, naturally. They're still being scooped out today.

Western Omelette

*J*UNIOR'S MAKES OMELETTES with the freshest of eggs (delivered every day). The chefs whisk the eggs just enough, not too much.

They start cooking the omelettes in a skillet, then skillfully flip them over to cook the other side. I've cooked this one the easier way, just by tilting the skillet while lifting up the cooked edges of the omelette and letting the uncooked eggs flow to the bottom of the skillet.

MAKES ONE 3-EGG OMELETTE

3 tablespoons unsalted butter

⅓ cup minced onion

⅓ cup minced green bell pepper

½ cup chopped baked sugar-cured ham

3 extra-large eggs

The Junior's Way—
When mixing up the omelette, use only eggs—don't mix them with water or milk. Use a whisk, not an electric beater. And whisk the eggs just until they're golden and airy, not until they are light and thick.

1. Melt 1 tablespoon of the butter in a medium-size skillet over medium-high heat. Add the onion and bell pepper and sauté until the vegetables start to soften. Add the ham and cook until the vegetables are tender, about 5 minutes in all. Transfer the vegetables and ham to a bowl and set aside.

2. Melt the remaining 2 tablespoons of butter in the same skillet over medium heat just until the butter is foamy and starts to brown, about 1 minute. Whisk the eggs in a small bowl until frothy, then pour them all-at-once into the skillet, tilting the skillet slightly to spread out the eggs. As the eggs start to cook, lift up the cooked edges with a spatula, while tilting the skillet at the same time to let the uncooked eggs flow to the bottom of the skillet. Cook the omelette until the top is lightly set, no uncooked batter appears (very important), and the eggs look set, about 3 minutes.

3. Spoon the vegetable-ham filling on the half of the omelette closest to you, leaving a ½-inch border around the sides. To fold the omelette, tilt and tap the skillet toward you while easing the other half on top of the filling. Fold the omelette only once, forming a semicircle.

4. At this point, the chef at Junior's turns the omelette onto a hot buttered griddle to finish the cooking, but at home, it's fine to just leave it in the skillet. Let the omelette cook just long enough to heat the filling, about 30 seconds more (or pop it under a preheated broiler for a few seconds). Serve the omelette immediately while it's still piping hot.

Old-Fashioned French Toast

A MORNING RITUAL FOR many of the "Regulars" at Junior's is their French toast—grilled to a perfect golden brown, moist on the inside, crispy on the outside.

It's made from thick slices of freshly baked Challah bread. First it's dipped in a flavored egg batter. Then it's covered with a crumb coating, made from another breakfast favorite—cornflakes.

MAKES 6 SERVINGS

FOR THE BATTER

5 extra-large eggs

¼ cup water

1 tablespoon sugar

1 tablespoon pure vanilla extract

¼ teaspoon salt

1 tablespoon vegetable oil

2 teaspoons pure vanilla extract

FOR THE FRENCH TOAST

6 slices very fresh Challah Bread (page 32) or white toasting bread, 1 inch thick

1 cup cornflake crumbs (look for them in the bread section near the containers of bread crumbs)

3 to 4 tablespoons unsalted butter

Maple syrup, warm

Apple and Raisin Preserves (page 126), warm

The Junior's Way—Use very fresh bread, preferably from a loaf that's been baked fresh the same day. Challah bread is one of the best, since it's so rich in eggs and sugar that it quickly browns perfectly and evenly. Soak the bread in the batter, first on one side, then the other, until the batter soaks completely through. This usually takes about 15 minutes for a piece of bread that's sliced 1 inch thick.

continued

1. Whisk all of the ingredients for the batter together in a small bowl until frothy.

2. Place the slices of bread in a single layer in a large shallow dish and pour all of the batter over them. Let the bread stand until the batter's soaked all the way through, turning each slice over once. This usually takes about 15 minutes to soak up all of the batter.

3. Spread out the cornflake crumbs in a shallow dish. Working with one slice of soaked bread at a time, coat the bread with the crumbs on both sides and on the edges of the crust. Press the crumbs down slightly with your hands (the crumbs will cover the bread completely).

4. Melt the butter in a large skillet over medium-high heat. Pan-fry the bread slices, turning each slice just once, until the French toast is crisp and golden brown on both sides, about 8 minutes in all. Serve the toast slices with warm maple syrup and the Apple and Raisin Preserves.

Griddle Cakes

*T*HE GRIDDLE'S ALWAYS going at Junior's from sun up right on down to closing time. A stack of these cakes tastes "just like more" anytime of the day. These griddle cakes cook up golden brown because of a little sugar in the batter . . . light and puffy because of the baking powder and eggs . . . rich in flavor because of the milk, butter, and vanilla.

MAKES A DOZEN 4-INCH GRIDDLE CAKES

1½ cups all-purpose flour

2 tablespoons sugar

1 tablespoon baking powder

½ teaspoon salt

1½ cups milk

The Junior's Way—When baking pancakes, let the tops fill with bubbles before turning them over. This indicates the cakes are evenly cooked all over. Flip the cakes over only once, no more.

2 extra-large eggs

3 tablespoons unsalted butter, melted

1 tablespoon vegetable oil, plus extra for brushing on the griddle

2 teaspoons pure vanilla extract

FOR THE SERVE-ALONGS

Unsalted butter, melted and kept hot

Maple syrup, warmed

Apple and Raisin Preserves (page 126), warmed

1. Preheat the griddle according to the manufacturer's directions. If you do not have a griddle, preheat a large nonstick skillet over medium heat. As you cook the cakes, watch the heat closely so the skillet does not get too hot.

2. In a large bowl, mix the flour, sugar, baking powder, and salt together, then set aside.

3. Using an electric mixer set on high, beat the milk and eggs until light yellow, then beat in the butter, 1 tablespoon of oil, and the vanilla. Turn off the mixer, add the flour mixture, and beat on low just until blended and smooth, 1 to 2 minutes (do not overbeat at this stage or the pancakes can be tough).

4. To cook the griddle cakes: Brush the preheated griddle or skillet with enough vegetable oil to coat it well. For each cake, pour a scant ¼ cup of the batter onto the hot griddle, making 4-inch cakes, about 1 inch apart. Let the cakes cook until the tops are covered with bubbles and the edges look done, about 3 minutes. Quickly flip over the cakes and cook the opposite sides until golden, about 2 minutes more. Serve immediately with hot melted butter, warm syrup, and warm Apple and Raisin Preserves.

Apple and Raisin Preserves

ORDER FRENCH TOAST or pancakes at Junior's and a little dish of these preserves arrives too—warm, fruity, sweet, and slightly spicy. They're the type of preserves that are also perfect to serve with roast pork or freshly baked ham.

MAKES 1 QUART PRESERVES

2 cups apple cider

1 cup sugar

1/2 teaspoon ground cinnamon

1/8 teaspoon salt

2 pounds firm red cooking apples, peeled, cored, and cut into slices 1/4 inch thick

2/3 cup dark raisins

3 tablespoons cornstarch

1/4 cup water

2 teaspoons pure vanilla extract

1/4 teaspoon lemon extract

> *The Junior's Way—*
> Pick firm apples that will hold their shape while they are simmering and poaching in the sweet cider syrup. Look for Rome Beauty, Delicious, or Cortland.

1. Combine the cider, sugar, cinnamon, and salt in a heavy saucepan and bring to a full boil over high heat. Let the syrup boil for 5 minutes.

2. Add the apples and raisins, reduce the heat to medium, and continue to simmer until the apples are tender and the raisins plump up, about 15 minutes. Watch closely and stir the preserves occasionally to keep the apples from sticking.

3. Mix the cornstarch and the water together in a small bowl until the cornstarch thoroughly dissolves. Whisk in a little hot cider sauce, then drizzle this mixture into the hot cider mixture in the saucepan while stirring constantly.

4. Bring the mixture to a full boil and let it continue to boil until it thickens slightly, about 2 minutes. Remove the preserves from the heat and stir in the vanilla and lemon extracts. Serve as hot preserves with pancakes or French toast, or as a warm conserve with roasted pork or freshly baked ham.

Homemade Potato
Pancakes

*T*HE MENU AT Junior's still features many specialties one expects to find at a Jewish deli—and luckily, it probably always will.

So, I wasn't surprised to find authentic potato pancakes being served every day. As expected, they're made the traditional way, from potatoes that have been put through an old-fashioned grinder, the type you churn by hand.

If you don't have one, just grate them by hand on a box grater or in a food processor, using the grating disk.

MAKES A DOZEN 4-INCH PANCAKES

2 pounds all-purpose boiling potatoes

1 cup grated onions

½ cup all-purpose flour

1 tablespoon baking powder

1 tablespoon sugar

1 tablespoon salt

½ teaspoon ground white pepper

2 extra-large eggs, beaten

3 tablespoons unsalted butter

1 tablespoon vegetable oil

Sour cream or applesauce

The Junior's Way—
When making these pancakes, use all-purpose boiling potatoes, which are high in starch and low in moisture.

1. Peel and grate or finely shred the potatoes (you need 4 cups of potatoes) and let them stand in ice water for 15 minutes.

2. Fill a medium-sized pan half-full with water and bring it to a boil over high heat. Drop in the potatoes and onions and blanch for 2 minutes. Pour the vegetables through a colander and squeeze out the excess water; pat dry on paper towels, then transfer to a large bowl.

continued

3. Mix the flour, baking powder, sugar, salt, and pepper together in a cup and toss with the potatoes and onions. Fold in the eggs just until the potatoes are coated. Do not overmix the batter at this stage, as this can make the pancakes tough and heavy.

4. Heat the butter and oil in a large nonstick skillet over medium heat until the butter melts. For each cake, scoop about ⅓ cup of the batter onto the hot griddle, making 4-inch cakes about 1 inch apart. Fry the cakes until golden brown and crispy on both sides, about 6 minutes in all. Watch the heat closely so the skillet does not get too hot; you want the pancakes to fry just fast enough to turn a golden brown on the outside (no darker) and cook the potatoes on the inside. Serve the pancakes immediately with sour cream or applesauce.

Freezing Tip—If you have some potato pancakes left over, slip them into self-sealing freezer bags and keep them in the freezer for up to 1 month. To serve, preheat the oven to 375°F. Place the frozen potato cakes directly on the middle oven rack and heat until hot and sizzling, about 8 minutes.

Blueberry Muffins

*A*S YOU MIGHT expect, Junior's muffins are towering peaks of sweet heaven. These fresh blueberry ones even have some mashed berries in the batter, giving more fresh berry flavor in every bite. Serve them piping hot, right out of the oven as Junior's often does. Or, halve them and grill them in a skillet with a little melted butter.

MAKES 6 JUMBO OR A DOZEN STANDARD TOWERING MUFFINS

2¼ cups all-purpose flour

1 tablespoon baking powder

½ teaspoon salt

½ teaspoon ground cinnamon

½ cup (1 stick) unsalted butter, at room temperature

1¼ cups sugar

The Junior's Way—Mix only half of the whole blueberries into the muffin batter. Save the rest for dropping on top of the muffins right before they go into the oven. This technique helps prevent the berries from sinking to the bottom and keeps them evenly suspended in the muffins as they bake.

2 extra-large eggs

1 tablespoon pure vanilla extract

3 cups fresh blueberries

½ cup milk

1. Preheat the oven to 400°F. Line 6 jumbo or 12 standard muffin tins with paper liners or butter them well. Mix the flour, baking powder, salt, and cinnamon together in a medium-size bowl and set aside.

2. Cream the butter in a large bowl with an electric mixer on high for 2 minutes. Then, with the mixer still running, gradually add the sugar, then the eggs, one at a time. Continue beating until the mixture is creamy and light yellow. Beat in the vanilla. Mash ⅔ cup of the berries and beat them into the batter.

3. Reduce the speed of the mixer to medium. Beat in one third of the flour mixture, half of the milk, then one third more of the flour, the remaining milk, and the rest of the flour. Beat the batter until airy and well combined, about 1 minute more. Gently fold in half of the remaining whole berries with a large spoon.

4. Fill the muffin cups with the batter almost up to the top. Drop the rest of the whole berries on top of the muffins. Bake the muffins at 400°F for 10 minutes. Reduce the oven temperature to 375°F and continue baking until the muffins are golden brown and set in the center, about 15 minutes more. These muffins are "at their best" when served freshly baked, hot from the oven.

Rugelach

*Y*OU DON'T HAVE to wait for Hanukkah to enjoy this traditional holiday specialty. Rugelach are baked every day at Junior's. My favorite ones are these rolled up with cinnamon, raisins, and walnuts inside. Naturally, they begin with the traditional rich cream-cheese-and-butter pastry. For some reason, though, rugelach made at Junior's taste richer, more moist, more buttery, more cinnamony, and just better than any others I can remember.

MAKES 40 PASTRIES

FOR THE CREAM CHEESE PASTRY

2 cups all-purpose flour

1 teaspoon salt

1/4 teaspoon ground mace

1 cup (2 sticks) unsalted butter, at room temperature

1 8-ounce package cream cheese (the regular variety, not light Neufchâtel cream cheese)

1/2 cup confectioners' sugar

2 extra-large eggs

2 teaspoons pure vanilla extract

FOR THE RAISIN AND WALNUT FILLING

2 cups dark raisins

2 cups very finely chopped walnuts (not chopped so fine that they look powdery)

1 cup fine crumbs (macaroons, yellow cake, or vanilla wafers)

FOR THE CINNAMON SUGAR

1/2 cup granulated sugar

1 tablespoon cinnamon

FOR THE GLAZE

1 extra-large egg

1 tablespoon water

The Junior's Way—

The bakers at Junior's save everything—and they find a way they can use it. Cake crumbs or macaroon crumbs are the start of this rugelach filling. If you don't have any cookies or yellow cake, crumble up a few slices of pound cake (it's usually easy to buy at the bakery). Granulated walnuts, which are walnuts that have been chopped very, very fine, but not to the point they are powdery, are also an important ingredient.

1. Mix the flour, salt, and mace together in a medium-size bowl and set aside.

2. Place the butter and cream cheese in a large bowl and beat with a mixer on high until light yellow and creamy. While the motor is still running, gradually add the confectioners' sugar. Beat in the eggs, one at a time, then blend in the vanilla.

3. Using a wooden spoon, stir in the flour mixture just until it disappears. Turn the pastry onto a lightly floured board and shape into a 6-inch disk, then wrap it in plastic wrap and refrigerate for 30 minutes.

4. Meanwhile, preheat the oven to 375°F and butter 2 baking sheets. Make the filling by tossing the raisins, walnuts, and crumbs in a medium-size bowl. Toss the granulated sugar and cinnamon together in a cup. Whisk the egg with the water to make the glaze in a small bowl.

5. To shape the rugelach: Roll out the pastry into a rectangle that's 20 inches wide and 18 inches long. Brush the pastry with about half of the egg glaze. Evenly spoon on all of the raisin filling, then sprinkle with all of the cinnamon-sugar mixture.

6. Using a pastry cutter or sharp knife, cut the pastry lengthwise into 10 rows, each 2 inches wide and 18 inches long. Cut each row crosswise into four equal pieces. You will have 40 pieces, each 4½ inches long and 2 inches wide. Starting with the narrow end of each pastry, roll up the rugelach jelly-roll-style and place seam-side-down on the baking sheets. Brush the rugelach with the remaining egg glaze and bake them for 15 minutes or just until light brown. Cool on wire racks. These store great in the freezer for up to 1 month.

Golden Corn Muffins

*S*OME CORN MUFFINS come out dry with a coarse grain—not so at Junior's. Instead, Junior's muffins are so tender with such a fine grain that they're almost cakelike. But they still have that golden corn look and taste, plus enough baking powder and beating, to let them rise up high and stately in the oven.

MAKES 6 JUMBO OR A DOZEN STANDARD TOWERING MUFFINS

1½ cups all-purpose flour

½ cup yellow cornmeal

1 tablespoon baking powder

1 teaspoon salt

½ cup (1 stick) unsalted butter, at room temperature

¼ cup vegetable shortening

½ cup sugar

2 extra-large eggs

1 tablespoon pure vanilla extract

1 cup milk

The Junior's Way—
To get muffins with high peaks, bake them in a hot oven (400°F) for a few minutes. This burst of heat gives the baking powder and eggs extra rising power, causing the muffins to peak up high in the center.

1. Preheat the oven to 400°F. Line 6 jumbo or 12 regular muffin tins with paper liners or butter them well. Mix the flour, cornmeal, baking powder, and salt together in a medium-sized bowl and set aside.

2. Cream the butter and shortening in a large bowl with an electric mixer on high for 2 minutes. Then, with the mixer still running, gradually add the sugar, then the eggs, one at a time. Continue beating until the batter is creamy and light yellow. Beat in the vanilla.

3. Reduce the speed of the mixer to low. Beat in half of the flour mixture, then half of the milk, beating about 1 minute after adding each. Repeat, beating in the rest of the flour mixture, then the rest of the milk. Beat the batter until well blended, about 1 minute more, then spoon it into the muffin cups, almost up to the top.

4. Bake the muffins at 400°F for 10 minutes. Reduce the oven temperature to 375°F and continue baking until the muffins are light golden brown and set in the center, about 15 minutes more.

Cornbread

STOP BY JUNIOR'S any time of day and you'll be greeted with your own personal basket overflowing with fresh bread. Almost always there will be squares of just-baked cornbread tucked inside. It's not like any other cornbread I've ever tasted—this one has that perfect combination of flour and cornmeal and rises light and high in the oven. And thanks to a batter using both oil and butter, this cornbread is exceptionally tender and melts-in-your-mouth, while still having that great buttery flavor. This recipe makes enough so everyone can have seconds, just like at Junior's.

MAKES A DOZEN 3-INCH SQUARES OF CORNBREAD

3 cups all-purpose flour

1¼ cups yellow cornmeal

¾ cup sugar

2 tablespoons baking powder

1 tablespoon salt

4 extra-large eggs

1 cup milk

1 cup water

½ cup (1 stick) unsalted butter, melted

⅓ cup vegetable oil

1 teaspoon pure vanilla extract

The Junior's Way—
Add a little vanilla to the batter to bring out the corn and butter flavors. Be sure to preheat the baking pan enough so the batter sizzles when it's added to the pan and forms a light brown crust as the cornbread bakes.

continued

1. Butter a 13 × 9 × 2-inch baking pan and place it on an oven rack in the middle of the oven. Preheat the oven to 400°F.

2. Mix the flour, cornmeal, sugar, baking powder, and salt together in a large bowl and make a well in the center of these dry ingredients with a spoon.

3. Beat the eggs in another large bowl with an electric mixer on high until they're light yellow and slightly thickened, about 3 minutes. Beat in the milk, water, butter, oil, and vanilla.

4. Pour this egg mixture all at once into the well in the dry ingredients. Stir the dry ingredients into the wet ones just until it comes together in a batter (do not overmix at this stage, or the cornbread can become tough).

5. Pour the batter into the hot baking pan (it should sizzle!) and bake until the cornbread is slightly golden brown, about 25 minutes. Cut the cornbread into twelve 3-inch squares. Stack the squares up high in a basket (just like they do at Junior's) and serve hot or warm.

Welcome to Junior's!

Vienna Rolls

EARLY EVERY MORNING and several times throughout the day, the bakers are busy baking these heavenly rolls. They knead the dough the easy way, with a dough-hook attachment on their giant mixer. It mixes and kneads the dough at the same time, automatically.

Shaping rolls in the Junior's bakery is as simple as pressing a button. They have a special roll-shaping machine that shapes a dozen perfect rolls in less than half a minute. But even if you don't have this machine, or maybe not even a dough hook on your mixer, try these rolls. They're easy. Better yet, make a double recipe, as they disappear fast.

Serve them warm, as is, with a bowl of steaming soup, or use them to make overstuffed corned beef or pastrami sandwiches as they do at Junior's. These are the rolls that you get free with every bowl of soup and every salad you order.

MAKES A DOZEN ROLLS ABOUT 4 INCHES IN DIAMETER (THIS RECIPE DOUBLES EASILY)

3¼ cups unbleached all-purpose flour

4 tablespoons sugar

2 tablespoons malted milk powder

1 tablespoon salt

1 cup water (105° to 115°F)

2 ¼-ounce packages active dry yeast

1 extra-large egg

⅓ cup vegetable oil

FOR GLAZING THE ROLLS

1 extra-large egg

½ teaspoon vegetable oil

The Junior's Way—

The secret to the fine grain of these rolls is to knead them for fifteen minutes, but no longer. Be sure to stop the machine before the machine action warms up the dough. If the temperature of the dough gets warmer than 115°F, it can kill the yeast.

continued

1950s—Up from Brooklyn's Turbulent Change . . . Junior's

1. In a medium-sized bowl, mix together the flour, 3 tablespoons of the sugar, the malted milk powder, and salt and set aside.

2. Next make the yeast sponge: Stir the water, both packages of the yeast, and the remaining tablespoon of sugar in a small bowl until dissolved. Let the mixture stand until it is foamy and light, about 5 minutes.

3. Meanwhile, using an electric mixer equipped with a dough hook or a paddle, beat the egg and the ⅓ cup oil in a large bowl on high until light yellow. Reduce the speed to low and beat in the yeast mixture, then the flour mixture. "Knead" in the flour mixture by beating the dough on high for 15 minutes (the dough will be smooth and elastic).

4. Transfer the dough to a well-buttered bowl, turning it over once to coat it well with the butter (the dough will be sticky). Cover the dough and let it rise at room temperature until it's double in size (this will probably take about 1 hour).

5. Preheat the oven to 400°F and butter a baking sheet. Punch the dough down with your fist to deflate it, then turn it out onto a lightly floured surface. Flour your hands and lightly knead the dough until it's no longer sticky, about 2 minutes.

6. Using kitchen shears, cut the dough into 4 equal pieces, then each piece into 3 more equal pieces, making 12 little mounds of dough, all the same size. Flour your hands well. Pick up each piece of dough in the palm of your hand and shape it into a rounded roll with a smooth top. Place the rolls about 2 inches apart on the baking sheet.

7. To make the glaze: Whisk the other egg with the ½ teaspoon oil and brush on top of each roll. Cover the rolls and let them rise until they're light and doubled in size, about 30 minutes more. Bake the rolls until they are golden and set, about 10 minutes. Be sure to watch the rolls closely as they bake, as this dough is very rich and can brown quickly. The rolls should bake only until they are golden brown, not dark brown. Serve the rolls warm or at room temperature or use them to make overstuffed sandwiches filled with roast beef, corned beef, or chicken or shrimp salad.

Welcome to Junior's!

Poppyseed Rolls

THESE ROLLS MAKE perfect sandwich buns, especially when they're spread with a spicy mustard and stuffed with pastrami, corned beef, or roast beef. Start with the basic recipe for Vienna Rolls. Then sprinkle the rolls generously with poppy seeds before baking.

MAKES A DOZEN ROLLS, ABOUT 4 INCHES IN DIAMETER (THIS RECIPE DOUBLES EASILY)

1 recipe Vienna Rolls (page 135)
¼ cup poppy seeds

1. Mix, knead, and shape the dough into 12 little mounds of dough, as for Vienna Rolls.

2. Glaze the rolls with the egg wash, as for Vienna Rolls, then generously sprinkle the tops with poppy seeds (you will need about 1 teaspoon of poppy seeds for each roll).

3. Preheat the oven to 375°F. Cover the rolls and let them rise until they're light and doubled in size, about 30 minutes. Bake the rolls until golden and set, about 10 minutes. Be sure to watch carefully, as the poppy seeds may cause the tops to brown fast.

The Junior's Way—
Sprinkle the rolls with poppy seeds, leaving some dough peeking through. You can also make sesame seed rolls by substituting the same amount of sesame seeds for the poppy seeds.

1950s—Up from Brooklyn's Turbulent Change . . . Junior's

Creamy Cole Slaw

EVEN COLE SLAW is different at Junior's. It's coarsely shredded so it stays crisp and slightly crunchy until you eat it. Plus there are strips of carrots that add an extra touch of color. But you see the real difference when you take a bite: The flavors of cabbage and carrots come right through—they're not masked by the dressing.

The dressing's just creamy enough to coat the vegetables. It has a very subtle bite of vinegar with the mildest hint of garlic, and a little sprinkling of sugar to smooth out the flavors.

Come to Junior's after eleven o'clock in the morning and, up until closing, you'll find a bowl of cole slaw on your table or in front of you at the counter. Serve yourself as much as you want.

When the slaw in the bowl gets low, a waiter's sure to notice it before you do, and fill the bowl again until it's brimming over with more freshly made slaw.

MAKES 3 QUARTS COLE SLAW

FOR THE MAYONNAISE DRESSING

2 cups *Hellmann's* Real Mayonnaise (not the light variety)

2 tablespoons cider vinegar

2 tablespoons sugar

1 teaspoon minced garlic

1 teaspoon ground white pepper

1 teaspoon salt

FOR THE VEGETABLES

5 large carrots (½ pound), peeled

1 head green cabbage (2 pounds)

The Junior's Way—
Make the mayonnaise dressing first so it's ready to toss on the slaw vegetables as soon as they are shredded. Cut the carrots first, then the cabbage, and quickly toss them with the dressing to keep the cabbage from turning brown.

1. Measure all of the dressing ingredients into a small glass bowl, then stir until mixed well.

2. Coarsely shred the carrots in the food processor, using the medium-coarse shredding blade, or shred them with a box grater or carrot peeler into long thin strips about ¼ inch wide (you will need about 2 cups). Wash the cabbage and remove the core with the point of a sharp knife. Coarsely shred it in a food processor that's fitted with a medium shredding blade, or cut the head with a sharp knife into thin long strips about ¼ inch wide (you will have about 12 cups).

3. Toss the cabbage and carrots together in your largest salad bowl. Quickly pour over the dressing and toss until all of the vegetables are well coated. Cover the bowl and refrigerate until the vegetables wilt a little, about 15 minutes. The flavors blend even better if you let the slaw marinate in the refrigerator for about an hour. Just toss again before serving to redistribute any dressing that might be in the bottom of the bowl.

1950s—Up from Brooklyn's Turbulent Change . . . Junior's

Pickled Beets

ONCE LUNCHTIME ROLLS around, a bowl of these beets is always nearby, right alongside the cole slaw, pickles, onions, and pickled peppers.

These beets are just like they should be—juicy, bright reddish-purple, slightly spicy, pleasantly pickled, with just a hint of sugar.

Eat as many as you like . . . they go with almost anything, from a chef's salad to meat loaf to a deli sandwich. And when the bowl gets empty, there's always a waiter nearby who fills it up again before you even notice.

MAKES 1 QUART BEETS

3 pounds trimmed fresh beets, unpeeled

1 tablespoon pickling spices

1 tablespoon salt

FOR THE SAUCE

3 cups sugar

2½ cups water

2 cups distilled white vinegar

2 cups slivered white onions

The Junior's Way—
To peel beets the easy way, cook them first. Then just rinse them under cold water and slip off their skins with your fingers.

1. Place the beets in a large saucepan, add enough water to cover, and sprinkle in the pickling spices and salt. Bring to a boil over high heat, reduce the heat to medium, and cook the beets, without covering them, until they're tender, about 30 minutes. Transfer the beets with a slotted spoon to a colander and rinse with cold water. Discard the cooking water and pickling spices.

2. When the beets are cool enough to handle, slip off their skins with your fingers and slice them ¼ inch thick (you will have about 4 cups).

3. In the same saucepan, combine all of the ingredients for the sauce. Bring to a boil over high heat and cook until the sugar dissolves completely, about 5 minutes.

4. Reduce the heat to medium, add the beets, and simmer in the open pan for 15 minutes until the sauce has reduced about a third and has thickened slightly.

5. Let the beets cool in the sauce for 30 minutes at room temperature, then transfer them with the sauce to a bowl. Cover the beets and let them marinate in the refrigerator a few hours or overnight. These pickled beets taste their best when they're chilled. If you have any left over, they'll keep just fine in a covered container in the refrigerator for up to 2 weeks.

Mac and Cheese Pie

COMFORT FOOD— Junior's-style. Nothing fancy, just good ol' creamy macaroni and cheese like Grandma used to make, provided you were as lucky as I to have a grandma who could really cook!

Here's a new twist to Junior's Mac and Cheese—it's baked in a pie plate with bread crumbs as a crust, then served up in a slice, just like a pie.

MAKES ONE 9-INCH DEEP-DISH PIE

¼ cup plain dry bread crumbs

1½ teaspoons salt

1 teaspoon olive oil

2 cups (8 ounces) uncooked macaroni

6 tablespoons (¾ stick) unsalted butter

½ cup chopped onion

⅓ cup flour

¾ teaspoon dry mustard

½ teaspoon ground white pepper

¼ teaspoon ground nutmeg

2½ cups milk

2½ cups (12 ounces) shredded sharp Cheddar cheese

1 drop red food coloring (optional)

1 drop yellow food coloring (optional)

Paprika

The Junior's Way—

Let the Mac and Cheese Pie stand until set, about fifteen minutes after it comes out of the oven. This is just long enough for the pie to firm up so you can slice it easily.

continued

1. Preheat the oven to 375°F and butter a 9-inch deep-dish pie plate. Sprinkle the bottom and the sides with the bread crumbs.

2. Fill a large pot half-full with water, add ½ teaspoon of the salt and the oil, and bring it to a boil over high heat. Stir in the macaroni and cook without covering the pot for about 15 minutes or just until the macaroni is almost tender. Transfer the macaroni to a colander, rinse with cold water, and drain well (you need 5 cups).

3. Meanwhile, melt the butter in a large skillet over medium-high heat. Add the onion and sauté until soft, about 5 minutes. Stir in the flour, the remaining teaspoon of salt, the mustard, pepper, and nutmeg, then cook until bubbly, about 1 minute.

4. Gradually stir in all of the milk, and continue to cook and stir until the sauce simmers and thickens. Add 2 cups of the cheese, plus the red and yellow food colorings, if you wish, and stir until completely melted and blended (the color of the sauce should be light golden). Remove the sauce from the heat and fold in the macaroni. Spoon the macaroni into the pie plate, mounding it high in the center, top with the remaining ½ cup of cheese, and sprinkle generously with the paprika.

5. Bake the pie until golden brown and bubbly, about 25 minutes. Let the pie stand on a wire rack until set, about 15 minutes, then slice it into wedges. Store any leftover pie in the refrigerator.

Baked Meat Loaf

S TART WITH ONLY good beef chuck and ask the butcher to put it through the grinder twice," says the chef. "Mix it with sautéed vegetables, seasonings, crumbs, and spices.

"Then shape it into a loaf and sprinkle with onions. The real secret is the way I bake it: surrounded with water with more onions sprinkled around and on top of the meat loaf. Each loaf comes out of the oven moist and juicy, yet just firm enough to make it easy to slice."

MAKES ONE MEAT LOAF, ABOUT 12 INCHES LONG
AND 6 INCHES WIDE

2 tablespoons (¼ stick) unsalted butter

2 tablespoons vegetable oil

2 extra-large yellow onions, chopped (2½ cups)

1 large green bell pepper, seeded and chopped (1½ cups)

3 large cloves garlic, minced

3 pounds ground beef chuck (ask the butcher to grind
    it twice)

⅓ cup seasoned bread crumbs

¼ cup A.1. Steak Sauce

1 tablespoon salt

1 teaspoon ground white pepper

3 extra-large eggs

FOR THE SAUCE

1 recipe Mushroom Sauce (optional) (page 78)

The Junior's Way—

To bake a moist meat loaf, shape it in a baking pan with 2- to 3-inch sides. Pat the loaf, leaving some space all around the sides. Surround the loaf with water and sprinkle onions on top of the loaf and in the water for some extra flavor. After baking the loaf, resist the temptation to slice it right away. Pour off the water and let it stand about ten minutes to let it set up, which makes it much easier to slice.

1. Preheat the oven to 350°F and butter a 13 × 9 × 3-inch baking pan.

2. Heat the butter and oil in a large skillet over medium-high heat until the butter melts. Add 1½ cups of the onions, the green pepper, and garlic and sauté until crisp-tender, about 5 minutes, then transfer to a large bowl.

3. Add the beef, bread crumbs, steak sauce, salt, and pepper and mix thoroughly. Whisk the eggs until frothy and mix with the beef mixture until they disappear.

4. Transfer this meat mixture to the baking dish and shape into a loaf about 12 inches long, 6 inches wide, and 3 inches high, mounding it slightly in the center. Top the loaf with one-third of the remaining onions. Fill the dish half-full with water and sprinkle the rest of the onions in the water.

5. Bake the meat loaf until it is firm in the center, 45 minutes to 1 hour, depending on the height of the loaf. Pour off the water and let the loaf stand until it firms up, about 10 minutes before slicing. Serve with Mushroom Sauce, if you wish.

Home Fries

AS YOU MIGHT expect, home fries are the real authentic thing at Junior's—and they always come out the same. The potatoes are snow-white (not off-white or gray), perfectly cubed, and cooked to a golden brown.

Take a bite and enjoy their fresh buttery potato flavor with just a hint of garlic. Naturally, you'll also find slivers of onions sprinkled throughout.

MAKES 4 SERVINGS

3 pounds all-purpose potatoes

1 teaspoon salt

½ cup (1 stick) unsalted butter

2 tablespoons vegetable oil

1 extra-large yellow onion, cut into thin strips

1 tablespoon minced garlic

Paprika

The Junior's Way—First sauté the onion and garlic in a little butter and oil on the griddle or in a skillet just until they begin to soften. Then place the potatoes on top of the onion and scramble them with a spatula to mix well. This way, all of the ingredients are ready to serve at the same time.

1. Peel the potatoes and cut them into ½-inch dice. Fill a large saucepan half-full with water. Add the potatoes and ½ teaspoon of the salt and bring the mixture to a boil over high heat.

2. Reduce the heat to medium and simmer the potatoes until they are crisp-tender when tested with a fork, about 10 to 13 minutes (be sure to remove them from the heat before they start breaking apart). Transfer the potatoes to a colander and rinse with cold water. Be sure to drain the potatoes well (you need 8 cups of potatoes).

3. Heat half of the butter and all of the oil on a griddle or in a large skillet. Add the onion and garlic and cook until the vegetables soften, about 5 minutes. Leave them on the griddle.

4. Spoon the potatoes on top of the onion mixture and sprinkle generously with paprika. Using a metal spatula, toss the home fries continuously until they are well mixed. Cook, turning often and adding the remaining butter as needed. The potatoes are ready to serve when they are golden brown and slightly crunchy on the edges, usually after about 15 minutes of cooking.

Welcome to Junior's!

Toasted Coconut
Custard Pie

*I*F YOU LIKE a creamy custard pie and you love coconut, you're in for a real
treat.

Junior's has been baking coconut custard pies for over forty years—and each
one always comes out perfectly set and creamy, with chunks of coconut in every bite.
Look closely—the top of the pie has been generously showered with coconut, which
toasts and gives the pie a delicious golden glow when it comes out of the oven.

MAKES ONE 9-INCH DEEP-DISH PIE

½ recipe Pie Pastry, enough for a single-crust pie (page 40)

4 extra-large eggs

⅔ cup sugar

1 teaspoon cornstarch

¼ teaspoon salt

1⅓ cups heavy cream

1 cup milk

1 tablespoon pure vanilla extract

1½ cups flaked coconut

2 tablespoons unsalted butter, cut into small pieces

¼ teaspoon ground nutmeg

The Junior's Way—
Be sure to save ¼ cup of the
coconut to sprinkle on the
top. It bakes up golden and
toasty, giving a little crunch
in every bite.

1. Preheat the oven to 425°F and butter a 9-inch deep-dish pie plate.

2. Mix and chill the pastry. Roll it out ⅛ inch thick on a lightly floured surface and trim to a 15-inch circle. Transfer the pastry to the pie plate, leaving a 1½-
inch overhang. Fold under the edge to stand up 1 inch high and flute. Prick it all over
with the tines of a fork. Place the unbaked shell in the freezer for 15 minutes.

3. To partially bake the shell before filling it, place a piece of foil in the center and weigh it down with pie weights, uncooked beans, or rice. Blind-bake the
crust just until it begins to set, about 8 minutes; remove the foil and pie weights and

return the shell to the oven until it starts to brown, about 4 minutes more. Transfer the crust from the oven to a cooling rack, then reduce the oven temperature to 325°F.

4. While the crust is baking, make the coconut custard filling. Using an electric mixer set on high, beat the eggs in a large bowl until thick and light yellow, about 5 minutes. Mix the sugar, cornstarch, and salt together in a small bowl and beat this mixture into the eggs until thoroughly mixed. Reduce the speed of the mixer to medium. Add the cream, milk, and vanilla and beat the filling until light and frothy, about 3 minutes more. Stir in 1¼ cups of the coconut. Pour the filling into the partially baked crust, dot with the butter, and sprinkle with the nutmeg.

5. Bake the pie for 30 minutes, sprinkle with the remaining ¼ cup of coconut, and continue baking the pie until the filling is golden, the coconut is toasty, and the filling jiggles only slightly in the center, about 20 to 30 minutes more. The pie is ready to come out of the oven when a knife inserted in the center comes out clean. Cool the pie on a wire rack for 1 hour. Serve the pie at room temperature or refrigerate until it's cold. Store any leftover pie in the refrigerator.

Welcome to Junior's!

CHAPTER FOUR

1960s— When Brooklyn . . . Rumbled

THE WHOLE COUNTRY suffered through ten years of nonstop up-and-down emotions—hope and excitement, terror and grief, anger, surprise—even shock. We survived broken traditions and painful divisions between young and old, black and white, hawks and doves. There was nothing mediocre about the decade of the 1960s; it was intense. Every day of it.

Brooklyn did not escape the mix-up that the country

went through. No way. We were a microcosm of it. By New Year's Eve in 1970, neighborhood changes, racial tensions, and urban redevelopment had put "the good old days" far behind us.

The decade was just in its infancy when a catastrophic omen crashed down on Brooklyn—literally shattering any sense of security we had. In the winter of 1960 a commercial jetliner demolished a congested neighborhood of brownstones and shops in Park Slope. It was December 12 and the United DC-8 was the first commercial jet carrying passengers to crash anywhere in the United States. With eighty-five people aboard, it had been struggling to stay aloft after a collision with another aircraft over Staten Island. Short of Idlewild Airport by a few miles, the pilot tried to keep the nose up for the few hundred yards he needed to make an emergency landing in Long Meadow in Prospect Park. It was 10:30 on a foggy morning; the air was dense with falling snow.

The crippled liner hit Park Slope near the corner of Flatbush and Seventh Avenues, amid homes and shops, two blocks short of Long Meadow, about a twenty-minute walk from Junior's front door. To people eight and ten blocks away, it felt like an earthquake as the jet crashed and broke apart. The fuselage skidded into a church and the impact killed the caretaker there. The tail section slid down Seventh Avenue toward Flatbush, taking the lives of five more men—a sanitation worker who was removing snow, two men selling Christmas trees on the sidewalk, a dentist, and a butcher—before it came to a stop. One wing took the roof off a house on Sterling Place. When everything stopped moving, the wing tip was inside the fourth-floor bedroom of the house next door. No one in either house was hurt, but I think once damages were estimated, United had to pay one of those home owners something like $2,500, a huge settlement at that time.

Sadly, all passengers and crew, except for a twelve-year-old boy, died within minutes of the crash. An outpouring of prayers, flowers, and donations from Brooklynites couldn't pull the boy through and he passed away at Park Slope's Methodist Hospital a few days afterward. Brooklyn had suffered tragedy before—serious trolley collisions, subway wrecks, electrical fires. But never had havoc fallen on us from the sky. The plane was filled with people coming to New York for the holidays.

Welcome to Junior's!

Getting to the "New Frontier" Was Rough

President Kennedy made his famous "Ask not what your country can do for you" inaugural speech a few weeks later in 1961 and there seemed to be a new burst of optimism. Our college graduates signed up for the new Peace Corps in droves. We believed things would settle down in Brooklyn, and the United States was going to be the first to fly to the moon, the New Frontier.

Then the Berlin Wall that separated communists from the free world made the Cold War colder and the Soviets came off as bigger bullies than ever. In Alabama, Mississippi, and Georgia, the Reverend Martin Luther King, Jr., started a

Civil rights demonstrators became as common a sight in downtown Brooklyn as anywhere else during the 1960s. This demonstration was not too far from Junior's on Court Street. Courtesy of the Brooklyn Historical Society

1960s—When Brooklyn . . . Rumbled

nonviolent war—something we had never seen before. But his peaceful protests against laws that for years had discriminated against blacks were met with brutal and humiliating violence. The images from those days as they came to us on television are unforgettable. Ordinary black people sat at a "white-only" lunch counter and angry whites taunted them—poured what looked like Cream of Wheat all over them. The black people didn't fight back, didn't retaliate.

It was amazing to us in Brooklyn where even today conversation can be a contact sport. Differences of opinion in those days were often settled with fists. These peaceful demonstrations continued in spite of violent retaliation by southern lawmen who wielded clubs, unleashed dogs, and opened fire hoses on demonstrators until long after the Civil Rights Act was passed later in the decade.

When President Kennedy was assassinated in 1963, the mood of Brooklynites, the majority of whom had supported the Irish-Catholic presidential nominee, spiraled from optimism into shock and sadness. Junior's was closed, as were all businesses throughout the city, during his funeral.

Soon, the Vietnam War escalated under President Johnson. Some young men began to resist the draft in obvious objection to the war early in 1964. The first ever ghetto riot astounded us as L.A.'s Watts burned up in racial and economic protests. Also around that time, Cassius Clay emerged. He was the unstoppable African-American boxer and 1960 Olympic light-heavyweight champion who later became Muhammad Ali. He was radical, loudmouthed, poetic, colorful—a different kind of hero. He danced like a butterfly and stung big Sonny Liston like a bee for the heavyweight boxing title of the world in 1964. He was, as he told everyone, "the greatest." In 1967, he was the first sports hero to resist the draft. For that he was stripped of his title. And we were again without a champion.

Sometimes a Sad Song Just Won't Get Better

Throughout the turmoil of the 1960s, Brooklynites endured the aforementioned plane crash, a hundred-day-plus newspaper strike in late 1962, the embarrassing rookie season for the New York Mets in which the team lost 120 games, and a subway strike in 1966 that stranded everyone for twelve days. We also endured the first major blackout in 1965. It trapped hundreds of thousands underground in subways, and here at Junior's we had no lights, no radio, no TV. We also had no way of finding out what had happened. We lit hundreds of candles and kept cooking on the gas flames. The place was full of smoke from the grill and packed with people who were drinking and eating freely because we all thought the world was coming to an end.

We survived the Beatles, too. They landed in New York in 1964, took *The Ed Sullivan Show* by storm, and then packed Shea Stadium as the Mets could not. They had an irreverent style, a melodic rock sound, and a kind of innocence or naiveté that I guess everyone needed. Anyone less than twenty-five years old gravitated to them like floundering sailors who head for a buoy.

The Beatles had hair, too! Lots and lots of it. By 1966, most clean-shaven, short-haired young men who went to college in the neighborhood and ordered something at Junior's counter every day had turned into Beatle-like, long-haired, bearded guys with sideburns wearing tie-dyed T-shirts. Young, well-groomed girls who had once emulated Jackie Kennedy, wearing slim-line dresses and pillbox hats, turned into psychedelic Pocahontases in long bright dresses, beads, and sandals. They were the look of the peace movement that rejected the government's pro-war efforts from a platform of flower power. Make Love Not War. Still, the war went on.

President Johnson bowed out of the reelection fight in 1968. Whoever heard of a Democrat doing that? Our New York senator Robert Kennedy ran for the nomination that year. He had been a friend to the working people of Brooklyn and had tried to keep the Navy Yard open when the Defense Department threatened to close it. He had run for the Senate in 1965 and had a big slice of cheesecake at Junior's while campaigning. Brooklyn was pro-Bobby. When he was also felled by an assassin in June of 1968, only two months after Martin Luther King, Jr., had been murdered in Atlanta, shock, bitterness, and cynicism about the war hung over the November elections. Richard Nixon, more a hawk than a dove, won the presidency, even while the first ever antiwar rock musical, *Hair*, was selling out on Broadway.

Meanwhile . . . Downtown Where?

The new breed of stay-at-home TV fans changed the theater life of downtown Brooklyn. They stopped coming here for movies, and the Paramount Theater was the first to close its doors after its last shows in 1963. Long Island University leased the entire

building and turned it into Metcalfe Hall, part of their campus. But the place is still an attraction. The baroque orchestra seating and proscenium became a gymnasium, which is still in use today. The Wurlitzer organ remains—it blasts triumphantly for awards ceremonies and convocations.

The lobby, a copy of the Great Hall of Mirrors of Versailles, is a student cafeteria now. Even though the tables are Formica and not imported marble, it's one of the more ornate student eateries anywhere. And the grand winding staircase with its antique brass railings leads to the spacious mezzanine which once welcomed audience members to the balcony. The mezzanine is simply a lounge area these days where students rest, read, or play cards. Vintage movie posters and photos of the original Paramount facade adorn the walls. What used to be balcony seating is the academic office area.

The Fox Theater closed too, but not until it hosted an Easter vacation rock 'n' roll show that debuted Little Stevie Wonder in 1963. Like the Paramount, the Fox couldn't make enough to pay its bills and closed in 1966. There's not even a brick of the

The Brooklyn Paramount had been the second-largest movie house in New York. By 1963 it had become a most unusual gymnasium for Long Island University. The conversion kept the ninety-foot ceilings, marble drinking fountains, ornate statuary, and Wurlitzer organ which still rises up from beneath a maple wood floor.
Courtesy of the Brooklyn Historical Society

original building left today. The Fulton-Nevins Street corner is now dominated by the new Con Edison building.

Until the Fox closed, we enjoyed a thriving, noisy business of teenagers who swarmed downtown for the school vacation shows. Junior's had a big fountain counter in those days—thirty-seven stools to accommodate a post-show rush (as compared to the fifteen that we have today). An egg cream cost thirty cents; a malted, forty cents; a Coke was a dime. Students from L.I.U. found refuge from cafeteria food here at Junior's and they've been coming ever since—our steakburger platters with fries and onion rings are one of their favorites.

The Albee Theater remained, attracting audiences for first-run movies. Until the mid-1970s when it did finally close, movie-goers there would still stop in at Junior's for dinner before or after a show. The Loew's Metropolitan down on Fulton

Welcome to Junior's!

remained open even into the 1980s. And smaller stores were moving into downtown, taking advantage of the thousands of people who worked in or lived near the area. Two larger stores, A&S and Martin's, were also doing good business.

The Navy Yard closed in 1966, even though Brooklyn borough powers and thousands of residents fought hard to keep it. In 1964 when word was out that the Defense Department would close the place, bus caravans of Brooklynites traveled to D.C. to try to save the Yard. There were posters, flyers, and handouts here in the restaurant for patrons to take home if they wanted to get involved in the fight.

"The shipyard earned 6 navy 'Es' given during World War II for excellence for work. On June 30 her last E will mark END for the Brooklyn Navy Yard."

—World-Telegram and Sun, February 1, 1966

In 1965 Bobby Kennedy visited the Yard and pledged his efforts to help protect the eleven thousand civilian jobs there. However, the Defense Department was

Bobby Kennedy campaigned for the Senate and for the presidential nomination in Brooklyn. Here he is in 1965 when he pledged to help keep the Navy Yard open. Courtesy of the Brooklyn Historical Society

having its day with cutbacks and it was so much cheaper to do ship work elsewhere. We lost the Yard, the jobs, three hundred acres of waterfront action, not to mention the business it meant to Junior's. It all seemed a continuation of the industry exodus that had begun in the 1950s. Even Mergenthaler Linotype, the company that made most of the world's typesetting machines, moved to Long Island. Other companies moved south, or to New Jersey, or anywhere taxes were lower.

Down on the Boardwalk?

In Coney Island, Luna Park burned down in 1962. They did not rebuild. Steeplechase Park closed in 1965. It could not keep up with rising property taxes as operating expenses went up, too. The place used to be twenty-some blocks long, dazzling with bright lights, and packed with people crowding the boardwalk, hotels, restaurants, beaches, and amusements. By the end of the 1960s there were three blocks left of Coney, plus, to our delight, the Parachute Jump, which the Lifesaver Candy Company had built for the 1939 World's Fair and moved to Coney in 1941. Large high-rise public housing replaced much of the strip. The place still attracts five million a year—a far cry from one million a day in the 1940s.

HEART OF THE MATTER

"Coney Island wasn't just a place, it was an emotion."

—Cousin Brucie Morrow, radio and TV personality

Let's Go to Junior's

Now, more than ever, Junior's became a destination. After the Paramount closed, we were the main attraction on the corner. Both of us were working here full time with my father during the sixties and we were raising our own families. But there was no way that we were removed from what was happening around us. When you run a restaurant, you may not be able to go out into the world much, but the world comes to you, day in and day out. Every race and every political issue comes through the door, sits down at the counter, and orders a slice of cheesecake, a cup of coffee, something.

Welcome to Junior's!

Politicians such as New York mayor John Lindsay, who was elected in 1965, and Bobby Kennedy, who campaigned for the New York Senate, made stops at Junior's complete with an entourage and photographers. Student protesters, marching workers, strikers, Long Island University student organizers, civil rights workers, working parents trying to envision a future, lawyers, borough politicians, and bureaucrats from the federal buildings nearby, teachers, nurses from Brooklyn Hospital down on DeKalb, salespeople, taxi drivers, ordinary downtown workers, the bewildered, and the adamant all found a home in Junior's. We became neutral ground where an irresistible bite of cheesecake attracted the bureaucrat, the radical student, the black teacher, and the white taxi driver.

"We lived on Avenue R in Flatbush. Whenever we went to visit our relatives in New Jersey, all four of us kids, my father, and my mother would pile into the car. On the way to Jersey, my father would swing by Junior's. We waited in the car until Mom came out with the two precious boxes. We didn't have to ask what was inside each one. We knew. It was a Junior's cheesecake. We never complained about going to see the relatives because we knew the day would end with a great big slice of Junior's cheesecake."

—Renée Nahas

Old Neighbors

For sixty years, Brooklyn had absorbed floods of immigrants who had created little villages of neighborhood life. They put down roots and became educators and leaders, builders, craftsmen, longshoremen, factory workers, restaurateurs, vaudevillians, opera stars, inventors, businesspeople, actors, artists, scientists, taxi drivers, civil servants, waiters, waitresses, cooks. They thrived here much as the ailanthus tree of Brooklyn does. If you live here, you come to know this tree, which mysteriously grows in backyards and vacant lots without ever being planted and without much help from anyone.

The Wonder Wheel, Parachute Jump, and some of Steeplechase Park are visible over the rooftop of Nathan's Famous Hot Dog stand on the corner of Surf and Stillwell in 1962. Steeplechase closed permanently soon after this picture was taken. Photo by Mike Zwerling, courtesy of the Brooklyn Historical Society

"The neighborhood watched over us from upstairs windows. It fed us, our friends, and most of our relatives. It observed every rite of passage. . . . In different languages and diverse cultural styles, neighborhoods blossomed."

—*Old New York*, WLIW-TV

Immigrants had built a Brooklyn culture of neighborhoods with strong multiethnic traditions of working families—Sunday suppers, block parties, baseball, unions, street games, religious celebrations, higher education, courtships at Coney Island, and marriages in local churches. Neighborhood streets teemed with activity and spontaneous sounds as diverse as doo-wop, bagpipes, opera, and oompah bands. Churches by the hundreds spilled forth sounds of Bach and gospel.

Bye-Bye, Brooklyn

When the first Brooklynites left in the 1950s, it was because they jumped at a chance to expand into a house with a yard at a mortgage rate that was unbeatable out in the new suburban housing tracts that were popping up east of us on Long Island.

They were the young Irish, Jewish, Italian, or German families, weary of cramped apartments over their fathers' or grandfathers' shoe repair shops in Bensonhurst or barber shops in New Utrecht or Brownsville. Who could blame them? They went to greener pastures and left behind friends and vacant apartments.

New Neighbors

The new immigrants—African Americans from the South, Puerto Ricans, Dominicans, Jamaicans, Trinidadians, some South Americans, all came just as others had—looking to better their lives. But what they encountered was a Brooklyn manipulated by a greed machine.

Bankers, real estate developers, and mortgage lenders controlled property values by redlining certain areas of Brooklyn. They unofficially agreed (by actually drawing red lines around neighborhoods on a Brooklyn map) which predominantly white areas would be targeted for growth so as to increase property values, and which neighborhoods would be ignored.

According to this practice, which was widely common before the Fair Housing Act in the late 1960s, a black family who owned a brownstone in redlined Bedford-Stuyvesant, for example, could not get a loan to repair or renovate—nor could black landlords there get loans to repair buildings. Redlined sections, beautiful neighborhoods such as Fort Greene, Bed-Stuy, Clinton Hill, parts of Park Slope, Prospect Heights, Crown Heights, East New York, and Brownsville extended low rents to the working poor but had no economic support for growth. All these neighborhoods began to decline quickly. Home owners who were white and had money to move did so. Others were trapped because they couldn't (due to race and economic status) get a mortgage in a finer Brooklyn neighborhood. As low-income immigrants flooded the redlined areas, they overwhelmed the areas and sped up the decay.

Redlining created ghettos of racial and economic differences that Brooklyn had never known. The fissure between white and black, between haves and have-nots grew. And so did hostility. Neighborhoods became closed off from one another—self-protective—fearful.

By the mid-1960s, a huge second wave of Brooklynites left—not because they wanted to, but because they were angry and afraid. Many lovely tree-lined neighborhoods that had been targeted for growth, Coney Island, for example, were bulldozed by developers who put up high-rises of own-your-own apartments. This was a strange notion to Brooklyn people who were most familiar with renting. Why buy an

1960s—When Brooklyn . . . Rumbled

apartment for $250 a month in fees, when you're already living in a lovely seven-room apartment for $30 a month? Often these resisters were "encouraged" to buy when landlords let buildings go unattended—without paint jobs or basic repairs. Broken windows left unmended would be the first sign. Someone would say, "It's time to go," and whole families would pick up and leave Brooklyn.

What never diminished during these upsetting changes was the urge to survive as neighborhoods. Each neighborhood kept or developed its religious festivals, block parties, community centers, parades—the activities that bind people together. And still, just as in the old days, one group stepped aside for the other group's parade. In declining places, which had no economic support from the city, some neighbors organized and rallied the best they could—turning littered vacant lots into gardens and painting and renovating their churches and homes.

Strength in Numbers

They were called the Gowanus Dukes, Kane Street Stompers, Mau Mau Chaplins, Corsair Lords, Saints, and Ambassadors among many other names. They wore their names scripted on the backs of their satin jackets. Gangs had sprouted up in the late 1950s as more or less social groupings of teenagers. These guys wore their hair *Grease*-style, in pompadours and ducktails. They gathered on the corners or in front of the candy store. They were never noted for acts of vandalism any more serious than turning over trash cans.

In the 1960s, gangs became a little tougher. They saw themselves as the protectors of their neighborhood turf, a way for the haves and have-nots to secure an identity, protect what they had from further decay or from infiltration. Families, the elderly, children, and shop owners were never at risk. Gangs had high regard for their neighborhoods and they coexisted with respect for other gangs. There might be a group of Hispanic guys on one corner, black guys on another, Italians on the other, but much of the time gangs had less to do with race—and more to do with the makeup of the neighborhood. The Red Hook Rebels, for example, were a gang of black, white, Japanese, and Hispanic boys. The Rebelettes were their girlfriends.

Fulton Street without the El was wider and brighter for sure. The Horn & Hardart was always packed during the week. That's Borough Hall in the distance. Courtesy of the Brooklyn Historical Society

If gang members became rough, it was with another gang that may have violated a boundary, affected the neighborhood or somebody in it in some way. Schoolyard rumbles late at night would settle the dispute—there were no drive-by shootings or sneak attacks. When there was nothing to rumble over, gang members were likely to hang out at Jahn's ice cream parlor or Garfield's cafeteria, as would any other teenager on a Friday night.

A Little Cheesecake Helps

We all saw the changes in Brooklyn and were disturbed by them, but my father never thought for a moment that Junior's would join the exodus from downtown. This area was in fact one of the last remaining galvanizers—where everybody could intermingle, interact. This is where all races and classes came to work, shop, do government business, go to school. We saw clearly that Junior's belonged to everyone! We were smack in between two strikingly different neighborhoods— Fort Greene, which had been redlined and which was filling up with an integrated, low-income population of African Americans, Hispanics, and whites, and Brooklyn Heights, a predominately well-off neighborhood which had itself declared a historic landmark in 1966.

Junior's in the 1960s was a place where all colors of people in all styles of dress could gather without tensions. No matter who came through the door, they were treated well. Good food and good service became the great equalizer. We started to expand the menu again—featuring some southern specialties such as roasted meats and barbeque, chicken and shrimp and southern-style fried chicken. We included other ethnic favorites, too, such as Shrimp Parmigiana, baked ziti, and calamari with marinara as an appetizer. We found, however, that the new Brooklynites enjoyed what Junior's did best—our huge deli sandwiches, our pancake or French toast breakfasts, blintzes, steaks, and most of all, our cheesecake.

My father was always a keen competitor and when it came to Junior's cheesecake, he was determined to have *the best in Brooklyn*. He was so adamant that we excel, and so confident that we could, that once in a while, if he noticed a slackening in sales, he'd send one of our office employees to scout the competition— the Brass Rail Restaurant, for example. My father's spy would sit down, order, see if they had added something to the menu, or added a topping to their cheesecake.

Our baker Eigel Peterson and my father had perfected a cheesecake recipe as we went into the sixties. And by the mid-1960s we had a very popular dessert. We were serving slices of plain, cherry, and strawberry cheesecake for dessert at breakfast, lunch, or dinner and people were taking slices home. From the bakery counter, we were packing up slices to go and selling whole cheesecakes in small, medium, and large sizes. We were also baking large special-order cakes for parties.

The Place to Party

The Albee Bowling Alley had been our downstairs neighbor for thirty years. It occupied the basement space and its several lanes stretched under the eight hundred square feet of Junior's dining rooms and kitchens. I can't tell you how many times over the years someone from the alley would run upstairs and tell us that another kitchen leak was dripping water down below. It got to the point that they'd have to hang buckets over the lanes to keep them and everybody else dry because spills and leaks are the nature of a restaurant kitchen. Soon after the alley closed in 1960 my father leased the space and converted it into a large banquet room.

Junior's Burgundy Room opened in 1961 and we catered hundreds, maybe thousands, of special-occasion parties over the next twenty years. There were bar mitzvahs, weddings, graduations, first communions, retirement parties, sweet-sixteen parties, award ceremonies, birthdays, club meetings, wedding anniversaries, and Passover seders downstairs in the Burgundy Room. If you called to make Mother's Day or Thanksgiving Day reservations, you were also seated in the Burgundy Room. There were two entrances: One was inside the restaurant down a wide stairway lit by a huge chandelier; the other was an outside entrance marked by a wine-colored awning on DeKalb Avenue. So many people enjoyed that room that almost every day someone

"You ask me, do I go to Junior's! I had my graduation party there. My daughter's graduation party was there. When my mother graduated from old Girls High School, she had her party there. So, yes, I go to Junior's."

—Elijah Mayrant

The Joe Franklin show featured a different restaurant every week. Marvin guested to talk about all the "new" soft mixers available at Junior's bar. Courtesy of the Rosen family

comes up to me, someone who is now grown up, and tells me how he or she will never forget their graduation party here or their wedding reception.

Who Was Who in Brooklyn

Great humor comes from hard times. Comedian Eddie Murphy was born in Bushwick in 1961. Another comic, Gabe Kaplan, was going to New Utrecht High School during the late sixties. Brooklyn-born Lenny Bruce was banned from New York nightclubs in the 1960s for using obscenity that nowadays would seem tame. Actress Rhea Perlman was growing up in Bensonhurst, as was playwright/actor, Harvey Fierstein. Steve Guttenberg was just five.

Young Arlo Guthrie, born in Coney Island in 1947, was just coming of age in the 1960s. Brooklyn-born Lou Reed and his Velvet Underground were already performing in clubs in the Village. He was well known for his Brooklyn pride—during each show he'd shout out into the crowd, "Who here's from Brooklyn?"

The rock star Pat Benatar was ten years old in Brooklyn in 1963 and Barry Manilow was living in Williamsburg. He turned eighteen in 1964, the year Beatlemania swept the country. Brooklyn's 1960s also brought us *NYPD Blue*'s actor Jimmy Smits.

Who Was Who at Junior's

Camille Russo, a young lady who was working the cash box at the Paramount in 1959, saw our sign *"cashier wanted"* in the window and came to work for us in 1960. She's still behind the counter selling cheesecakes, pies, cookies, and other freshly baked goods and taking cash for checks. She has more energy than most of us and has a way with customers that makes them feel like her favorite. We've traveled as far away as Alaska, Japan, and Australia and it never fails, there's always a fellow traveler who finds out we're from Junior's of Brooklyn. First thing he asks—"How's Camille?" She definitely makes a lasting impression. Has a smile for everyone. When you ask if she wants to retire, she merely says she'll do this until she doesn't want to anymore. Until then, Camille is still here from 5:30 A.M. until about 2:30 in the afternoon.

The 1960s also brought Mary Blevins to Junior's. She walked through the door in 1962, a young red-headed girl from the Virginia mountains via Norfolk. She wasn't familiar with popular northeastern foods, let alone ethnic specialties. Bagels, homemade cheese blintzes, chopped liver, matzoh ball soup, fresh brisket of beef sandwich on Challah or rye, even cheesecake, were part of the new food language she had to learn quickly. My father hired her as a waitress for the main floor, but after a while asked her to work the counter. She was thrilled. With thirty-seven seats at the counter and a fast turnover of "Regulars," her new position was like a promotion. Mary's been at the counter ever since, working the breakfast-lunch shift—6:30 A.M. to 2:30. She's put three kids through college. When and if Mary leaves Junior's, it will be for those childhood mountains of Virginia.

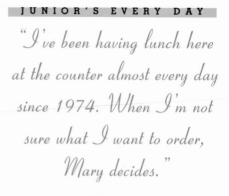

Our own families grew like vines in the 1960s. Marvin's daughters Sheri and Beth and his son Jeffery and Walter's sons—Brett, Kevin, and Alan—were like stair steps in that decade. Meanwhile, the senior Rosen, my father, Harry, once he felt Junior's was thriving, began to turn more of the business over to us. By 1968, he who had started everything from a sandwich shop here on the corner of Flatbush and DeKalb turned the thriving business over to us and concentrated a little more on his golf. Not to say that he didn't keep his hand in the running of the place; when he wasn't in Florida, he was here at Junior's. But by 1969, the day-to-day responsibilities now belonged to the next generation of Rosens.

1960s—Melting Pot

AS THE NUMBER and nationalities of the customers grew in the sixties, so did the menu. No longer was Junior's known just for its overstuffed sandwiches and stacked-up sundaes. It became known as the meeting place for Brooklynites who had lived here many years, plus those just moving in—from the South, the West, wherever, even from many countries across the seas. Junior's fast became a place for the intermingling of regional flavors, ethnic specialties, national favorites.

There was fried chicken and Virginia ham from the South . . . big meatballs in marinara sauce from our Italian immigrants . . . old-fashioned turkey 'n' dressing from the Midwest . . . shrimps, crabs, and fish-du-jour from our seashores.

Everyone took for granted that these foods would always be on the menu. They were in the sixties—and they still are today.

Homemade Chili

WHEN IT'S WINDY and snowy in Brooklyn, the locals head for Junior's. A bowl of their steaming homemade chili is all they need to warm them up. It's chock-full of kidney beans and flavored with just enough chili powder to make it authentic. Junior's serves its chili over rice, then tops it with plenty of chopped onions, if you like.

One big bowlful, plus some hot cornbread, will easily fill you up.

MAKES 2 QUARTS

2 pounds ground beef chuck (ask the butcher to grind it twice)

¼ cup (½ stick) unsalted butter

2 large yellow onions, chopped (2 cups)

1 large green bell pepper, seeded and chopped (1½ cups)

2 large cloves garlic, minced

2 tablespoons chili powder

1 tablespoon salt

1 teaspoon ground black pepper

1 28-ounce can crushed tomatoes

1 28-ounce can tomato paste

1 28-ounce can tomato purée

2 cups drained, canned kidney beans

1 teaspoon hot pepper sauce, or to taste

The Junior's Way— **Always simmer chili in an open pot. This lets the excess moisture boil away, leaving the chili with a delicious intense flavor—never watery or diluted.**

FOR THE GO-ALONGS

6 cups cooked white rice (2 cups uncooked)

¾ cup chopped onions (1 medium)

1. Brown the beef in a large stockpot or Dutch oven over medium-high heat until the pink disappears. Using a slotted spoon, remove to paper towels to drain. Drain off all but 3 tablespoons of the drippings.

continued

2. Melt the butter in the drippings. Add the onions, bell pepper, garlic, chili powder, salt, and black pepper. Sauté until the vegetables are tender. Return the beef to the pot.

3. Add the tomatoes, tomato paste, tomato purée, and kidney beans. Season to taste with the hot pepper sauce.

4. Bring the chili to a boil. Reduce the heat to low and simmer in the open pot, until the flavors are well blended and the chili has thickened slightly, about 30 minutes. Stir frequently to keep the chili from sticking. Serve chili piping hot over the cooked rice and sprinkle with the chopped onions.

Junior's Famous 10 Oz. Steakburgers

FROM THE VERY first day Junior's opened its doors, charbroiled steakburgers have been one of their most famous sandwiches. But in those days, it was called a charcoal-broiled hamburger steak and was served with onion rings and two vegetables—all for $2.75! But whatever its name and however it comes, the meat's the same: ten ounces of fresh chopped beef chuck, ground not once but twice, making it extra juicy and tender.

When "working the burger line" one day with the short-order chef, I quickly learned the language—one C Burger, that means a cheeseburger only, no fries or onion rings; two E burgers, that means no cheese on the burger but served with "the works" of lettuce, tomato, fries, and onion rings.

But whichever burger you choose, it's guaranteed to be hot off the grill and freshly cooked only for you, just the way you like it.

MAKES ONE LARGE BURGER

To Shape Steakburger the Junior's Way—Pat each steakburger into a rectangle, about 4 by 3 inches and at least 1½ inches thick. Then charbroil it, just to each customer's liking (be sure to turn it only once). Serve the burger immediately the Junior's Way, with "the works": open-faced with the grilled steakburger on the bottom half of a large warm hamburger roll, plus a deep-green curly lettuce leaf, and a red tomato slice arranged on the cut-side of the top of the roll. Stack up thick-cut French fries alongside and top the fries with two giant French Fried Onion Rings (page 175). The extra fixings are some of the best part—they vary according to the burger you choose.

Broiled Steakburgers the Junior's Way

The A Burger—Broiled Steakburger with Melted Muenster Cheese: Place two slices of Muenster cheese, one on the bottom of the bun and one on the top (about 2 ounces in all), then run them under the broiler until melted and bubbly. Place the charbroiled steakburger on top of the melted cheese on the bottom bun. Serve it open-faced, the Junior's Way, with "the works," that is, lettuce and tomato on the top bun, plus French fries and two giant French Fried Onion Rings alongside (page 175). Serve it up with a small bowl of Sautéed Mushrooms (page 174).

The B Burger—Broiled Steakburger with Smothered Onions or Italian Red Onion: Serve the charbroiled steakburger open-faced, the Junior's Way, with "the works," that is, the burger on the bottom of the bun and lettuce and tomato on the top bun, plus French fries and two giant French Fried Onion Rings (page 175) alongside. Place a thick-cut, raw Italian red onion on the steakburger—or a small bowl of Smothered Onions on-the-side (page 84).

The C Burger—Broiled Cheeseburger: Place two slices of American cheese, one on the bottom of the bun and one on the top (about 2 ounces in all), then run them under the broiler until melted and bubbly. Place the charbroiled steakburger on top of the melted cheese on the bottom bun. Serve the burger open-faced, the Junior's Way, with only the lettuce leaf and tomato slice on the top bun—no French fries or onion rings, please.

The D Burger—Broiled Cheeseburger: Place two slices of American cheese, one on the bottom of the bun and one on the top (about 2 ounces in all), then run them under the broiler until melted and bubbly. Place the charbroiled steakburger on top of the melted cheese on the bottom bun. Serve the burger open-faced, the Junior's Way, with "the works," that is, lettuce and tomato on the top bun, plus French fries and two giant French Fried Onion Rings alongside (page 175).

The E Burger—Broiled Steakburger: Serve a plain charbroiled steakburger open-faced, the Junior's Way, with "the works," that is, the burger on the bottom of the bun, and lettuce and tomato on the top bun, plus French fries and two giant French Fried Onion Rings alongside (page 175).

The F Burger—Broiled Bacon Cheeseburger: Place two slices of American cheese, one on the bottom of the bun and one on the top (about 2 ounces in all), then run them under the broiler until melted and bubbly. Place the charbroiled steakburger on top of the melted cheese on the bottom bun, then lay two crisp bacon strips on top of the burger. Serve it open-faced, the Junior's Way, with "the works," that is, lettuce and tomato on the top bun, plus French fries and two giant French Fried Onion Rings alongside (page 175).

Sautéed Mushrooms

ORDER HAMBURGER A at Junior's and you'll get a ten-ounce charbroiled burger topped with Muenster, served with "the works," and a side dish of these sautéed mushrooms. The chef begins with large white cultivated mushrooms—plus ample butter for sautéing, of course. "Nothing substitutes for butter, especially when cooking mushrooms. If possible, clarify the butter first."

MAKES 2 CUPS

1 pound white mushrooms
½ cup (1 stick) unsalted butter

1. Wash the mushrooms and pat them dry with paper towels. Trim off about ¼ of an inch of the stems. Using a sharp paring knife, slice the mushrooms vertically, ⅛ to ¼ inch thick (you will have about 6 cups of sliced mushrooms).

The Junior's Way—
Use plenty of butter, a large skillet, and high heat. These three "ingredients" are essential when cooking mushrooms in order to get that golden-brown color and the tasty sautéed flavor. If the skillet is not large enough to give ample cooking surface, the mushrooms end up stewing and simmering in their own juices, resulting in soft poached mushrooms instead of flavorful sautéed ones.

Welcome to Junior's!

2. Melt the butter in a large skillet over medium-high heat (use an iron skillet if you have one).

3. Add the mushrooms and cook them quickly, turning them constantly with a spatula until the mushrooms are golden brown and tender, about 5 minutes. Great with hamburgers or steaks.

French Fried Onion Rings

AS YOU MIGHT expect, these onion rings are the real large, thick, crispy, crunchy ones—the kind that were famous in the fifties. They're also the kind that folks at home usually don't try. But by adding an extra coating of flour before frying, you'll find they are easy and foolproof to make.

MAKES ABOUT 2 QUARTS ONION RINGS

1 recipe Dipping Batter (page 188)
4 cups all-purpose flour
2 tablespoons paprika
2 pounds extra-large Spanish onions
Vegetable shortening or oil

The Junior's Way—
Use the largest yellow onions you can find—preferably at least four inches in diameter. Buy Spanish onions if they are in the market. If not, choose large Bermuda onions. To fry the onion rings, the chef recommends buying solid vegetable shortening and melting it. If it's not handy, vegetable oil works OK too.

1. Make the Dipping Batter and let it stand for 15 minutes. Mix the flour and paprika in a large shallow dish.

2. Peel the onions and cut them horizontally into ½-inch slices. Separate the rings, being careful not to tear them.

3. Dip the onion rings in the batter, then coat them completely, on both sides, with the flour mixture. Refrigerate the onion rings for 15 minutes to set the coating.

4. Meanwhile melt enough shortening or heat enough oil to give 1 inch of cooking fat in a large skillet (an iron one is great). Slide the onion rings into the hot oil in a single layer and fry them on both sides until golden and crispy, about 6 minutes total. Or if you prefer, use a deep-fat fryer according to the manufacturer's directions. Transfer the fried onion rings to a cooling rack to drain. Serve hot!

1960s—When Brooklyn . . . Rumbled

Big Meatballs
with Spaghetti

MEATBALLS AND SPAGHETTI seem like ordinary fare—but not at Junior's. There's nothing ordinary about the flavor of these meatballs with their hint of Parmesan and fresh parsley. And there's nothing ordinary about their size either—each one is almost the size of a baseball.

MAKES 6 SERVINGS OF 2 MEATBALLS EACH

FOR THE SAUCE

1 recipe Chef's Marinara Sauce (178)

FOR THE MEATBALLS

2 tablespoons (¼ stick) unsalted butter

2 tablespoons vegetable oil

1 cup chopped yellow onion

1 cup chopped green bell pepper

3 large cloves garlic, minced

3 pounds ground beef chuck (ask your butcher to grind it twice)

½ cup seasoned dry bread crumbs

½ cup minced fresh parsley

⅓ cup freshly grated Parmesan cheese

¼ cup A.1. Steak Sauce

1 tablespoon salt

1 teaspoon ground black pepper

4 extra-large eggs

1 pound uncooked spaghetti

The Junior's Way—
To shape the meatballs, pick up about half-a-cup of the meat mixture in your hands. Press and shape into a ball, then roll it on a flat surface into a firm round ball, about the size of a baseball.

1. Assemble the Chef's Marinara Sauce in a large saucepan, but simmer the sauce slowly while you're making the meatballs.

2. To make and shape the meatballs, heat 1 tablespoon each of the butter and the oil in a large skillet over medium-high heat until the butter melts. Add the onion, green pepper, and garlic and sauté until crisp-tender, about 5 minutes. Transfer to a large bowl.

3. Add the beef, bread crumbs, parsley, cheese, steak sauce, salt, and pepper and mix thoroughly. Whisk the eggs until frothy and mix with the beef mixture. Shape into 2½-inch meatballs (you should have about 12).

4. Heat the remaining butter and oil in the skillet over medium-high heat. Brown the meatballs, turning them constantly, then transfer them to the pan containing the sauce. Bring the sauce and meatballs to a rolling boil, then reduce the heat to low and simmer until the meatballs are cooked through, about 30 minutes.

5. While the sauce is simmering, cook and drain the spaghetti according to the manufacturer's directions. To serve, make a nest of spaghetti on each plate, then top with 2 meatballs, and ladle over plenty of sauce.

Chef's Marinara Sauce

HERE IS ONE of those tomato sauces that tastes like it has simmered for hours, but it actually takes only thirty minutes of cooking. The reason? It's made from canned crushed tomatoes that have already been cooked before you buy them.

Technically, it is a typical Italian marinara, meaning it is spiced with onions, garlic, and oregano.

MAKES 2 QUARTS MARINARA SAUCE

2 tablespoons (¼ stick) unsalted butter

2 tablespoons olive oil

2 cups chopped yellow onions

1½ cups chopped green bell pepper

6 large cloves garlic, minced

1 tablespoon dried oregano leaves

2 teaspoons salt

1 teaspoon ground black pepper

2 28-ounce cans crushed tomatoes in purée, undrained

¼ cup tomato paste

¾ cup slivered fresh basil leaves

½ cup water

1 teaspoon sugar

2 bay leaves

The Junior's Way—
The secret to a good sauce is in the cooking. Simmer on low, not high, heat, in an open skillet. Stir it often, making certain it does not stick or burn.

1. Heat the butter and oil in a large pot over medium-high heat until the butter melts. Add the onions, green pepper, garlic, oregano, salt, and pepper and sauté until the vegetables are crisp-tender, about 5 minutes.

2. Add both cans of the crushed tomatoes and their purée, the tomato paste, basil, water, sugar, and bay leaves. Bring to a simmer, then reduce the heat to low. Cook the sauce in the skillet, without covering it, until the flavors are blended and it has thickened slightly, about 30 minutes. Stir frequently to make sure the sauce does not burn or stick to the bottom of the pot, adding a little more water if necessary.

3. Remove the sauce from the heat and discard the bay leaves. Ladle generous helpings of sauce on hot steaming spaghetti or your favorite cooked pasta.

Baked Virginia Ham

I WAS IN THE Junior's kitchen talking with the chef one morning, listening carefully as he told me how he glazes those delicious hams. "Maple syrup . . . that's it. Why do anything else, when that's all you need?" Well, I tried it. And he's right.

It coats the ham, giving it a wonderful shiny look. But as the ham bakes, the syrup also caramelizes into a slightly sweet complex flavor that makes you think you want another bite, then another. Try it, but don't skimp on the ingredients.

Buy a sugar-cured ham, plump, pink, and fully cooked. For the best flavor, choose one that's still on-the-bone. For the syrup, make sure it's 100% maple syrup—not the imitation kind.

That's the best, the chef assures me.

**MAKES 20 TO 24 SERVINGS (WHOLE HAM)
OR 10 TO 12 SERVINGS (HALF HAM)**

*1 fully cooked smoked whole ham or the bone
(12 to 16 pounds) or 1 shank or butt half
of ham on the bone (6 to 8 pounds)*
Whole cloves (optional)
*100% pure maple syrup
(about 2 cups for whole
ham; 1 cup for half of ham)*

The Junior's Way—Buy only a fully cooked sugar-cured ham and place it on a rack in a roasting pan with a little water. Roast it slowly at a low temperature until a thermometer inserted in the thickest part reads 135°F. Add more water to the pan as needed to keep the ham moist and juicy.

continued

1. Preheat the oven to 325°F. Fit a roasting pan with a rack. Carefully remove the net from the ham, if there is one, without tearing the fat on the ham. If you are roasting the ham for a company dinner, you might also want to score the fat into diamonds and stud each diamond with cloves. Place the ham, fat-side-up, on the rack and pour about 1 inch of hot water into the pan.

2. Bake the ham, without covering it, according to the directions that come with the ham or until a thermometer inserted in the center of the thickest part reads 135°F (the temperature will rise at least 5 degrees while standing after the ham comes out of the oven). Roasting will take 2¾ to 3 hours for a 16-pound whole ham; 2 to 2¼ hours for an 8-pound half of ham. Check frequently to be sure there is still water in the pan, adding more if necessary to keep about 1 inch in the pan at all times.

3. About 1 hour before the end of the roasting time, brush the top and sides of the ham generously with the maple syrup. Continue basting and glazing the ham every 15 minutes. The last 3 minutes, turn on the broiler and broil the ham until it's very glazed and bubbly (watch carefully!). Remove the ham from the oven and let it stand for 15 minutes, until the internal temperature reaches 140°F. If you have studded the ham with cloves, remove them before serving.

Stuffed Whole Broiled Flounder with Crabmeat

THE FIRST TIME I visited the upstairs kitchens where the hot dishes are made, I saw this delicious-looking dish—a whole little flounder, over-stuffed with crabmeat and bubbling under the broiler. It looked so good that I was sorry it was not yet time to break for lunch.

I since have found out this is one of Junior's most requested fish dishes. And no wonder—this seafood dish tastes even better than it looks, if that's possible.

MAKES 4 SERVINGS

1 recipe Crabmeat Stuffing (page 184)

4 fresh pan-dressed baby flounders, about 1 pound each

½ cup (1 stick) butter, preferably clarified (page 314)

¼ cup fresh lemon juice

Seasoned dry bread crumbs, for topping

Paprika

Wedges of fresh lemon

The Junior's Way—Ask your fishmonger to pan-dress the flounders, removing their heads and splitting them horizontally. Start at the belly of each fish and cut almost through to the backbone. Right before cooking, overstuff the belly of each flounder with crabmeat and broil them until the flesh turns opaque; this usually takes 15 to 20 minutes in all.

1. Preheat the broiler and smear a broiler pan or a shallow baking pan with 1-inch sides with butter.

2. Prepare the Crabmeat Stuffing.

3. Ask your fishmonger to pan-dress the flounder, removing the heads and leaving the tails on, if you wish.

4. Loosely stuff one-fourth of the stuffing into the body cavity of each flounder, pressing it in place with your fingers.

5. Heat the butter and lemon juice in a small saucepan over medium heat until the butter melts, whisking until it comes together into a thin sauce. Brush the lemon butter on both sides of the flounder (save the remaining butter mixture). Sprinkle both sides of the fish with bread crumbs and dust with paprika.

6. Broil the fish about 6 inches from the source of heat, first on one side and then the other. Baste frequently with the remaining lemon butter, until the flounders turn opaque, the flesh is firm to the touch, and the stuffing turns golden, 15 to 20 minutes. Garnish the fish with lemon wedges and serve immediately.

1960s—When Brooklyn . . . Rumbled

Baked Stuffed Jumbo Shrimps with Crabmeat

*T*HIS IS ONE of those dishes that looks much more difficult than it really is. The secret is to splurge at the fish market and buy the biggest jumbo shrimps you can find. And when you peel them, take a tip from the chef: "Leave the tails on to make them look their best on the platter."

MAKES 4 SERVINGS OF 6 SHRIMPS EACH

½ cup plus 2 tablespoons (1¼ sticks) unsalted
       butter, preferably clarified (page 314)
1 recipe Crabmeat Stuffing (page 184)
24 jumbo fresh shrimps in shells (about 2 pounds)
¼ cup fresh lemon juice
Seasoned dry bread crumbs, for topping
Paprika
Wedges of fresh lemon

The Junior's Way—Peel and clean the shrimps carefully, being sure to leave the tails on . . . some fish markets will do it for you, for a price. Use a thin pointed knife to split each shrimp, starting from the inside belly and cutting almost through to the curved back edge. Remove the veins; look carefully, as the veins can be both thin and dark or wide and opaque. Place the shrimps on a broiling pan, with their cut sides up and their tails pointed up in the air. Mound a generous helping of the crabmeat stuffing on top of each shrimp.

1. Preheat the oven to 400°F and smear a shallow baking pan (with sides) with 2 tablespoons of the butter.

2. Prepare the Crabmeat Stuffing.

3. Peel the shrimps (leaving the tails on), then devein them with a sharp paring knife. Butterfly the shrimps by cutting horizontally along the inside belly of the shrimp, down through the shrimp, almost but not completely through to the back side. Open each shrimp up like a book and remove any veins you see.

4. Heat ½ cup of the butter and lemon juice in a small saucepan over medium heat until the butter melts, whisking until it comes together into a thin sauce. Brush the lemon-butter on both sides of the shrimps (save the remaining butter mixture). Lay out the shrimps in the buttered baking pan, with the cut sides up and their tails sticking up.

5. Mound 2 heaping tablespoons of stuffing on the top of each shrimp, shaping it with your fingers. Sprinkle the stuffing with about a tablespoon of bread crumbs and dust with paprika.

6. Bake the shrimps, basting frequently with the remaining lemon-butter, until they turn opaque and the stuffing turns golden, about 12 to 15 minutes, depending on the size of the shrimps. Serve immediately with lemon wedges.

Crabmeat Stuffing

Have This Crabmeat stuffing any way you like—rolled inside a filet of sole, stuffed in a whole boneless flounder, baked on top of jumbo shrimps. This stuffing is guaranteed to be one of the best—with lumps and chunks of fresh crabmeat, pieces of bright tomatoes, plus the sweetness and spice of peppers and onions. What a great way to enjoy the daily catch, whether you're at Junior's or in your own home.

MAKES 4 CUPS STUFFING

1 pound crabmeat, preferably fresh, drained

2 tablespoons (¼ stick) unsalted butter

2 tablespoons vegetable oil

1 extra-large yellow onion, chopped (1½ cups)

1 medium-size green bell pepper, seeded and chopped (1 cup)

1 large clove garlic, minced

1 28-ounce can whole tomatoes, drained and chopped (2 cups)

⅔ cup seasoned dry bread crumbs

The Junior's Way—
If you can find fresh crabmeat and can afford it, by all means use it in this stuffing. Choose the snow-white lump crabmeat from the body of the crab, not the small bits of darker backfin meat that is mostly shredded.

1. Pick through the crabmeat for shells, leaving the meat in lumps (do not flake).

2. Heat the butter and oil in a large skillet over medium-high heat until the butter melts. Add the onion, bell pepper, and garlic and sauté until tender, about 5 minutes. Stir in the crabmeat and sauté 1 minute more, then transfer to a large bowl.

3. Add the drained tomatoes and bread crumbs to the crab mixture and toss just until it is well mixed (too much stirring can make the stuffing tough and gummy). If you wish, you may mince the mixture at this stage in a food processor (however, we left it nice and chunky and it worked just fine). Use in Stuffed Whole Broiled Flounder (page 180) or Baked Stuffed Jumbo Shrimps (page 182).

Roast Maryland Turkey
with Dressing

*I*T MAY NOT be November or December—but that doesn't matter. Turkey and dressing are always on the menu at Junior's, item Number 166.

As you might expect, this stuffing is the old-fashioned bread dressing, chock-full of seasonings and chestnuts. I often can't find chestnuts in the spring or summer, so I use pecans. However you mix this stuffing, it has that homespun taste.

MAKES 16 SERVINGS
MAKES 3 QUARTS STUFFING, ENOUGH TO STUFF A 16-POUND TURKEY WITH LEFTOVERS

1 16-pound turkey

FOR THE PANADE (SPONGE)

4 cups bread cubes (½ pound)

2 cups boiling water

¼ cup chicken stock seasoned base or 8 chicken bouillon
  cubes

FOR THE STUFFING

½ cup (1 stick) unsalted butter, preferably clarified (page 314)

6 large ribs celery with leaves, chopped (3 cups)

2 extra-large yellow onions, chopped (3 cups)

12 cups bread cubes, preferably a day old (1½ pounds)

2 cups dark raisins

2 cups coarsely chopped chestnuts (dry, not canned) or coarsely chopped pecans

1 tablespoon salt

1 teaspoon paprika, plus extra for sprinkling on top

1 teaspoon ground white pepper

The Junior's Way—
Chicken stock base is one of the secrets of this stuffing. It adds flavor and a wonderful golden color. Look for it in the spice section in your supermarket.

continued

1. Wash the turkey according to the directions that come with the bird, removing the neck and giblets.

2. To make the panade, place the 4 cups bread cubes in a large bowl. Stir the water and chicken base in a measuring cup until dissolved, then pour over the bread cubes. Let the bread stand until it soaks up most of the water. Squeeze out and discard any excess water.

3. To make the stuffing: Melt the butter in a large skillet over medium-high heat. Add the celery and onions and sauté until crisp-tender, about 8 minutes. Transfer the vegetables to the bowl with the panade.

4. Add the 12 cups bread cubes and all of the remaining ingredients for the stuffing. Toss well. Use to stuff the turkey and bake according to the directions for a stuffed bird that come with the turkey.

To bake the stuffing separately, preheat the oven to 350°F and butter a 13 × 9 × 2-inch baking dish. Spread the stuffing evenly into the dish and place it in a large shallow pan with hot water that comes about 1 inch up the sides of the baking dish. Sprinkle the top with some extra paprika. Bake the stuffing until it's golden and set, about 1 hour.

Golden Fried Chicken, Southern Style

NO MATTER WHICH southerner you ask, you will probably get a description of the only way to cook real southern fried chicken.

Talking to the chef at Junior's is no exception. The steps are simple—but specific: "Dip the chicken in the dipping batter—but don't let it soak. Then roll each piece in the poultry breader and fry until crisp and golden. Never change the method. Do it the same way, time after time."

At Junior's, they've been frying chicken ever since that opening day in 1950. At that time, $2.50 bought an entire Special Chicken Dinner: Southern Fried Chicken and all the fixings—including a tossed green salad, a crisp corn fritter, candied sweet potatoes, and real old-fashioned strawberry shortcake with mountains of whipped cream.

MAKES 6 SERVINGS

1 recipe Dipping Batter (page 188)

3 pounds chicken pieces on the bone, such as drumsticks,
     breasts, thighs, wings

Vegetable oil

FOR THE POULTRY BREADER

2 cups all-purpose flour

¼ cup whole wheat flour

¼ cup yellow cornmeal

2 tablespoons cornstarch

3 tablespoons fried chicken seasonings (look in the spice
     rack in your supermarket or gourmet store)

2 tablespoons dried thyme leaves

1 tablespoon paprika

1 teaspoon ground white pepper

The Junior's Way—

Buy chicken pieces or a cut-up whole chicken that is still on the bone. First dip the pieces into a thick egg batter, then coat with a breader. This is simply a seasoned flour mixture that covers the batter, holding the batter on the chicken during frying and making a golden-brown crispy crust. Chill the coated chicken pieces for a few minutes before frying to set the coating.

1. Make the Dipping Batter and let it stand for 15 minutes.

2. Meanwhile, rinse the chicken and pat it dry with paper towels.

3. Mix all of the ingredients for the poultry breader in a large shallow dish.

4. Dip the chicken pieces in the batter, then roll them in the breader, coating each piece evenly. Place in the refrigerator for 15 minutes to set the coating.

5. Meanwhile, heat about 1 inch of oil in a large skillet (an iron skillet is great). Or use a deep-fat fryer according to the manufacturer's directions. Fry the chicken, a few pieces at a time, turning them occasionally, until golden brown and the juices run clear when pierced with a fork, about 20 to 30 minutes. Transfer to a cooling rack to drain. Best when served piping hot or at room temperature.

Dipping Batter

WHEN I WALKED into the chef's kitchen one day, I saw a giant bowl sitting on the counter. It held a golden, thick, rich mixture, looking as if it contained many eggs and milk.

"That's just batter," he said. "Whether I'm frying chicken, onion rings, shrimps, or any kind of fish, I dip them in this first.

"The ingredients are simple—eggs, milk, flour, a little cornmeal, a few seasonings. The batter must be just thick enough to adhere to the food, but not too thick, or it falls off in the pan during frying. I season it lightly, just enough so it works with almost anything you want to batter up."

MAKES ABOUT 4 CUPS BATTER

2 cups all-purpose flour

¼ cup yellow cornmeal

2 tablespoons seasoning salt

1 tablespoon baking powder

½ teaspoon ground white pepper

5 extra-large eggs

1½ cups milk

The Junior's Way—
Let the batter stand fifteen minutes before using. This thickens up the batter so it coats the food better.

1. Mix the flour, cornmeal, salt, baking powder, and white pepper together in a small bowl.

2. Whisk the eggs and milk in a medium-sized bowl until thick and light yellow, about 2 minutes.

3. Add the flour mixture to the egg mixture and whisk the batter just until the flour disappears and the batter is smooth, about 1 minute. Let the batter stand for 15 minutes before using as a dipping batter for Golden Fried Chicken, Southern Style (page 186), Fried Seafood Combination (page 189), and French Fried Onion Rings (page 175).

Fried Seafood Combination: Butterflied Shrimps, Sea Scallops, Filets of Sole

*I*N THE 1950s, when Junior's first opened its doors, a mere $1.35 could buy you a heaping platter of fried filet of sole—fresh, battered, golden, crispy, and right out of the fryer. It came with "the works"—cole slaw, French fried Idahos, and tartar sauce. For a few pennies more, sixty-five pennies to be exact, you could also have your choice of appetizer, dessert, and coffee, tea, or milk.

Today, fried filet of sole is still on the menu. You can get it any day by itself or in combination, as here, with fried butterflied shrimps and sea scallops. Either way you order, it still comes with "the works."

MAKES 6 SERVINGS

1 recipe Dipping Batter (page 188)
1 recipe Tartar Sauce (page 191)
1½ pounds fresh filets of sole
½ pound fresh sea scallops
1½ pounds extra-large fresh shrimps, in shells
Vegetable oil

FOR THE SEAFOOD BREADER

2¼ cups all-purpose flour
1½ cups yellow cornmeal
3 tablespoons cornstarch
¼ cup seafood seasonings (look in the spice rack in your supermarket or gourmet store)

The Junior's Way—
Nothing takes the place of fresh fish. Buy it the morning of the day you're cooking it. Shop at a fish market, if there's one nearby. We use a breader that has a substantial amount of cornmeal, since it's the natural complement to fish and seafood in both texture and flavor.

continued

1. Make the Dipping Batter and let it stand for 15 minutes. Prepare the Tartar Sauce and refrigerate.

2. Meanwhile, rinse the sole filets; if they are exceptionally large, cut them into irregular pieces about 4 inches long and 2 or 3 inches wide. Rinse the scallops, making certain all of the sand from the crevices of the scallops is washed away. Shell, devein, and butterfly the shrimps (see page 182). Spread out the seafood on paper towels and pat dry.

3. Mix all of the ingredients for the seafood breader in a large shallow dish.

4. Prepare the seafood for frying: Keep the seafood separate, coating first the filets of sole, then the scallops, then the shrimps. Dip the seafood in the batter, then roll in the breader, coating evenly on all sides. Place in the refrigerator for 15 minutes to set the coating.

5. Meanwhile, preheat the oven to 200°F (this warm oven is for keeping the fried seafood hot while you're frying the rest). Line a large shallow pan with paper towels and place a cooling rack on top of the towels.

6. Heat at least an inch of oil in a large skillet (an iron skillet is great). Or use a deep-fat fryer according to the manufacturer's directions. Fry the seafood a few pieces at a time: first the filets of sole, then the scallops, then the shrimps, until puffy and golden brown, about 3 to 4 minutes per side, turning each piece only once. When the seafood is done, transfer it from the hot oil to the cooling rack in the pan with a slotted spoon and place the pan in the warm oven. Serve seafood piping hot with the Tartar Sauce.

Welcome to Junior's!

Tartar Sauce

FRIED SEAFOOD AND tartar sauce just seem to go together—especially at Junior's. Whatever you order—fried filet of sole, shrimps, scallops, or the seafood combo—tartar sauce arrives, too. Traditionally, tartar sauce is made with capers. But forget the capers. This version is well worth making.

The best part: It has only four ingredients and is so-o-o simple, yet it tastes so complex, making you think it's much more difficult to make than it really is.

MAKES ABOUT 1 CUP

¼ cup minced green bell pepper

⅓ cup minced onion

¼ cup finely chopped dill pickle

¾ cup *Hellmann's Real Mayonnaise (not the light variety)*

The Junior's Way—
Mince the bell pepper and onion very fine, about ⅛-inch dice, for this sauce.

1. Mix the bell pepper, onion, and pickle together in a small bowl.

2. Fold in the mayonnaise. Store any leftover sauce in the refrigerator.

1960s—When Brooklyn . . . Rumbled

Junior's Shrimp Salad

AS YOU MIGHT expect, Junior's shrimp salad is the real thing! Every bite is chock-full of fresh cooked shrimp—no canned baby shrimps for this salad. Like their chicken salad, its dressing has that extra creaminess from sour cream, a tangy flavor bite from Dijon mustard, and a hint of hotness from white pepper.

MAKES 5 CUPS

FOR THE SHRIMP SALAD

1 extra-large lemon

Celery leaves

1 tablespoon pickling spices

1 teaspoon salt

1/8 teaspoon ground white pepper

3 pounds medium-size fresh uncooked shrimps in their shells, or 2 1/2 pounds cooked, shelled fresh shrimps (5 cups cooked)

1 tablespoon fresh lemon juice

1 cup celery, cut into 1/4-inch dice

1 to 2 teaspoons snipped fresh dill, according to your taste

FOR THE SOUR CREAM DRESSING

*2/3 cup **Hellmann's** Real Mayonnaise (not the light variety)*

1/2 cup sour cream

1 tablespoon Dijon mustard

3/4 teaspoon salt

1/4 teaspoon ground white pepper

1/4 teaspoon garlic powder

> ### The Junior's Way—
> Buy the medium-size of fresh shrimps for this salad. They are less expensive than the large or jumbo ones but just as flavorful. In most cities, there are fish markets that do the boiling, shelling, and cleaning for you (for a price). If you buy the less expensive uncooked shrimp, boil them in salted water and pickling spices for extra flavor.

1. To cook the shrimps: Half-fill a large saucepan with water. Squeeze the juice from the lemon into the water and toss in the rind. Add a few celery leaves, the pickling spices, salt, and white pepper and bring to a boil over high heat. Drop in the shrimps in their shells and boil them just until they turn pinkish-white and opaque, about 4 minutes. Using a slotted spoon, transfer the shrimps to a colander and rinse immediately with cold water to stop the cooking. Peel and devein the shrimps, discarding all of the pickling spices. Cut the shrimps into bite-sized pieces (you need 5 cups of shrimps).

2. To use precooked shrimps, buy 2½ pounds, or 5 cups, of cooked, shelled, deveined shrimps from the fish market.

3. Place the cooked shrimps in a medium-size bowl, sprinkle with the lemon juice, and toss well. Add the celery and dill and toss again.

4. Mix all of the ingredients for the dressing in a small bowl. Spoon the dressing over the shrimp mixture and stir until all of the shrimps and celery are well coated. Great for making sandwiches on thick slices of white or Challah Bread (page 32), or simply as a salad on curly lettuce leaves. Refrigerate any leftovers and use within 2 days.

Pecan Pie

IN THE SOUTH, where pecan orchards line the highways, you can always seem to find a slice of homemade pecan pie—from the deep dark dense pie at a Mom-and-Pop café along a country road to the light golden custardy type with whipped-cream rosettes at the fanciest city restaurant. At Junior's, they are famous for their old-fashioned recipe—the pie where you can see the pecans on top, with a rich, sweet filling made with plenty of dark corn syrup, brown sugar, butter, and eggs.

MAKES ONE 9-INCH DEEP-DISH PIE

½ recipe Pie Pastry, enough for a single-crust pie (page 40)

5 extra-large eggs

1¼ cups packed light brown sugar

1 cup dark corn syrup

½ cup (1 stick) unsalted butter, melted

1 teaspoon pure vanilla extract

½ teaspoon salt

1½ cups pecan halves (large pecan pieces, not finely chopped)

The Junior's Way—
Mix the filling just enough to whip the eggs and blend in all of the other ingredients. Over-mixing can prevent the pecans from rising to the top of the pie during baking.

1. Preheat the oven to 375°F and butter a 9-inch deep-dish pie plate.

2. Roll out the pastry ⅛ inch thick on a lightly floured surface and trim to a 15-inch circle. Transfer the pastry to the pie plate, leaving a 1½-inch overhang. Fold under the edge to stand up 1 inch high and flute. Do not prick the crust.

3. Using an electric mixer set on high, beat the eggs just until frothy, about 2 minutes. Reduce the speed to low and blend in the sugar, corn syrup, butter, vanilla, and salt. Stir in the pecans and pour the filling into the unbaked shell.

4. Bake the pie until the filling is golden and puffy and jiggles only slightly in the center, 45 to 50 minutes. Cool the pie on a wire rack for 1 hour. This pie is at its best when served at room temperature. Be sure to store any leftover pie in the refrigerator.

1970s—In a Can't-Do World
. . . Brooklyn Starts Doing

IN 1969 BROOKLYN, you couldn't walk or drive anywhere without seeing signs of deterioration. On one corner, it might be a once beautiful apartment building abandoned and covered with graffiti, or around the corner, an entire block of turn-of-the-century row houses burned out and boarded up. (Fire became the only way to pull money out of declining neighborhoods and arson was often for hire.) Small stores remained permanently closed on once active shopping streets, their marquees faded and iron gates covering their entrances. And big business continued to flee the rising cost of staying in Brooklyn; the last three major breweries—Piels, Schaefer, and Rheingold—all closed by 1973, ending a Brooklyn beer dynasty that had begun in 1900 when there were forty-five breweries and beer gardens.

As middle-class taxpayers kept leaving Brooklyn for the suburbs, and the new working poor kept coming, the city struggled for ways to survive. It wasn't good. There was no sign of growth anywhere in New York City—no new business, no obvious new construction except for the World Trade towers, which we could see from across the river when they went up in 1974. No money was being spent to bring our neighborhoods back from the progressive urban blight that began in the 1960s. What was worse was that nobody could imagine how to bring them back.

Newcomers kept moving in, especially after immigration laws eased for Latin Americans and Asians. Panamanians, Costa Ricans, Ecuadoreans, Argentines, Colombians, Indians, and Koreans added to the already huge wave of immigrants who were coming to build their lives in a city that was not able to support them. Crime was an increasingly big issue in all of New York ever since 1964, when Kitty Genovese cried out for help on the streets of Queens and thirty-eight people said they had heard her but were too afraid to get involved. Her murder was national news and New York topped the list of the meanest, scariest places to live.

What Was What

In the summer of 1969 things began to look up. Literally. We all watched our televisions as Neil Armstrong planted the Stars and Stripes on the moon. We had made it to our first stop into the New Frontier. And the 1969 New York Mets finally won big. They even managed to win over a few diehard Brooklyn Dodger fans when they took the World Series. That wouldn't happen again until 1986.

Labor strikes aggravated life in the 1970s. Strikes were big, in fact. In winter 1971 police walked out on strike. It was an illegal mini-strike, of course, and the cops returned in a few days. Thank God it was so cold. We had record-breaking zero temperatures that seemed to keep criminals inside. There was also a garbage pickup strike. And doctors went on strike at city hospitals.

Another power shortage caused a blackout that shut the city down. But this time not all people huddled with one another around candles at home or in restaurants. Many took to the streets with flashlights and looted.

Disco was *the* big sound and discos were *the* big businesses. The fever caught on so fast that the number of discos nationally and locally more than tripled from 1975 to 1977. Studio 54 in Manhattan got most of the hype with its bouncers out front guarding the door. But you didn't have to go into the city for disco. Dozens had sprung up in Brooklyn neighborhoods overnight. Disco was the mood elevator of the day. It seemed to blitz the 1970s sadness and unsolved problems with wild strobe lights, mirror balls, and pulsating beats.

Who Was Who

Mayor John Lindsay was popular enough to get reelected in 1969 running against (among others) Brooklyn Heights resident, novelist, and "Regular" at Junior's Norman Mailer. All candidates—Democrat, Republican, Independent—promised they could deliver the city from growing crime, urban decay, and huge fiscal problems.

The real Frank Serpico blew the whistle in 1971 on hidden and widespread police corruption that affected every borough.

President Nixon finally succumbed to public pressure and pulled our soldiers out of the ten-year war in Vietnam. The United States left unvictorious in 1973— our people sped out of Saigon in getaway helicopters much as Nixon had left Washington after the Watergate scandal a year later.

Brooklyn-born Abe Beame took the mayoral seat from John Lindsay in 1973, pledging to do something about crime and the dismal financial situation of the city. Lindsay had overspent city coffers on ineffectual Band-Aid social programs aimed at helping neighborhoods. The city was nearly broke. Abe Beame was a "Regular" here at Junior's. Some say he ran the city from the corner table in the back. But try as he might, it was Abe's unfortunate place in history to be the one to solicit guaranteed loans from Washington when New York faced bankruptcy in 1974. President Gerald Ford, after taking office from Nixon, who had recently resigned, became the villain when he said no to Mayor Beame. The headline of the *Daily News* said "Ford to City: Drop Dead."

In 1976 the Democrats hosted their convention at Madison Square Garden and eventually put Jimmy Carter in the White House. When Carter took the presidency away from Ford, there wasn't a wet eye in Brooklyn.

Mayor Ed Koch succeeded Beame in 1977 and was successful in getting federal loans to bail the city out of ruin in 1978. His popularity soared.

David Berkowitz didn't help our national image or our mood as he terrorized the whole city as Son of Sam in the mid-1970s. I know there have been worse serial killings since Berkowitz's string of five murders, but for us and the whole country it was a first and it was terrifying.

The film director Spike Lee went off to college in 1975. He left Fort Greene and went to his dad's (Bill Lee, the musician) alma mater, Morehouse in Atlanta. He would be back, though. Once he finished film school at NYU, he would come back to Brooklyn.

John Travolta, an unknown then, just might have been the most positive psychological image to hit Brooklyn in the '70s. Although not Brooklyn-born, he played an Italian kid from Brooklyn in *Saturday Night Fever*. It was his exhilarating walk during the opening credits of the film as the Bee Gees beat out the lyrics to "Stayin' Alive" that caught our attention and didn't let go. It was a strut and a glide. He led with a strong shoulder and followed with the smooth shifting gait of a young guy who looked as if he could step off the pavement and fly if he wanted to. But he didn't want to. All he wanted to do was dance and rule his world of disco. He wanted to be the best. He was youth, strength, desire, and talent. Brooklynites recognized him. He was us—or what we used to be—a guy who used everything he had of himself to make his dream happen. He gave us a way of seeing ourselves again.

Stayin' Alive

The fact was that Brooklyn had never been in such severe economic trouble—not even during the Depression. Our neighborhoods, which were falling apart, and our

By 1979, fine old neighborhoods of row houses like these in Park Slope began to revive through the efforts of new homeowners who bought cheap and renovated. Courtesy of the Brooklyn Historical Society

businesses, which were leaving by the truckloads, had always taken care of us. For a few years we felt paralyzed by the instability, crime, and decay. It became evident, however, that if Brooklyn was to regain its vitality, we would have to preserve what we had from further decay and start rebuilding what we had lost. And it would have to happen not from on high but one person, one neighborhood at a time.

Brooklyn Heights was the first neighborhood to begin to fight back early in 1966. By declaring it a historic district—the first in all of New York—the Heights residents moved to protect their architecture and nineteenth-century character. Today,

1970s—In a Can't-Do World . . . Brooklyn Starts Doing

the Heights, among many other fine areas, is a historical landmark. To walk the tiny streets and alleys there—down Pierrepont where the Historical Society occupies a Victorian mansion on the corner of Clinton, up Willow past Truman Capote's old residence, past dozens of brick and stone houses with four floors of handsome bay windows and ironwork trim, some with attached carriage houses—you can feel transported in time. It's as if Walt Whitman or Hart Crane could turn the corner any minute.

Other fine neighborhoods such as Cobble Hill, Fort Greene, Park Slope, and Prospect Heights began to act to preserve the look and feel of the rich character of the streets. Hundreds of the working poor began to see opportunity in renovating old brownstones and row houses.

Literally dozens of community-housing groups sprang up during the early and late 1970s. They got funding and organized themselves to revitalize the failing neighborhoods of low- and medium-income people. One of the first to start up in 1974 was Williamsburg's People's Firehouse. They organized tenants and helped them buy and rebuild abandoned homes, buildings, and row houses before the arsonist's torch could beat them to it.

East Brooklyn Churches was a nonprofit, bootstrap coalition of mostly black churches that started up in the late 1970s. They organized neighborhoods and private and public monies, too, which resulted in new and renovated homes in burned-out sections. Another group based in local churches was the Nehemiah Program in Brownsville and East New York, which was affiliated with the great urban activist Saul Alinsky. The Nehemiah Group organized funds and neighbors to reclaim property, to renovate or build new homes, enabling people to get out of deteriorating housing. Soon after in 1979, the Brooklyn Economic Development Corporation formed. It was another nonprofit group that focused on revitalizing neighborhood merchants and shopping.

A Melting Pot of Flavors

No matter what race or nation of origin, no matter what hardship people were suffering, Brooklyn families continued to gather for a weekly meal together. Their kitchens and tables provided spiritual—not just nutritional—boosts. There were Irish fries after Sunday mass in Red Hook, Park Slope, Flatbush, and even nowadays in Gerritsen Beach and Marine Park. Families and friends sat down to huge breakfasts of sausage, roast meats, potatoes, soda bread, and eggs.

And on Saturday nights from Jewish households in Bensonhurst or Williamsburg came the aromas of mushroom barley soup, kreplach and potalajella, pot roast or brisket. When the black Baptist churches emptied on Sunday afternoons, two and three generations of a family might walk over to Junior's for lox and eggs or turkey and trimmings. Others went home for stuffed game hens, or smothered chicken and dumplings, cornbread, and greens with egg pie or sweet potato pie.

Puerto Ricans in Sunset Park and West Indians in Flatbush put out platters and bowls of beans and rice, sweet-and-sour vegetables, crabmeat salads, codfish cakes, or fish stew with plantain dumplings. In Greenpoint, Polish families served up brick-oven breads and pastries, kielbasa, pierogi. The Italians in Park Slope and Bensonhurst sat everyone down to several courses beginning with antipasto and progressing to fresh homemade pasta, chicken cacciatore, biscotti, ricotta cake. The Greeks in Bay Ridge and the Egyptians and Yemenites near Atlantic Avenue served hummus, dolmas, roasted lemon chicken, baklava, and other fine pastries in phyllo dough.

We became aware of ourselves as a stewing pot as much as a melting pot. As new immigrants poured in, longtime residents might at first be a little wary of the different smells and tastes of another people's food. But after one taste of Middle Eastern falafel, Dominican *mofongo*, Puerto Rican fried plantains, Indian curry, Italian scampi, or Polish stuffed cabbage, Brooklynites braved the fear of new neighborhoods and crime to get to restaurants, food festivals, and street fairs just to taste calzone, kielbasa, barbequed ribs, sweet potato pie. Brooklynites eventually developed a massive appetite for the great variety of tastes and textures of one another's foods.

Come to the Party

One Brooklyn festival received world attention in the 1970s because of its spectacle and its ability to bring one neighborhood together with others. The festival of Our Lady of Mount Carmel and Saint Paulinas in July had been a yearly event since 1949 that bonded the Williamsburg Italians to each other and their mother-country roots. But by the 1970s the festival was also medicine that healed the community there,

This is a great picture of the dancing of the *giglio* (lily). It was taken in the early 1960s, but by 1970 the feast had swelled to a million-plus people who crammed the streets of Williamsburg every July. The procession of the *giglio* honors Saint Paulinas and Our Lady of Mount Carmel. Courtesy of the Brooklyn Historical Society

which had been split and broken by construction of the Brooklyn-Queens Expressway. The Mount Carmel parish church, a fixture for the Williamsburg Italians who had always lived among the Jews, Poles, Russians, Germans, and black Americans, was literally destroyed. A new one had to be built.

The feast started in 1903 on the banks of the East River where the first Italian immigrants put down roots in 1880. During World War I and World War II, the festival was dormant, but since 1949 it has rallied and thrived. By the 1970s it was a very big event because of its tradition, its spectacle, and its food. More than a million people cram into the neighborhood each year.

Besides the open-air food stalls, which send up pungent smells of grilled sausage and peppers, steak and onions, and display rows and rows of fresh calzone, the procession, nicknamed "dancing the *giglio*," is the main event. The *giglio* is an eighty-five-foot wooden and plaster tower sculpture covered with painted casts of lilies and angels. Statues of Saint Paulinas and Our Lady of Mount Carmel are significantly placed on the top and in the center of the *giglio*.

The word *giglio* is Italian for "lily." And the giant lily commemorates a medieval event when Saint Paulinas returned to his town after a heroic deed. Each person welcomed him by waving a lily. The Brooklyn *giglio* weighs about three tons. At the base is a platform on which sits an eight-piece band. During the procession, 120-some men lift the entire structure (band and all) and dance it, dip it, and turn it round while the band plays "Lily of Paradise." The men can dance the *giglio* for only three or four minutes at a time.

During the rests, thousands of observers lean into one of many food stalls that border the procession and buy freshly made sausage and pepper heros, sodas, and Italian pastries. When the band begins again, everybody knows it's time to watch the *giglio* lunge and "cha-cha" down the street. Literally thousands gather without incident for the ceremony, the camaraderie, and the food. Since the sustained popularity of the feast of Mount Carmel, dozens and dozens of block parties, church festivals, parades, and street fairs have careened into popularity all over Brooklyn.

Where They Can Meet and Eat All Day, All Night

Today, cafeterias have all but disappeared from the eastern cityscape. Although, I hear, in Texas and California they're still big business. But in the seventies they were still thriving here. So if there wasn't a festival or street fair to get people together, there was always Dubrows on Eastern Parkway or Kings Highway or Garfield's Cafeteria on Flatbush or any one of our competitor cafeterias downtown. These were all safe places to go and for the minimum of fifty cents, the price of fries and a Coke, you could stay all night. They were large friendly places—clean, bright, white-tiled and chromed—cavernous places that welcomed everybody—old and young in the early mornings, families and teens at night, taxi drivers, UPS deliverers and dockworkers just before dawn. They were places where different people could meet and feel safe with one another.

Ice cream parlors, too—every neighborhood had one—would stay open to 2:00 A.M. Teenagers would descend after dates, play the jukebox and share the house specialty, which at the famous Jahn's parlors was a giant concoction of fifteen different flavors of ice cream and as many toppings—cherries, syrups, nuts, fruits.

1970s—In a Can't-Do World . . . Brooklyn Starts Doing

1973 – When the World Discovered Junior's

Junior's made its place as . . . well, a place downtown where you could feel safe and at home, still a part of old Brooklyn. We expanded our menu. We added outdoor lighting. We stayed open until 1:30 A.M. on weeknights and 4:00 A.M. on weekends.

WORD IS OUT

"Most American cities with large Jewish populations have their Junior's late-night, brightly lit delis featuring overstuffed combination cold-cut sandwiches, but nowhere outside of Brooklyn will you find kibitzing raised to the art it is at Junior's; and nowhere in the world can you eat cheesecake like this . . . thicker than most, barely gummy, so dense that it requires some effort of mouth to wrench it from the tines of the fork. Coffee, preferably black, helps float it down."

—Jane and Michael Stern, food and travel writers

In 1973, Junior's style, charm, and reputation for good food day or night were catapulted to citywide celebrity on a pastrami sandwich and a forkful of cheesecake. Frankly, life has never been the same. Through publicity (which we never generated) during the winter, summer, and fall of 1973, Junior's became more than a favorite for Brooklynites. We became one good reason jaded Manhattanites ventured across the East River and why tourists in Midtown would explain to the taxi driver that they wanted to go to Brooklyn. Here's how it all happened.

In the winter of 1973, the Underground Gourmet of *New York* magazine secretly taste-tested New York's pastrami-sandwich offerings. There were eighteen eateries in the competition, only one in the Bronx and one (Junior's) in Brooklyn. We came in fifth place, beating out, among others, the Carnegie Deli, Second Avenue Deli, the Stage Deli, and Katz's. Out of all, we piled the most meat on, giving you 6¾ ounces of pastrami for less money than, for example, the Carnegie's 5¼-ounce sandwich.

Then, in the summer of 1973, the *Village Voice* ran a long article challenging

With cheesecake success doubling our sales after 1973, we had this holiday postcard rendered. Courtesy of the Rosen family

Happy Holidays from Brooklyn, home of world-famous Junior's cheesecakes.

On Valentine's Day, 1974, there was a line around the block. For what? Junior's Cheesecake, naturally! Courtesy of the Rosen family

Loves me.

Loves me not.

Loves me.

Loves me not.

Loves me.

Say it with Junior's Cheesecake.

205

This picture with Bob Lape, the food columnist; Paul, the head baker at Junior's; Marvin on the extreme left; and Walter on the right was taken in our bakery in 1973 shortly after Junior's cheesecake had been family proclaimed the best in New York by *New York* magazine. Lape was trying to get the secret. Courtesy of the Rosen family

anyone anywhere to find a better cheesecake than the one at Junior's. The writer, Ron Rosenbaum, had such a profoundly pleasant experience here that he went on and on for four columns.

In the fall of 1973, *New York* magazine published the results of their secret cheesecake contest. A panel of six judges voted Junior's cheesecake the best in all of New York, beating out the famous Stage Delicatessen and Ratner's Dairy Restaurant.

We were elated! Since New Yorkers then reportedly ate an estimated ten thousand cheesecakes a day (about twenty-five thousand pounds), being voted the best was not only an obvious honor but great free advertising. We had never been much for promotion. We had just done our work and let our reputation spread by word of melt-in-your-mouth. My father, of course, was thrilled! This had been his goal—to make and sell the best cheesecake in the world. He was also quick to remind us that it's harder to keep a good reputation than it is to get one.

Because of the need to pose for photographs, we knew the contest results about one month before the public did. We ordered orange-colored *We're # 1* buttons, which our staff wore beginning the day the magazine hit the stands. And one week after the *New York* magazine article, we had begun to double business. An average day saw two thousand customers between the restaurant and the retail bakery. About five hundred cakes went out over the counter and about five hundred slices were served to diners. Our head baker and his staff of eight worked round the clock to keep up with the demand for cheesecakes. By 1977, our bakers were producing five thousand cheesecakes weekly.

Junior's started to be included in New York City tour guides—what to see and where to go in New York. Politicians, such as Mayor Abe Beame and, later on, Ed Koch, made Junior's their unofficial Brooklyn headquarters. And why not? What place could be better for a politician to sit down to a pastrami on rye or a dinner of salmon croquettes and visit with a large number of his constituency?

It was, and still is, always politically correct to drop in at Junior's. Borough President Howard Golden had (still has) a number of political breakfasts here throughout the year. So do city attorneys, prominent businessmen and women, professors and students. It seems that a real cross section of modern society—from Buddy Holly and Elvis Presley back in the 1950s to the Reverend Al Sharpton, Joe Torre, Robert DeNiro, and Evander Holyfield—have made Junior's their place to meet and eat as well.

The Faces of Junior's

Kevin Rosen and Alan Rosen, Walter's young sons, began to spend time in the restaurant helping out during the 1970s. They took to it almost too enthusiastically. Kevin, at five years old, helped Camille at the bakery counter, placing Danish on the tray. He'd eat one for every one he placed. When he had eaten enough, Camille would assign him to doily-separation duty.

Fred Morgan, third from the top in the longevity list of employees here (after Camille Russo, who came in 1960, and Mary Blevins, in 1962), came to work for us in 1972, just in time for what would become known as the cheesecake boom of 1973. Fred was from Panama and a waiter well trained in what my father, Harry Rosen, called the "talent of good service." To this day, Fred is there with the coffee refill before you can form the thought of wanting more. He knows that you're having decaf without a reminder, and when you come back on another day, he's got the steaming cup waiting as you sit down. He's that good! And he's one of the reasons customers will choose to sit at the counter rather than at a table.

Downtown and Down the Block

Outside and down the street from Junior's, more changes were affecting downtown. In 1976, the beautiful Albee Theater came down. The Albee had been a consummate vaudeville and first-run movie palace, then later, the RKO Albee. Al Jolson and Bill Robinson, among hundreds of others, had performed there early on. A friend of ours took his first date there in the late 1930s. They heard Jack Benny play violin and crack jokes before Spike Jones and his crazy band of noisemakers took over with their slide-whistling and banjo-banging antics. If the Paramount had been the diamond of downtown, the Albee, one block away, had been pure gold. It was a warm and stately place with a backstage so large it could care for the traveling vaudevillian with a laundry, a tailor, a nursery for child care, rooms with kitchenettes, a recreation room, and a safe to store valuables.

As with the other theaters, the Albee could not compete with suburban movie houses and television, and it closed in 1976. The house, which seated 3,200, on closing day could draw no more than three hundred people.

Welcome to Junior's!

The following year, after the Albee was razed, an indoor tri-level shopping mall with food court was erected on the old property. It was named, appropriately, the Albee Square Mall. Nowadays it's got a longer and, I guess, a glitzier name—the MetroTech Gallery at Albee Square Mall. To get an idea of how large the theater space once was, one need only walk through the mall today. There are more than two dozen retail shops—shoe stores, clothiers, optometrists—several pushcart vendors selling small specialties such as picture frames, stuffed toys, and costume jewelry, and nearly all the fast-food eateries a shopper could desire.

The mall was a good idea. It helped spur the slow comeback of downtown shopping, which had been slacking off. We began to get the feeling that downtown and all of Brooklyn could come back. In fact it was well on its way.

This is the Cyclone in 1970, and it's still diving, whipping, rolling, and terrifying riders today. Photo by Milton Berger, courtesy of the Kingsborough Historical Society

1970s—Specialties of the House

COMFORT FOOD . . . THAT'S what folks needed in the seventies, for that's when things were deteriorating all around Brooklyn. Those who lived and worked there turned to family, friends, familiar faces, and places to pull them through. Mealtimes were good times—in some cases, the *only* good times in a day. The more food, the better. The bigger the portions, the better. In those hard times, Junior's just kept doing what it does best: offering a safe haven where you knew you could always get an overstuffed pastrami sandwich. But not just any pastrami sandwich—one that was rated by the Underground Gourmet for piling on the most meat for the money.

And anytime you really needed a big treat, all you had to do was stop into Junior's for a slice of cheesecake. There were so many flavors to choose from, it was always a little hard to decide. Still is. And what better place to go? After all, all of us in Brooklyn knew it was Number 1, as far as cheesecakes go. But then in the fall of 1973, *New York* magazine made it official by publishing the results of their secret cheesecake-tasting contest. They voted Junior's cheesecake the best of the best in New York.

The Deli

WHAT'S FOR LUNCH? Walk right up to Junior's deli take-out window or sit down at the counter and pick your favorite. If you want the real thing—the authentic deli sandwich—this is the place. Pastrami, corned beef, roast beef—whatever you like, and on whatever you like, from an onion rye roll to a pumpernickel round or a slab of Challah.

Originally, the word *deli* comes as an abbreviation of *delicatessen*, derived from the German word *Delikatesse*, meaning "delicacy." In Germany during the 1880s, *deli* referred to preserved foods.

After the Civil War, many Jews emigrated to America and set up butcher shops, known as *schlacht* stores. But gradually, store after store added more items to their shelves until they were called an appetizing store or a delicatessen store, later shortened to *deli* or *delly*. Often foods served there were referred to by the same name.

At Junior's, many favorites of the Jewish culture are served daily—from pastrami to potato salad, sauerkraut, pickles, beets, and rye bread. High on the list is a collection of overstuffed, freshly cooked, expertly spiced, and professionally sliced deli sandwiches. Take the hints and tips from Junior's and try these famous deli combinations.

A Deli Sandwich the Junior's Way

The Meats—cook, simmer, spice, and slice it up right

- *Roast beef*—At least one steamship of beef, weighing about twenty pounds, is roasted, sliced, and served every day at Junior's. Ask your butcher for a tender roasting cut, such as a standing rib roast or a rib eye roast—the less cooking needed to tenderize the meat, the juicier the meat. Before placing the meat in the oven to roast, layer the outside generously with coarse kosher salt. Baste the beef frequently with the pan juices during roasting.

- *Corned beef*—As with all Jewish-style corned beef, Junior's serves only corned beef made from brisket of beef. Long ago, the brisket was cured in cement tanks and wooden barrels, but today that's not permitted in the United States. Instead, flavorings are injected into the meat, then the brisket is cured in a flavored brine for several days. Finally, it's trimmed by hand, then expertly cooked by the chef. He slowly simmers it for several hours until it's tender and spicy in a pot of cooking water sometimes flavored with onions, carrots, spices, and a little vinegar. While it's still warm, the staff professionally slices it across the grain about ½ inch thick, then stuffs it into Junior's famous corned beef sandwiches.

- *Pastrami*—In the olden days, the term *pastrami* referred to any cut of meat that was cured and smoked. But at Junior's, pastrami always means cured and smoked *beef*—no other kind. At the smokehouse, the meat is first soaked in a liquid brine with flavorings and seasonings for four or five days minimum (the longer, the better). Then it's removed from the brine and flavored again, this time with a spice blend that includes allspice, coriander, and garlic. It then travels by conveyor belt to racks in the smokehouse to slowly smoke for 4½ hours over hard hickory wood. It's then refrigerated overnight, and transported by refrigerated trucks to Junior's to be warmed, sliced, and stuffed into sandwiches. On request, a stack of pastrami is covered with cheese, then melted under the broiler before being made into a "pastrami melt."

- *Breast of turkey*—As might be expected, only natural oven-roasted turkey breast is served at Junior's—with no extras (such as salt, sugar, or water) added. You get only the real thing when you order a white meat sliced turkey sandwich or a hot turkey sandwich with gravy, cranberry sauce, and French fried potatoes.

Welcome to Junior's!

- *Baked Virginia ham*—Only the more moist, milder, sugar-cured hams are sliced at Junior's, not the drier salty country hams. To bake and glaze hams their way, see page 179.

- *Breads—Freshly baked every day.* Have any sandwich your way—on whatever bread or roll you like. Choose Vienna rolls, plain, sesame, or poppyseed; onion rye rolls; pumpernickel rolls; Challah (little twisted rolls with sesame seeds, or a sandwich loaf, or the traditional braid). Or use your favorite bread—pumpernickel, rye, whole wheat, or white.

There's a lot of know-how in the slicing of deli meats! For the tenderest cut, slice across the grain. Use a slicer (the knife with the long straight-edged blade) and, above all, keep it sharp. When making sandwiches, slice the meat thin and stack the slices up high.

Junior's Sandwich Board

- *Corned beef and pastrami* on onion rolls
- *Fresh roasted beef* on onion rye rolls
- *Baked Virginia ham and turkey* on Challah
- *Something Else*—Rumanian beef tenderloin (that's tenderloin sliced very thin), grilled just the way you like, on club rye bread, served with a slice of fresh tomato and curly leaf lettuce. Heap up some French fries alongside.
- *Brisket Melt*—Freshly roasted beef brisket, sliced thin, and stacked on a slice of Challah. Smothered Onions (page 213) are piled on top, then covered with 2 slices of Muenster cheese. The second slice of Challah gets 2 more cheese slices, then both are broiled until the cheese melts. It's all served open-faced with a hefty helping of French fries.
- *Something Different*—Freshly roasted beef brisket stuffed between 2 potato pancakes and served with applesauce on the side (page 320)
- *Hot Open Sandwiches*—Serve sandwiches open-faced with gravy and French fried potatoes. Try these combos at home, the day after you've roasted a roast or baked a ham. Make them on Challah if you have time to bake some, or old-fashioned white, wheat, or rye:
  - Open prime roast beef with beef gravy
  - Open brisket of beef with beef gravy

1970s—In a Can't-Do World . . . Brooklyn Starts Doing

- Open baked Virginia ham with gravy

- Open roast turkey with giblet gravy and cranberry sauce

- *Hickory-smoked turkey, Black Forest ham, and Brie cheese* stuffed into an onion rye baguette spread with honey mustard

- *BAR B-Q brisket of beef* on twin rolls, served with French fries alongside

- *Sliced turkey, baked Virginia ham, Swiss cheese, and cole slaw*, on Challah with Russian dressing (page 89) on the side

- *Egg salad and bacon* on Challah

- *BLT*—The bacon's always crisp, the tomatoes red-ripe, the lettuce curly and crisp— on white toast (both sides are toasted)

- *Junior's Famous 10 oz. Steakburgers* on oven-toasted buns with "the works" (page 172)

- *Melted American cheese and bacon* (3 thick slices), served open-faced on thick slices of Challah

- *Nova Scotia salmon and cream cheese* served open-faced on a bagel with fresh tomato, curly leaf lettuce, and a slice of Bermuda onion

- *Chopped chicken liver* on rye bread with a slice of fresh tomato, curly leaf lettuce, and a slice of Bermuda onion

- *Baked Virginia ham and Swiss* on sesame seed Vienna rolls with Creamy Cole Slaw (page 138) and Russian dressing

- *Beef tongue and Swiss* on club rye bread with Creamy Cole Slaw and Russian dressing

- *Fresh roasted turkey and Swiss* on poppyseed rolls with Creamy Cole Slaw and Russian dressing

- *Junior's chicken salad and bacon* served open-faced on thick slices of whole wheat

- *Corned beef and chopped liver* on club rye

- *Corned beef and melted Swiss cheese* with Creamy Cole Slaw on pumpernickel

- *Turkey, corned beef, and pastrami* on twin rye rolls

- *Virginia ham, Swiss cheese, and turkey* on Challah

214

Welcome to Junior's!

The Deli Board

THE DELI BOARD —Great sandwiches and salads start with the freshest ingredients—and the Sandwich Board at Junior's is always well stocked. **Here are some things you'll always find:**

- Pickled red pepper strips
- Fresh broccoli florets (blanched a few minutes)
- Fresh ripe tomato slices
- Red onion slices
- Red pickled peppers
- Garbanzo beans (canned, well drained)
- Creamy cottage cheese
- Pickled Beets (page 140)
- Freshly made Creamy Cole Slaw (page 138)
- Freshly made Red Potato Salad (page 321)
- Freshly made egg salad
- Freshly made White Meat Chicken Salad à la Junior's (page 30)
- Freshly made Junior's Shrimp Salad (page 192)
- Professionally sliced meats—turkey, pastrami, corned beef, roast beef
- Grilled white meat of chicken (cut in strips)
- Bacon strips, cooked until crispy, drained
- Cheeses (slices and strips)—Swiss, American   Jack
- Julienned carrot strips
- Hard-boiled eggs, peeled and cut in wedges
- Green beans, blanched and chilled
- Stuffed green olives
- Spreads—Hellmann's *Real* Mayonnaise, Dijon mustard, Russian Dressing (page 89)
- Corn, onion, and red bean salad
- Sautéed Mushrooms (page 174)
- Grilled Peppers and Onions (page 76)

1970s—In a Can't-Do World . . . Brooklyn Starts Doing

Onion Rye Rolls

ALMOST EVERY TIME the giant ovens are baking away in the bake shoppe, I see at least a dozen pans of these rolls on the revolving shelves, with thirty-five rolls on each pan. That's at least 420 of these rolls, rising and baking almost any time of day. Each one of these rolls is the size of an oversized hamburger bun, unless the bakers are baking the smaller twin onion rye rolls, as they often do, which are only three inches in diameter instead of four.

There's good reason for making so many of these rolls. They are the most asked-for roll that Junior's makes and are used in its most popular sandwich: Corned Beef and Pastrami Combo on Onion Rye Rolls.

MAKES A DOZEN ROLLS ABOUT 4 INCHES IN DIAMETER OR 2 DOZEN TWIN ROLLS, ABOUT 3 INCHES IN DIAMETER

3¾ cups unbleached all-purpose flour

⅓ cup rye flour

4 tablespoons sugar

2 tablespoons malted milk powder

1 tablespoon salt

2 teaspoons caraway seeds

1 cup water (105° to 115°F)

2 ¼-ounce packages active dry yeast

1 extra-large egg

⅓ cup vegetable oil

1½ cups coarsely chopped yellow onions

FOR GLAZING THE ROLLS

1 extra-large egg

½ teaspoon vegetable oil

The Junior's Way—

Place the rolls about two inches apart, not touching, on the baking sheet. As they rise and bake, the rolls are far enough apart to give rising room, and not close enough to touch their neighboring rolls in the oven. Before placing each pan of rolls in the oven, generously sprinkle the tops of the rolls with coarsely chopped onions.

1. Mix together both flours, 3 tablespoons of the sugar, the malted milk powder, salt, and caraway seeds in a medium-sized bowl. Set aside.

2. Make the yeast sponge: Stir the water, yeast, and the remaining tablespoon of sugar in a small bowl until dissolved. Let the mixture stand until it is foamy and light, about 5 minutes.

3. Meanwhile, using an electric mixer equipped with a dough hook or a paddle, beat the egg and ⅓ cup oil in a large bowl on high until light yellow. Reduce the speed to low and beat in the yeast mixture, then the flour mixture, then 1 cup of the onions.

4. Knead the flour mixture by beating the dough on high for 15 minutes (the dough will be smooth and elastic).

5. Transfer the dough to a well-buttered bowl and turn over the dough once to coat it well with the butter (the dough will be sticky). Cover the dough and let it rise at room temperature until it's double its size (this will probably take about 1 hour).

6. Preheat the oven to 400°F and butter 2 baking sheets. Punch the dough down with your fist to deflate it. Turn out the dough onto a lightly floured surface. Flour your hands and lightly knead the dough until it's no longer sticky, about 2 minutes.

7. To make dinner-size 4-inch rolls: Cut the dough into 4 equal pieces, then each piece into 3 more equal pieces, using kitchen shears. You will have 12 little mounds of dough. (For smaller twin rolls, divide the dough into 24 equal pieces.) Flour your hands well. Pick up each piece of dough in the palm of your hand and shape it into a rounded roll with a smooth top. Place the rolls about 2 inches apart on the baking sheets.

8. Whisk the egg with the ½ teaspoon oil and brush this glaze on top of each roll. Sprinkle with the remaining ½ cup onions. Cover the rolls and let them rise until light and doubled in size, about 30 minutes more. Bake the rolls until they are golden and set, about 10 to 12 minutes for the twin rolls, 13 to 15 minutes for the buns. Serve them warm or at room temperature or use for overstuffed sandwiches. These are outstanding when filled with layers of freshly sliced warm corned beef on the bottom and sliced pastrami on top.

History of the Cheesecake

AS FAR BACK in history as 2000 B.C., folks have been making cheese, as documented by the discovery of cheese molds at that time. Although the origin of the cheesecake is unknown and obscure, it is widely accepted that these popular cakes made from cheese originated in ancient Greece. It's a fact that this delicacy was served to the athletes in the first Olympic Games in 776 B.C., and the island of Samos was famous for its cheesecake. In 500 B.C., the Greek playwright Mayris described a deep-fried honey-covered version of the cheesecake. And later, the Greek scholar and social historian Athenseus recorded a cheesecake recipe in his writings.

Following the conquest of Greece by the Roman Empire, the cheesecake began spreading fast across Europe. In fact, the Romans soon discovered that many cultures were already familiar with cheese making. As they entered each new country, culinary techniques and the local customs mixed to develop many new cheesecake creations throughout Europe.

As European immigrants arrived in America, they brought their cheesecake *receipts* (recipes) and knowledge of making these delicacies with them. When American dairymen tried to duplicate the popular French cheese Neufchâtel in 1872, they created cream cheese. Then James L. Kraft developed the method of pasteurizing cheese in 1912. The mass distribution of Philadelphia brand cream cheese followed, making it possible for homemakers throughout America to bake heavenly cheesecake creations.

Welcome to Junior's!

The Birth of Junior's Cheesecake

THERE'S ONLY ONE way to make a cheesecake—the Harry Rosen way . . . the Junior's Way . . . the right way. The real recipe has remained a family secret for over fifty years. My father was a perfectionist in everything he did, especially when it came to Junior's food and particularly when it came to baking cheesecakes.

It was 1950 and Junior's was just about to open its doors. My father hired Eigel Peterson, a Danish baker, and together they began creating menu items. Everywhere he went, Father never came back empty-handed. Whether in Manhattan or traveling in far-away places, he was always stopping in at neighborhood bakeries and cafés to taste anything that looked extra-good, and choosing the best slice of cake or just-baked roll, he'd bring it back to Junior's. Back home, he'd go up to the bakery and help Eigel and his bakers mix and bake, then mix and bake again, until they duplicated it. Then they'd start baking some more to make it even better.

That was the way it was with the cheesecake. In those days, just like today, New Yorkers loved their cheesecake. There was lots of competition—Lindy's, Reuben's, even the local diner down the street. The Brass Rail nearby had an excellent cheesecake. Some were dense, creamy, and rich . . . others, towering, airy, and a little crumbly . . . still others quickly melted-in-your-mouth, but without that rich creamy taste. Father would bring slices of cheesecake back to the restaurant, then start stirring up batters with Eigel. Father was a hands-on creative boss; he could be seen beating and stirring up the batters alongside his bakers at any hour of the day.

Finally a cheesecake came out of the oven that pleased my father. It had a delicious layer of buttery light sponge cake on the bottom, instead of the usual graham cracker crust. It's the same one we use today but it always stays fresh and moist until the cheesecake is eaten (it never gets soggy like graham cracker crusts often do).

The filling my father and Eigel developed had all of the things one wants in a bite of cheesecake—creamy but not heavy, light without falling apart as you take a forkful, and of course that rich cheesy flavor with just a hint of lemon. Most of all, the cheesecake tasted great—better than any others my father had ever tasted. We still make that same cheesecake today. Nothing has changed.

In 1973, without our knowing it, an editor from *New York* magazine ordered one of Junior's cheesecakes for a taste-off by six cool-headed food professionals (real cheesecake lovers!). They rated twelve Jewish-style plain cheesecakes for freshness, quality of ingredients, and just plain good taste and enjoyment.

After the last slice was eaten and the scores were tallied, Junior's emerged the winner—the BEST of the BEST! Maybe it was the high-quality cream cheese, fresh eggs, heavy cream, and sugar that are used. Or maybe it was the sensitive blending of those ingredients. But whatever the reasons, that article, and many others since then, began telling the Junior's story. Years later, millions are fast to agree—Junior's cheesecake deserves all the fame, fortune, and happy customers it continues to receive.

Welcome to Junior's!

Junior's Famous No. 1 Pure Cream Cheesecake— The Best of the Best!

"THERE NEVER WILL be a better cheesecake than the cheesecake they serve at Junior's on Flatbush Avenue . . . it's the best cheesecake in New York," wrote Ron Rosenbaum (*Village Voice*, July 26, 1973). After that article, a jury of six cool-headed cheesecake lovers for *New York* magazine named Junior's the Champion Cheesecake in 1974. Through it all, many writers, celebrities, and just plain folks have tried to describe this best-of-the-best cheesecake—smooth and light, soft and creamy, heavenly and delicious, rather sweet, a complex play of many exciting and subtle flavor overloads. But there's nothing better than baking a cheesecake similar to the ones they make at Junior's. You'll soon be experiencing the taste of ecstasy.

MAKES ONE 9-INCH CAKE, ABOUT 2½ INCHES HIGH

1 recipe Thin Sponge Cake Layer for Cheesecake (page 223)

FOR THE CREAM CHEESE FILLING

*4 8-ounce packages cream cheese (the regular variety, not
      light Neufchâtel cream cheese), at room temperature*

1⅔ cups sugar

¼ cup cornstarch

1 tablespoon pure vanilla extract

2 extra-large eggs

¾ cup heavy whipping cream

> **The Junior's Way—**
> Let the cream cheese warm up to room temperature before making the filling. This lets you beat more air into the cheese mixture, making a lighter, higher, yet still creamy cheesecake.

1. Preheat the oven to 350°F and generously butter a 9-inch springform pan. Make the batter for the sponge cake as the recipe directs. Evenly spread the batter

1970s—In a Can't-Do World . . . Brooklyn Starts Doing

on the bottom of the pan, and bake just until set and golden, about 10 minutes. Place the cake on a wire rack to cool (do not remove it from the pan).

2. While the cake cools, make the cream cheese filling: Place one 8-ounce package of the cream cheese, ⅓ cup of the sugar, and the cornstarch in a large bowl. Beat with an electric mixer on low until creamy, about 3 minutes, then beat in the remaining 3 packages of cream cheese.

3. Increase the mixer speed to high and beat in the remaining 1⅓ cups of the sugar, then beat in the vanilla. Blend in the eggs, one at a time, beating the batter well after adding each one. Blend in the heavy cream. At this point, mix the filling only until completely blended (just like they do at Junior's). Be careful not to overmix the batter.

4. Gently spoon the cheese filling on top of the baked sponge cake layer. Place the springform pan in a large shallow pan containing hot water that comes about 1 inch up the sides of the pan. Bake the cheesecake until the center barely jiggles when you shake the pan, about 1 hour.

5. Cool the cake on a wire rack for 1 hour. Then cover the cake with plastic wrap and refrigerate until it's completely cold, at least 4 hours or overnight. Remove the sides of the springform pan. Slide the cake off of the bottom of the pan onto a serving plate. Or if you wish, simply leave the cake on the removable bottom of the pan and place it on a serving plate. If any cake is left over, cover it with plastic wrap and store in the refrigerator.

Welcome to Junior's!

Thin Sponge Cake Layer for Cheesecake

MOST CHEESECAKES ARE made with a graham cracker crust, which can get very soggy as the cake stands in the refrigerator waiting to be eaten.

Junior's has not only eliminated the soggy crust, they have created their cheesecake with a delicious light and airy sponge cake layer on the bottom that stays heavenly and moist until the last piece of cake is served.

The bakers on Flatbush Avenue make so many cheesecakes that they bake up sponge cake after sponge cake, then slice each cake into four layers, making enough light sponge for four cheesecakes.

Since you'll probably want to make only one cheesecake at a time, I've created this recipe from Junior's master recipe, which makes only enough sponge for one cheesecake. Bake the batter in the same springform pan you're using for the cheesecake, then spoon on the filling and bake the sponge layer again with the creamy cheesecake filling on top.

MAKES ONE 9-INCH SPONGE CAKE LAYER, ¾ INCH HIGH, ENOUGH FOR ONE CHEESECAKE

½ cup sifted cake flour

1 teaspoon baking powder

Pinch of salt

3 extra-large eggs, separated

⅓ cup plus 2 tablespoons sugar

1 teaspoon pure vanilla extract

3 drops pure lemon extract

3 tablespoons unsalted butter, melted

¼ teaspoon cream of tartar

The Junior's Way—
Watch this cake carefully while it's baking. There's not much batter, so it needs only about ten minutes of baking— only enough time for the cake to turn light golden and set on the top. The cake should not brown on top.

continued

1970s—In a Can't-Do World . . . Brooklyn Starts Doing

1. Preheat the oven to 350°F and generously butter a 9-inch springform pan. Sift the cake flour, baking powder, and salt together in a medium-sized bowl and set aside.

2. Beat the egg yolks together in a large bowl with an electric mixer on high for 3 minutes. Then, with the mixer still running, gradually add the ⅓ cup of sugar and continue beating until thick light-yellow ribbons form in the bowl, about 5 minutes more. Beat in the vanilla and lemon extracts.

3. Sift the flour mixture over the batter and stir it in by hand until no more white flecks appear. Then blend in the butter.

4. In a clean bowl, using clean dry beaters, beat the egg whites and cream of tartar together on high until frothy. Gradually add the remaining 2 tablespoons sugar and continue beating until stiff peaks form (the whites should stand up in stiff peaks, but not be dry). Stir about ⅓ cup of the whites into the batter, then gently fold in the remaining whites (don't worry if a few white specks remain).

5. Gently spoon the batter into the pan. Bake the cake just until the center of the cake springs back when lightly touched, only about 10 minutes (watch carefully!). Let the cake cool in the pan on a wire rack while you continue making the cheesecake filling. Do not remove the cake from the pan.

Fresh Strawberry Cheesecake

EVERY DAY OF the week, bakers in Junior's bake shoppe are busy making strawberry cheesecakes. One baker carefully washes, hulls, and picks through quarts and quarts of gorgeous strawberries. Only the best of the best berries, all similar in size and shape, get chosen to top Junior's famous cheesecakes. The rest of the berries are sliced by the afternoon crew for layering into Junior's Famous Fresh Strawberry Shortcakes and stirring into their famous strawberry sauce.

Another baker proudly prepares the sponge cake layer for the cheesecakes.

Welcome to Junior's!

Still another one whips up the filling. The fourth baker adds just the right amount of water to the baking pans to steam them perfectly and then monitors them as they go tediously round and round in the giant ovens. When the cakes are done, he transfers them onto tall baker's racks and wheels them into the walk-in refrigerator. Then, the baker who picked out all the berries begins decorating each cake. He arranges each berry carefully by hand—laying the berries side-by-side until each cake is covered.

Next he drizzles the cakes with a strawberry glaze, giving them a bright shine, and adds the finishing touch: a generous sprinkle of crunchy macaroon crumbs around the edge.

Since most of us do not have barrels of macaroon crumbs sitting around as they do at Junior's, I have substituted, at the master baker's suggestion, a mixture of toasted nuts and coconut. They work just fine.

MAKES ONE 9-INCH CAKE, ABOUT 2½ INCHES HIGH

1 recipe *Thin Sponge Cake Layer for Cheesecake (page 223)*
1 recipe *Junior's Famous No. 1 Pure Cream Cheesecake*
(page 221)

FOR THE MACAROON CRUNCH
½ cup chopped mixed nuts (almonds, pecans, and/or
walnuts)
⅓ cup angel flake coconut

FOR THE STRAWBERRY TOPPING
1 quart large ripe strawberries
1 cup strawberry jelly
⅓ cup apricot preserves

The Junior's Way—
Look for extra-large ripe strawberries, all about the same size. Look for the brightest, reddest ones in the market. When placing them on the top of the cake, take time to arrange them in a decorative way with ends pointing in the same direction, toward the edge.

1. Preheat the oven to 350°F and butter a 9-inch springform pan. Make and bake the sponge cake layer. Make the cheesecake filling and bake the cake as for Junior's Famous No. 1 Pure Cream Cheesecake. Transfer the baked cake to a wire rack to cool, about 1 hour.

continued

2. While the cake is baking and cooling, make the macaroon crunch: Spread the nuts and coconut on a baking sheet and toast in a 350°F oven until golden and crunchy, about 10 to 15 minutes. Set the crunch aside to cool.

3. To prepare the strawberries: Wash, hull, and sort through the strawberries, then pat them dry with paper towels. Starting at the outside edge of the cheesecake, arrange the berries on their sides, in rows, with ends pointing toward the edge of the cake. Continue until the top of the cake is completely covered by strawberries.

4. Now make the strawberry topping: Melt the strawberry jelly and apricot preserves together in a small saucepan over medium-low heat. Strain and drizzle the warm jelly over the berries.

5. Sprinkle the macaroon crunch in a 1½-inch border around the edge of the cheesecake, covering the berries around the outside edge. Loosely cover the entire cake with plastic wrap, being careful not to let the glaze stick to the wrap. Refrigerate the cake until it's completely cold, at least 4 hours or overnight. Remove the cake from the pan and serve it chilled. Wrap any leftover cake in plastic wrap and store in the refrigerator.

Blueberry Cheesecake

BLUEBERRIES AND CREAM go together naturally. The taste treat is even better when the blueberries are fresh and sweetened just enough by a sugary sauce. The cream, in this case, comes in the form of Junior's cheesecake. All in all, a grand combination you'll want to serve again and again.

MAKES ONE 9-INCH CAKE, ABOUT 2½ INCHES HIGH

1 recipe Thin Sponge Cake Layer for Cheesecake (page 223)
1 recipe Junior's Famous No. 1 Pure Cream Cheesecake (page 221)

FOR THE MACAROON CRUNCH
½ cup chopped mixed nuts (almonds, pecans, and/or walnuts)
⅓ cup angel flake coconut

FOR THE BLUEBERRY TOPPING

2 cups fresh blueberries, picked over for stems and

  bruises

1 cup blueberry syrup (usually found near the ice cream

  freezer in the supermarket)

1 cup cold water

¼ cup cornstarch

2 tablespoons fresh lemon juice

1 tablespoon unsalted butter

1 teaspoon pure vanilla extract

1. Preheat the oven to 350°F and butter a 9-inch springform pan. Make and bake the sponge cake layer. Make the cheesecake filling and bake the cake as for Junior's Famous No. 1 Pure Cream Cheesecake. Transfer the baked cake to a wire rack to cool, about 1 hour.

2. While the cake is baking and cooling, make the macaroon crunch: Spread the nuts and coconut on a baking sheet and toast in a 350°F oven until golden and crunchy, 10 to 15 minutes. Set the crunch aside to cool.

3. Now make the blueberry topping: Wash the blueberries, remove any stems, and discard any bruised berries. Pat the berries dry with paper towels. Stir the syrup, water, and cornstarch together in a medium-sized saucepan until the cornstarch is thoroughly dissolved. Bring this mixture to a full boil over high heat, stirring constantly, and boil for 2 minutes. Remove the syrup from the heat and stir in the lemon juice, butter, and vanilla. Gently fold in the blueberries. Let the blueberry topping cool for 15 minutes, then mound it on top of the cooled cake, covering the top of the cake completely.

4. Sprinkle the macaroon crunch in a 1½-inch border around the edge of the cheesecake, covering the berries around the outside edge. Loosely cover the entire cake with plastic wrap, being careful not to let the glaze stick to the wrap. Refrigerate the cake until it's completely cold, at least 4 hours or overnight. Remove the cake from the pan and serve it chilled. Wrap any leftover cake in plastic wrap and store in the refrigerator.

Pineapple Cheesecake

FOR THOSE WHO like pineapple, and most folks do, this recipe makes the perfect topping for one of Junior's cheesecakes. I like to add a little fresh pineapple too, but naturally that's not necessary. The canned pineapple works by itself just fine. But one caution: Don't use more fresh pineapple than the recipe calls for, as this can make the topping lose its stiffness.

MAKES ONE 9-INCH CAKE, ABOUT 2½ INCHES HIGH

1 recipe *Thin Sponge Cake Layer for Cheesecake (page 223)*

1 recipe *Junior's Famous No. 1 Pure Cream Cheesecake (page 221)*

FOR THE MACAROON CRUNCH

½ cup chopped mixed nuts (almonds, pecans, and/or walnuts)

⅓ cup angel flake coconut

FOR THE PINEAPPLE TOPPING

2 1-pound cans crushed pineapple in heavy syrup

3 tablespoons cornstarch

1 tablespoon fresh lemon juice

1 cup small fresh pineapple chunks (optional)

2 tablespoons unsalted butter, cut into small pieces

The Junior's Way— If you have the time, make this cheesecake the day before you plan on serving it, as they do at Junior's. Mound the pineapple topping on top of the cake. Then chill the cake overnight. It's easier to cut and serve this cake when it's completely chilled.

1. Preheat the oven to 350°F and butter a 9-inch springform pan. Make and bake the sponge cake layer. Make the cheesecake filling and bake the cake as for Junior's Famous No. 1 Pure Cream Cheesecake. Transfer the baked cake to a wire rack to cool, about 1 hour.

2. While the cake is baking and cooling, make the macaroon crunch: Spread the nuts and coconut on a baking sheet and toast in a 350°F oven until golden and crunchy, 10 to 15 minutes. Set the crunch aside to cool.

3. While the cake is cooling, make the pineapple filling: Drain the syrup from both cans of the pineapple into a measuring cup. Pour 1 cup of the syrup into a small saucepan and whisk in the cornstarch and lemon juice. Bring this mixture to a rolling boil over high heat and boil until thickened, about 2 minutes. Fold in the canned pineapple, plus the fresh pineapple, if you wish, and cook 1 minute more. Remove the topping from the heat and stir in the butter until melted. Pour the topping into a heatproof bowl and refrigerate until it's cold, about 30 minutes.

4. Mound the pineapple topping on top of the cooled cake, covering the top of the cake completely. Sprinkle the macaroon crunch in a 1½-inch border around the edge of the cheesecake, covering the fruit around the outside edge.

5. Loosely cover the entire cake with plastic wrap, being carefully not to let the glaze stick to the wrap. Refrigerate the cake until completely cold, at least 4 hours or overnight. Remove the cake from the pan and serve it chilled. Wrap any leftover cake in plastic wrap and store in the refrigerator.

Chocolate Swirl Cheesecake

*P*LAIN CHEESECAKE AT Junior's is always a treat.

But if you want something even more special, try this one with chocolate fudge swirled throughout. It resembles the marble cakes popular during the fifties. Those were made from butter-cake batter—half vanilla and the other half chocolate. The two batters were spooned alternately into cake pans, then swirled together before baking. When sliced, each piece resembled the swirling design that's found in colorful glass marbles that children love to play with.

This chocolate swirl cheesecake is even easier to create than the original marble cakes. All you need is a recipe of Junior's Famous No. 1 Cheesecake plus a jar of fudge ice cream topping. Simply swirl the fudge into the cake batter before baking. **When sliced and served, each piece is artistically swirled with deep rich fudge. Very impressive to serve—and a double treat in every bite.**

MAKES ONE 9-INCH CAKE, ABOUT 2 ½ INCHES HIGH

1 recipe Thin Sponge Cake Layer for Cheesecake
 (page 223)
1 recipe Junior's Famous No. 1 Pure Cream Cheesecake
 (page 221)
¾ cup fudge ice cream topping (the thick kind in a jar)

1. Preheat the oven to 350°F and butter a 9-inch springform pan. Make and bake the sponge cake layer.

2. Make the cheesecake filling and spread half of the batter on top of the baked sponge cake in the pan.

3. Warm the fudge ice cream topping in a small saucepan over low heat, stirring constantly. Watch carefully and do not let it boil. Drizzle the cheesecake batter in the pan with half of this warm fudge topping.

The Junior's Way—Be sure to buy the thick fudge ice cream topping, usually found in a jar near the ice cream freezer in the supermarket (the thinner type of chocolate syrup doesn't work well in this cake). The richer and thicker the topping, the better. Be sure to warm it before using it. And swirl it into the batter just until it's swirled throughout. Too much swirling will make the marble design disappear during baking.

4. Carefully spoon the remaining cheesecake filling on top and drizzle with the remaining fudge topping. Using a table knife, swirl the fudge topping into the batter, working in a circle and turning the knife constantly as you go. Swirl just until the fudge is marbled throughout—not enough to blend the colors.

5. Bake the cake in a water bath, as for Junior's Famous No. 1 Pure Cream Cheesecake, until the center barely jiggles when you shake the pan, about 1¼ hours. After the top of the cake sets and starts to brown, usually after about 45 minutes of baking, lay a piece of foil over the top of the cake for the remaining baking time. Cool, serve, and store the cake as directed for Junior's Famous No. 1 Pure Cream Cheesecake.

Apple Crumb Cheesecake

*T*AKE SLICES OF fresh apples tossed with cinnamon-sugar. Arrange them on top of a buttery sponge layer and cover with Junior's creamy cheesecake filling. Then circle the batter with more apples.

After baking, crown the cake with brown-sugar crumbs and shower it with powdered sugar. You'll have a creation that deserves all the raves and accolades it will undoubtedly receive.

MAKES ONE 10-INCH CAKE, ABOUT 2 ½ INCHES HIGH

1 recipe Thin Sponge Cake Layer for Cheesecake (page 223)
1 recipe Junior's Famous No. 1 Pure Cream Cheesecake (page 221)

FOR THE APPLE LAYER

½ cup granulated sugar

½ cup packed light brown sugar

2 tablespoons all-purpose flour

1 tablespoon cornstarch

½ teaspoon ground cinnamon

1½ pounds tart-sweet apples, such as McIntosh or
      Rome Beauty

1 tablespoon fresh lemon juice

FOR THE BROWN-SUGAR CRUMB TOPPING

1 cup all-purpose flour

½ cup packed light brown sugar

½ teaspoon ground cinnamon

6 tablespoons (¾ stick) cold unsalted butter, cut into small pieces

¼ cup vegetable shortening

¼ teaspoon lemon extract

⅓ cup sifted confectioners' sugar

The Junior's Way—
Take a little extra time to arrange the apples in the batter in a circular pattern. Place them so they stand up straight in the cake. You'll need twenty to twenty-five slices. This way, each slice will not only have apples on the bottom but throughout the cake.

continued

1. Preheat the oven to 350°F and butter a 10-inch springform pan. Make and bake the sponge cake layer. Make the cheesecake batter and refrigerate it while you prepare the apples.

2. To make the apple layer: Toss both of the sugars, the flour, cornstarch, and cinnamon in a small bowl. Peel, core, and slice the apples ¼ inch thick into a large bowl (you need 4 cups of apples). Drizzle the apples with the lemon juice and toss them gently with your hands to mix well. Sprinkle the cinnamon-sugar mixture over the apples and toss again until all of the apple slices are well coated. Spread about two-thirds of this apple mixture over the baked sponge cake layer. Set the remaining apples aside.

3. Gently spread the cheesecake filling over the apples in the pan. Using your fingers, place one of the remaining spiced apple slices straight down in the batter about 2 inches from the edge, pushing it down until almost but not completely covered by the batter. Continue placing about 20 more slices into the batter in a circular pattern.

4. Bake the cake in a water bath, as for Junior's Famous No. 1 Pure Cream Cheesecake (page 221), until the center barely jiggles when you shake the pan, about 1¼ hours. When the top sets and starts to brown, after about 50 minutes of baking, lay a piece of foil over the top of the cake for the rest of the baking.

5. While the cake bakes, make the brown-sugar crumb topping: Mix the flour, brown sugar, and cinnamon together in a medium-sized bowl. Work the butter and shortening into this flour mixture with your fingers or a pastry blender until the mixture looks like coarse crumbs about the size of small peas. Stir in the lemon extract.

6. Cool the cake on a wire rack for 30 minutes and chill until cold, about 4 hours. Top the cake with the crumb mixture and dust it completely with the confectioners' sugar. Cover the cake loosely with plastic wrap and refrigerate it until it's time to serve. Remove the cake from the springform ring and transfer to a platter (leave the cake on the bottom of the pan if you wish). Wrap any leftover cake in plastic wrap and store in the refrigerator.

Pumpkin Cheesecake

DINE AT JUNIOR'S on Thanksgiving and enjoy a slice of the Pumpkin Cheesecake, or order a whole cake by overnight mail if you're not near Brooklyn. You'll be glad you did. A slice of this cheesecake comes out just as light and creamy as Junior's famous plain cake, but with a faint yellowish orange in color.

Look closely and you'll also see specks of cinnamon. Take a bite and enjoy the taste of the creamiest cheesecake and subtle pumpkin-pie flavors, all in one. Before you finish the last scrumptious bite, you'll start counting the days until next Thanksgiving.

Better yet, don't wait until next year—follow our recipe and bake several pumpkin cheesecakes throughout the year, right at home.

MAKES ONE 9-INCH CAKE, ABOUT 2 ½ INCHES HIGH

1 recipe Thin Sponge Cake Layer for Cheesecake (page 223)
1 1½-pound pie pumpkin (such as sugar baby) or 1 cup
    canned solid pack pumpkin
¾ teaspoon ground cinnamon
1 recipe Junior's Famous No. 1 Pure Cream Cheesecake
    (page 221)

The Junior's Way—
For the delicate-tasting pumpkin cheesecake that Junior's is famous for, start with a fresh pie pumpkin, just like they do for their holiday pies at Junior's. It takes a little extra time to prepare a fresh pumpkin, but when you taste the cheesecake, you'll be glad you did.

1. Preheat the oven to 350°F and butter a 9-inch springform pan. Make and bake the sponge cake layer.

2. If you're using the fresh pumpkin: Cut the pumpkin into quarters, discarding the stem, seeds, and pith. Cook the pumpkin in boiling water until tender and transfer it with a slotted spoon to paper towels to drain and cool. Now scrape the pulp into a medium-sized bowl and beat with an electric mixer until smooth (you need 1 cup of pumpkin purée). Beat in the cinnamon until blended. If you're using canned pumpkin, blend it with the cinnamon.

3. Make the cheesecake filling. Add the spiced pumpkin after blending in the eggs in Step 3 of the Junior's Famous No. 1 Pure Cream Cheesecake recipe (page 222).

4. Bake the cake, remove it from the pan, then cool, serve, and store it as directed for Junior's Famous No. 1 Pure Cream Cheesecake (page 222).

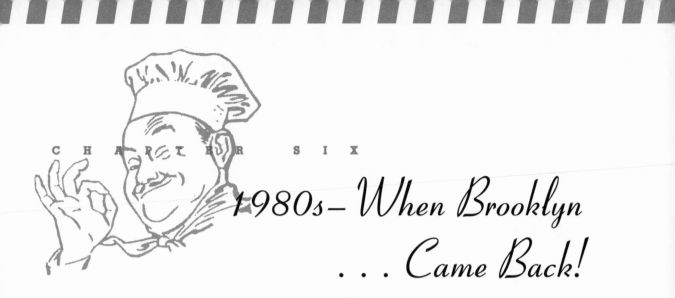

CHAPTER SIX

1980s – When Brooklyn . . . Came Back!

BROOKLYN'S STRUGGLE TO hold on to a sense of

independence and reestablish its innate character and

productivity took on an aggressive and political tone in the

early 1980s. Mayor Koch had been able to get Washington to

help bail New York City out of near bankruptcy in 1978.

Everybody in Brooklyn—from long-established shop owners

to the newest immigrant from Panama—pressed for monies

to help bring more small businesses back to neighborhoods,

This aerial shot of downtown and nearby neighborhoods shows the Brooklyn and Manhattan bridges and, at the arrow, the corner of DeKalb and Flatbush Avenue Extension, Junior's. Courtesy of the Brooklyn Historical Society

provide jobs for displaced manufacturing workers, take crime and drug problems off the streets, and help make Brooklyn neighborhoods feel safe. But the mayor's fiscal reforms mainly focused on tourism and revitalizing the Big Apple. There was the "I LOVE NY" campaign to bolster image and self-esteem, and the rebuilding of Midtown Manhattan so that corporations would want to return and investors would want to invest.

But it was widely thought that Mayor Koch's plans didn't foster community-wide prosperity—only prosperity for the upper-middle- and upper-class Manhattanites and corporate business. Meanwhile in Brooklyn and the other boroughs, impoverished African Americans, Hispanics, and low-income immigrants boarded up business districts while one or two merchants continued to struggle on their own.

Resentment began to brew here where we were still suffering from the bad decisions of the early 1960s. In 1981, three years after Washington bailed the city out of bankruptcy, our neighborhoods had ever-shrinking opportunities, more distress—more drugs on the streets, more violence and racial hostilities. There was still much to be done.

August 17, 1981, 1:00 A.M. Fire destroys the roof and top floor of Junior's. While firemen battle to save the restaurant, priceless records, photos, and memorabilia are destroyed. Courtesy of the *New York Post*—Lenore Davis/Corbis

Welcome to Junior's!

Just When You Think Things Couldn't Get Worse

Late on a hot Sunday, August 17, 1981, we had both gone home for the night. One of our waiters, Tony Seals, was upstairs in the employees' locker area at about closing time—1:30 A.M. Tony smelled something burning near the paper-goods room there on the second floor and he went to check it out. At the same time, down on the first floor, Roberto, our night manager, saw smoke drifting out of the air-conditioning vents and he sent someone up, too. A few seconds later Tony screamed for everyone to get out, while he and a couple others opened fire extinguishers into the heavy smoke they had discovered.

The second-floor smoke turned into violent flames in a matter of minutes. All fifty employees and seventy-five customers got out safely. Roberto called us right away, saying there was a fire but he didn't know how bad it was. It took three engine companies two and a half hours to contain the blaze, which by that time had brought the roof down in collapse. As firefighters shot water into the building, onlookers chanted: "Save the cheesecake, save the cheesecake!"

We arrived separately. Walter had to drive in from Great Neck. Marvin lived in Manhattan. Flatbush Avenue Extension was blocked off and the police were reluctant to let us through until they found out it was our restaurant that was burning. By the time we got there, most of the big damage was done. And it was worse than either of us had imagined. There was smoky night sky where our roof used to be.

The next morning, our counterman Marty Posner, who had worked for Junior's for twenty years, found out about the fire as he was getting on the bus to head down Flatbush for work. A neighbor happened to say to him, "Going to where you used to

---

ONE MORE BITE OF PIE

"It was orderly—the evacuation. Very calm. One patron said, 'Let me finish my pie à la mode.' And we let him finish his pie à la mode. Another man wanted to finish his cheese pie too, but when the smoke got heavier and the heat broke a lightbulb above him, he left fast—cheese pie, plate, fork, and all."

—Roberto, night manager, 1981

THE MORNING AFTER

Scene: A crowd of onlookers in front of Junior's. Smoke is still rising. A news crew meanders through the crowd. A reporter approaches a woman.

Reporter: *What brought you to Junior's this morning?*

Woman: *I'm shocked. I come here every morning for cheesecake and coffee on my way to work. Every morning. Not some mornings. Every morning!*

Reporter: *What are you going to do now?*

Woman: *I don't know.* (She looks at reporter squarely) *You're going to have to get the recipe. You are going to get the recipe and pass it on to us.*

(The crowd cheers.)

work?" When he got here, we were all standing outside the still-smoking building waiting until it was safe to enter. When I say we, there were the two of us, our families, and all the employees, too. I can't think of anyone who didn't stand out front with us on that Monday morning. No one could believe it. We stood in shock, staring at the charred remains of what were our offices and bakery. There were many others too—local TV news, camera crews, regular customers, and friends from the area.

Such a Mensch!

Arthur Ratner, who owned Albee Square Mall property, was a real mensch. The very next day, he led both of us over to a first-floor office space at the mall. He told us it was ours to use. We could have the space, the phones, whatever we needed until we reopened. He tore up a check we offered him for the rent. We are still grateful to Arthur. His was a supportive gesture that we really needed at the time. Neither one of us had ever had to come back from such a disaster.

Our employees were mensches, too. As soon as we could get into the space and start cleaning up, they were there. Many of our bakers, deli men, cooks, and waiters volunteered to step through rubble and carry boxes and equipment out. They knew they'd be out of work for months, but they pitched in anyway. They wore the *We're #1* buttons usually worn by the wait staff to advertise our status in the cheesecake world. Now, though, they were badges of loyalty.

Rumor Control

It took some time to assess the damage at about $1,000,000. Rumors started to fly that the fire was the work of an arsonist. An investigation never proved arson. And we always thought it was a cigarette butt— somebody smoking where they shouldn't have—that started the fire. No one ever came forward, but we think it was something careless like that.

Then there were more rumors—that we were leaving Brooklyn, that Junior's was relocating. We took every opportunity to assure the public that we would rebuild. Whenever a news crew came by or a reporter called, we told them with no uncertainty that we intended to rebuild. Junior's was a motherhouse, a place where everybody could come. It was known for its racial and economic integration. It was a landmark magnet that attracted office workers, families, and deal-making politicians. It was truly an everyman place. There was no way we were leaving.

"We intend to rebuild. We will be back. The cheesecake will return and be better than ever."

—Walter Rosen, *News 4 New York*, August 18, 1981

"Junior's is the pulse of the entire downtown area. With it—downtown ticks. This is our area. We've been here thirty years. We belong here and we feel obligated to rebuild."

—Marvin Rosen, New York *Daily News*, August 21, 1981

From out of the Ashes

The first order of business was literally to save the cheesecake! The old Barton Candy factory down on DeKalb had oven space and we started baking there and retailing through the candy distributor. We had a retail cheesecake kiosk in Albee Square Mall as well where customers could buy cheesecake by the slice or the cake. We put up signs on Junior's facade directing people down to the mall for cheesecake.

Kevin was a teenager then and he had an advertising group write and record a catchy jingle, "Here Comes the Dream Cheesecake from Junior's." He rigged speak-

There's a lot of cheesecake in the whole wide world, but there's only "one"
Number One.
Get ready, New York . . . for cheesecake at its best.
Here comes the dream cheesecake from Junior's.
Get ready, New York . . . We're a cut above the rest.
Here comes the dream cheesecake from Junior's.
Don't try to resist . . . Oh, Mama never baked a cake like this . . .
Get ready New York . . . for cheesecake at its best.
Here comes the dream cheesecake from Junior's . . .
Here comes the dream cheesecake from Junior's!

ers so that anyone could follow the sound of the jingle to the kiosk. When we weren't dealing with the heavy work of rebuilding Junior's, we were both down at the mall selling cheesecakes!

Most of the wait and cook staff took temporary jobs in other restaurants during the months of rebuilding. My father did not get involved in the reconstruction. Rather, he allowed us to make all of the decisions. After nine months and three days of slogging through renovation and day-to-day troubleshooting with equipment vendors and contractors, the two-million-dollar rebuilding was completed.

The Cheese Cakerie in the Albee Mall did a dynamite business for all the nine months and three days that Junior's was closed for renovation after the fire. Courtesy of the Rosen family

Welcome to Junior's!

The new Junior's—twenty-seven thousand square feet—nine thousand on each of three floors, looked like the old, but it was much bigger and better. We increased our seating by one hundred by adding a sidewalk café and bar which, even though it was the same orange-and-white color scheme as the main dining room, had a cozier feel and added even more character to the place. We closed the downstairs banquet room and turned it into storage and freezer space. But with the extra seating on the main floor at 450 instead of the 350 we used to seat, there was still plenty of room for parties. We updated all our kitchens, giving more space for a preparation kitchen, a short-order kitchen, salad preparation, a butcher department, and a catering department, and upstairs we added a refurbished bakery and office space.

The Champagne Flowed

Reopening day, May 27, 1982, was one huge party all afternoon. DeKalb Avenue was closed off. Dignitaries and friends and their families and our family filled the restaurant and spilled out into the street. There were speeches from Borough President Howard Golden and Mayor Koch. Golden proclaimed May 27 Junior's Day. Then he pointed to my father and said, "You're one of the people who has the true Brooklyn instinct—to come back again. If the Dodgers had done that, they'd have been smarter for it."

Senator Marty Markowitz said he'd lost seventeen pounds since the fire and was looking forward to growing back into his old suits. The Brooklyn Tech band

On reopening day in May 1982 people stood in line to get a seat in Junior's.

Courtesy of the *New York Post*—Lenore Davis/Corbis

LEFT: **Harry Rosen at the reopening of Junior's in 1982, thanking God, thanking Brooklyn, thanking everyone for coming. Borough President Howard Golden is on the right. Senator Marty Markowitz is on the left.** RIGHT: **Harry, Marvin, and Walter Rosen join Howard Golden as he presents a proclamation declaring May 27 as Junior's Day in Brooklyn!** Photos by Deborah Gardner, courtesy of the Rosen family

The line formed from early morning and went on late into the night. The only thing different about Junior's that day was the addition of the sidewalk café at left. Courtesy of the *New York Post*—Lenore Davis/Corbis

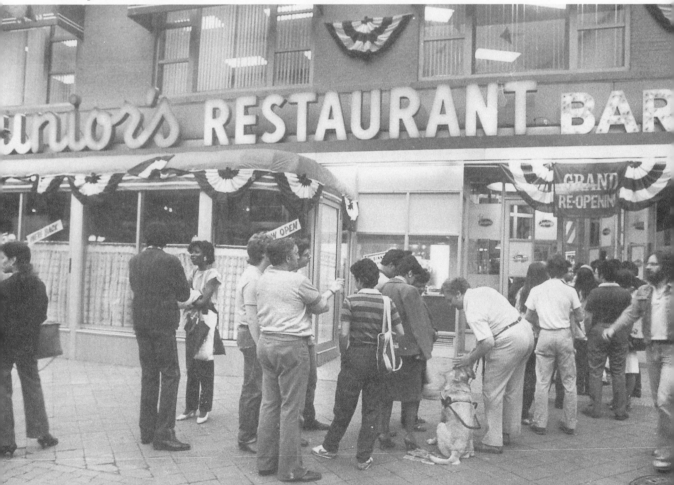

"When my wife, Judy, and I were courting, we would always stop at Junior's on our way home from PS 129 where we both taught. We would devour ice cream sodas. It was in Junior's where I first felt what in Sicily they call the "thunderbolt" and I told Judy of my love for her and took her hand in mine. We have friends who also courted at Junior's some thirty years ago. Whenever Judy and I would hear Petula Clark's hit 'Downtown,' it always meant Brooklyn, not Manhattan, and it always meant the heart of Brooklyn, Junior's."

—Nino Pantano, 1982

played. There were news crews. The Champagne flowed. But what was most gratifying was the joy on my father's face that day at seeing the hundreds of people fill up the booths and tables of Junior's.

It was true. People couldn't wait for us to return. The place was packed and still more people kept coming. Our feet were bleeding. We couldn't keep up. Everything went. We should have closed the doors at eight o'clock, telling everyone we were out of food. But that wouldn't be the Junior's Way. So we stayed open and did the best we could. Everyone just wanted to get back into Junior's. It was unbelievable! Even more gratifying was seeing our 150-strong staff back and working. We were finally back—same service, same food, same crowds.

More Good News

Brooklyn, let's face it, has always been considered the underdog, a kind of pet, by Manhattanites—not to be taken seriously as a viable city. We were stereotyped as the borough of working-class bums and eccentric characters à la Ed Norton from *The Honeymooners*. We were also known for bravado, street accents, and tough evil-deed-doers—a stereotype that went back to Al Capone and the Mad Bomber.

We seemed to be the only ones who treasured our cultural tradition—our own philharmonic, museums, gardens, theaters, one of the finest colleges in the country, and a litany of poets, writers, inventors, musicians, comics, actors, and directors that even these pages can't hold. But Manhattanites and much of the country stubbornly regarded us with disdain as Podunk. It was an attitude thing and we were used to it from across the river. It had been going on for more than a century. And we cheerfully reciprocated.

But in the early 1980s when young professionals and new artists, writers, actors, playwrights, opera singers, and musicians fled the high rents of Manhattan for the more affordable and architecturally interesting neighborhoods of Brooklyn, there was a surge of interest and respectful notice of Brooklyn by uppity Manhattanites.

Neighborhoods such as Cobble Hill, Fort Greene, Park Slope, Prospect Heights, Clinton Hill, and Bedford-Stuyvesant were well into slow but sure renovation through the efforts of local citizens and bootstrap organizations. And this was proving very attractive to those looking for interesting urban places to live. One such neighborhood—Park Slope—had been one of the most affluent communities in the United States at the turn of the century. Mansions and classic brownstones that crammed a large area just off Prospect Park had become rooming houses during the war—then were simply left with disinterest by the great exodus of the 1950s and 1960s. In 1979, it was possible to buy a hundred-year-old four-story brownstone with fine parquet floors and ornate moldings and leaded glass windows for fifty thousand dollars. In Bed-Stuy and Fort Greene, which also had large numbers of fine homes and buildings, the same vintage house went for forty thousand dollars.

Urban pioneers bought and began renovations, too. This contributed to the energy of renewal already begun in these neighborhoods. They were not in fact gentry, although they were gentrifying the neighborhoods. Most of them were ordinary people of all races, people on budgets who held jobs in the city and worked at renovating their houses on weekends. They rebuilt, renovated, and reclaimed the beauty of neighborhoods that had been neglected. Soon, more working professionals began to opt for the beauty of classic Brooklyn over the suburbs. And this contributed to the financial diversity of Brooklyn and gave a much longed for addition to New York's tax base.

Park Slope nowadays is an area where the rents are as high as what early pioneers sought to escape in Manhattan in the early 1980s. (Not always such a good thing for the old-timers struggling to keep up with property taxes.) The brownstone that one of our friends bought for fifty-six thousand dollars on Sterling Place in 1979 sold recently for over five hundred thousand dollars. Now, Park Slope is considered the Left Bank of Manhattan—housing a large population of successful writers, poets, scholars, actors.

Commercial Revival, Too

Business, too, began to come back—not necessarily big business but small business. Sunset Park along Fifth Avenue is another resurrection story. The neighborhood had been clobbered by the twenty-year exodus and the construction of the Prospect Expressway. The heavily Hispanic area organized a merchant association, brought in viable commerce, restaurants, shops. Fifth Avenue today has everything—colorful eateries, household-goods shops, lively commerce.

In Bed-Stuy, too, the Bedford-Stuyvesant Restoration Center took over the old Sheffield Farms building on Fulton Street in the late 1970s and during the 1980s provided training for residential rebuilding and rehab and construction, and employment programs, and health care. They also had an art center and theater.

Downtown got a big boost when the New Wave Festival took off at the Brooklyn Academy of Music. This provided a long-term use of the magnificent building. The newest, most provocative, and controversial artists in dance, theater, and performing art played to sold-out audiences at BAM. If you wanted to see the avantgarde work of Philip Glass, Robert Wilson, Pina Bausch, even Ingmar Bergman's live production of *Hamlet,* you had to ride fifteen minutes on the D-Train and come to where the great Caruso sang and where also once Eleanor Roosevelt lectured on social reform. You had to come to Brooklyn. In 1989 and 1990 the Majestic Theater was resurrected and restored as part of BAM. For some time in the mid-1990s, the Majestic became home for Garrison Keillor's live radio broadcasts for National Public Radio's *A Prairie Home Companion*. It was terrific to hear his opening, "We are coming to you live from the beautiful Majestic Theater in downtown Brooklyn."

Over at Fulton Landing something wonderful for business was taking place. The old Gair Sweeney building, a tall monolith on the river's edge that once manu-

The stately opera house in the Brooklyn Academy of Music and the Majestic Theater across the street from the Academy have been major legitimate houses since the late nineteenth century. In the late 1980s they offered the hottest ticket in New York. BAM became home to the Next Wave avant-garde performance festival and attracted new audiences and artists downtown. Courtesy of the Brooklyn Historical Society

factured cardboard goods, was restored and converted to office suites and lofts. Trying to attract business away from New Jersey, they called Fulton Landing the Un-Jersey. Fulton Landing was finally getting a glimmer of the feel the place must have had in 1882 when it unloaded passengers from ferries every few minutes, when it was a small port town in and of itself with eateries, saloons, and businesses that catered to the waterfront.

By the late 1980s, Fulton Landing was not only home to the refurbished Gair Sweeney but also the world renowned five-star restaurant the River Café. The café rests on a barge at the base of the Brooklyn Bridge and is a huge attraction. No one I know can merely walk the cobblestone entrance, through trees illuminated by thousands of tiny white lights, without stopping to admire the graceful bridge that rises overhead and sweeps across the river. Inside, the main dining room offers a view of Manhattan's skyline that draws as many people to the place as does the food.

Wanna Buy the Brooklyn Bridge?

Carol Bellamy, the New York City Council president in 1981, actually thought that it might be a good idea to look for a buyer for the Brooklyn Bridge, someone to manage it, take it off the city's hands. It appeared on her New Year's wish list for 1982 in the *Daily News* along with her wish that Junior's reopen. Well, she got her Junior's wish . . . but the bridge? Who could part with the Brooklyn Bridge?

On May 24, 1983, the city threw one of the most spectacular birthday parties for one of its most well-loved landmarks. The beautiful and functional symbol of strength and productivity, the longest suspension bridge of its day—the Brooklyn Bridge was one hundred years old.

It was destined to be an icon from opening day, May 24, 1883, judging from the way the big event was celebrated. For the hundredth birthday, the city tried to duplicate that original spectacle. At 9:00 P.M. with the huge shadowy monument stretched across the dark river, a fireworks extravaganza that went on and on lighted up the sky, the bridge, the river, and a fleet of boats.

At a fireworks finale hundreds, maybe thousands of rockets relentlessly pelted the sky red, gold, silver—like strobes making the bridge appear in relief—almost alive. Bells, gongs, and ship horns blew. What we added in 1993 was permanent lighting to enhance the beauty and majesty of the bridge at night.

In 1883 everyone hoped the bridge would spur growth and prosperity for Brooklyn. It did. In 1983, the celebration brought attention to Brooklyn's extraordinary past and its current residential and commercial renewal. More than a million visitors packed the water's edge at either end of the bridge for the spectacle. Boats of all sizes cruised the river, and planes and helicopters hovered above. Millions more watched on TV.

Being from Brooklyn was recognized as having emotional power, undaunted

---

THE GREATEST

"Indeed, as the longest suspension bridge ever built, with towers that dwarfed the Manhattan skyline, the Brooklyn Bridge was an extraordinary engineering feat. To the Victorians who watched from the shores as it rose, it both embodied the spirit of the age and symbolized U.S. progress."

—Ellen M. Snyder-Grenier, *Brooklyn!*

Welcome to Junior's!

The Brooklyn Bridge has been a well-maintained unofficial national treasure since its opening in 1883. By midcentury when these bridge painters were snapped, Manhattan had built a skyline to compete with the bridge towers. That's the Woolworth building far left. Courtesy of the Municipal Archives Department of Records and Information Services, City of New York

1980s—When Brooklyn . . . Came Back!

The Brooklyn Bridge centennial was a monthlong party that culminated on May 24, 1983, with a fireworks display that has yet to be matched in New York. Courtesy of the Brooklyn Historical Society

character, and yes, a kind of grace—just like the bridge. It was clear that the power of Brooklyn came from the cauldron of struggle. But, more important, it was clear that the entire country wanted to connect to a colorful and tough Brooklyn-ness, and it could do so actually or symbolically by way of the majestic Brooklyn Bridge.

Brooklyn's Spike Lee

His name is really Shelton J. Lee and he was born in Atlanta, Georgia, in 1957 but he moved to Brooklyn as an infant and has been here ever since. His father is the accomplished jazz musician-composer, Bill Lee. The family lived in Crown Heights and Cobble Hill for a while, then settled in Fort Greene, not more than a few blocks from Junior's. Spike's mother, Jacqueline Lee, a teacher, took Spike and his brothers and sister everywhere, exposed them to as much art, theater, and culture as possible. He was four years old when he saw Yul Brynner perform *The King and I* on Broadway. He may have had his first bite of Junior's cheesecake even earlier.

Spike went to school in Brooklyn, to college in Atlanta, film school at NYU, then he moved back to Brooklyn and claimed it as his home. He won an Oscar for his thesis project *Joe's Bed-Stuy Barbershop: We Cut Heads* in 1982. The success of the film helped him set up his own film production company, 40 Acres and a Mule Film Works, which is located right down the street from us on DeKalb Avenue. Then in 1986, he wrote, directed, and starred in *She's Gotta Have It*, a comedy about black single people in Brooklyn. The film, like his first film, was shot in the area and Lee used everybody in his family. His father scored the film, one brother did the still photography, his sister acted, another brother was assistant director.

Spike Lee's films are bold, funny, emotional, and most important—true. In *Do the Right Thing*, which opened in 1989, Lee showed the problems of power, racism, art, and economics on one small street in Bed-Stuy where an Italian pizzeria, a Korean grocer, and a predominantly black population integrated with whites and

Hispanics came into clashing conflict. Brooklyn streets again became the microcosm through which the country could get a clear view of the complex problems of racism and economic struggles that had plagued every urban neighborhood since the late 1960s. It was an honest, artful, and very funny film which made the black, white, Hispanic, and modern immigrant experience in Brooklyn accessible to everyone.

Spike likes Junior's. And we like Spike. He's been coming here most of his life. And he's an example of an artist committed to Brooklyn. We love having him in the neighborhood. We love what he and his artistic vision have done for Brooklyn.

A 1980s' Rosen Event

When Kevin Rosen turned twenty-two in 1988, he joined the family business. Of course we were very pleased. We had never pressured any of our children to take on the huge responsibility and sixteen-hour workdays that it took to run Junior's. We had been very careful, in fact, to encourage them all to go to college, study what they wanted, become what they wanted. We had not had such a choice. When Junior's was new and struggling and my father needed us to help keep the business going, there was no question about where we belonged. It was a done deal. We would work here. Not so in the 1980s. The business was thriving. Our kids could do what they wanted. Brett, Kevin's older brother, had already chosen insurance as his profession with our blessings.

With Kevin's new energy and that of his younger brother Alan, who at nineteen had already made his choice to join in and was champing at the bit to finish college first, we didn't know for sure what the 1990s held for us.

But whatever it would be, we had a good feeling it would thrive!

1980s—Bake Shoppe

FIRST THE DEVASTATING fire at Junior's . . . then reopening day, May 27, 1982. Everything inside seemed old, yet new at the same time.

As you waited in line to get inside, you could see meringue pies through the windows. They looked bigger and taller than ever. The aromas from the bake shoppe when you first walked inside the door seemed more delicious than ever.

The cakes appeared to be more towering too, though they were the same three layers as before. Even the racks of cheesecakes and pies seemed to be taller and stocked with more items than before. Only the rows and rows of neatly stacked cookies looked the same . . . there just seemed to be more of them.

Tea Biscuits

EVERY MORNING AT the take-out counter, provided you arrive early enough, there's a large baking pan of these golden tea biscuits that has just come out of the oven.

Their name is misleading, as tea biscuits are often small and dainty. Not at Junior's. Their tea biscuits are extra-big—over three inches round and almost as high. They're chock-full of richness and flavor—sour cream, butter, cream cheese, and raisins. These biscuits are great as is, just by themselves. But they're even better with a slab of cream cheese and a heaping spoonful of preserves.

MAKES 1 DOZEN TEA BISCUITS

3½ cups cake flour

2 cups all-purpose flour

3 tablespoons baking powder

1 tablespoon salt

½ cup (4 ounces) cream cheese (the regular variety, not light Neufchâtel cream cheese), at room temperature

¼ cup (½ stick) unsalted butter, at room temperature

¼ cup shortening, at room temperature

¾ cup sugar

4 extra-large eggs

1 tablespoon pure vanilla extract

2 cups sour cream

1 cup dark raisins

¼ teaspoon vegetable oil

FOR THE GO-ALONGS (OPTIONAL)

Cream cheese

Strawberry preserves

The Junior's Way—

Pat or roll out the dough two inches thick—no thinner. Then brush with beaten egg before baking; this gives these biscuits a golden shine.

1. Preheat the oven to 400°F and butter 2 baking sheets. Mix both of the flours, the baking powder, and salt in a medium-sized bowl and set aside.

2. Cream the cream cheese, butter, and shortening in a large bowl with an electric mixer on high for 2 minutes. Then, with the mixer still running, gradually add the sugar, then 3 of the eggs, one at a time. Continue beating until the mixture is creamy and light yellow, then beat in the vanilla.

3. With a spoon, stir in one-third of the flour mixture, then half of the sour cream, then another third of the flour mixture, the remaining sour cream, and then the rest of the flour. Stir until well blended (do not overmix at this stage, as the biscuits can become tough). Stir in the raisins.

4. Generously flour a flat surface and pat or roll out the dough 2 inches thick. Cut out the biscuits with a 3½-inch round cutter, rerolling the scraps as you go, and place them on the baking sheets, 2 inches apart. (You will have at least 12 biscuits.)

5. Whisk the remaining egg and the oil together and brush on the tops of the biscuits. Bake the biscuits until shiny and golden, 12 to 15 minutes. These biscuits are at their best when eaten piping hot or warm . . . even better when served with cream cheese and strawberry preserves.

257

1980s—When Brooklyn . . . Came Back!

Danish Dough

*T*HERE ALWAYS SEEMS to be a fresh batch of Danish coming out of Junior's bakery and being wheeled downstairs for sale. One hour it's twisted into their popular round **Almond Cinnamon Danish;** another hour it's rolled into long individual coffee breads called **Cigars;** another hour it's cut into squares, filled with spiced apples and folded into **Apple Turnovers.** It's one of those versatile doughs that sounds difficult to make, but really isn't, especially since it's mixed up quickly in the mixer.

MAKES ENOUGH DOUGH FOR ABOUT 2 ½ DOZEN DANISH

FOR THE BUTTER LAYERS

1 cup (2 sticks) unsalted butter, chilled

½ cup (1 stick) margarine, chilled

FOR THE YEAST SPONGE

1 cup water (105° to 115°F)

2 ¼-ounce packages active dry yeast

1 tablespoon sugar

FOR THE DOUGH

4½ cups all-purpose flour

½ cup sugar

2 tablespoons malted milk powder

2 teaspoons salt

2 extra-large eggs

½ cup (1 stick) unsalted butter, at room temperature

6 tablespoons margarine, at room temperature

1 tablespoon pure vanilla extract

½ teaspoon lemon extract

The Junior's Way—
Use a combination of butter and margarine to layer into this Danish dough. Let them both stand at room temperature just long enough to make them pliable enough to cream into a mixture—but not long enough to make them soft and warm.

Welcome to Junior's!

1. Make the butter layers: Cut the 1 cup butter and the ½ cup margarine for the butter layers into small pieces, then mix them together in a medium-sized bowl. Using an electric mixer set on high, cream this butter mixture just until smooth (do not overbeat). Let stand at room temperature while you make the dough.

2. Now, make the yeast sponge: Stir the water, both packages of yeast, and the tablespoon of sugar in a small bowl until the yeast and sugar have dissolved. Let the mixture stand until it is foamy and light, about 5 minutes.

3. Meanwhile, begin making the Danish dough: Mix the flour, the ½ cup of sugar, malted milk powder, and salt together in a large bowl. Set aside.

4. Using the mixer equipped with a dough hook or a paddle, beat the eggs, the ½ cup butter, the 6 tablespoons margarine, and the vanilla and lemon extracts on high in a large bowl until light yellow, about 5 minutes. The mixture will look slightly curdled, but don't worry, it should.

5. Reduce the mixer speed to low and beat in the yeast mixture, then the flour mixture. Knead in the flour mixture by beating the dough on high for 5 minutes (the dough will be smooth and elastic). Transfer the dough to a lightly floured surface to rest for 10 minutes.

6. Flour your hands. Starting from the center and working out to all 4 edges, push, pat, and roll the dough with your hands into a 24-inch square. Then spread the creamy butter mixture evenly over the dough, stopping within ½ inch of the edges.

7. Fold the dough into thirds: First fold one end over the middle; then fold the other end on top, forming a rectangle 24 × 8 inches. Now fold the 24-inch length into thirds, in the same way, making an 8-inch square. Wrap tightly in plastic wrap and refrigerate for at least 1 hour.

8. Use the dough to make Almond Cinnamon Danish (page 260), Cigars (page 261), or Apple Turnovers (page 263). Or, keep the dough wrapped tightly in plastic wrap in the refrigerator for up to 2 days or in the freezer for up to 1 month.

1980s—When Brooklyn . . . Came Back!

Almond Cinnamon Danish

MANY "REGULARS" AT Junior's start their day with one of these freshly baked Danish and a cup of coffee. One's plenty for most folks. But you'll probably want another the next day—cinnamony, nutty, rich, and buttery. That's Junior's Danish!

MAKES 15 DANISH
(THIS RECIPE DOUBLES EASILY)

½ recipe Danish Dough (page 258)

1 recipe Smear (page 261)

⅔ cup sugar

3 tablespoons ground cinnamon

⅔ cup cake crumbs

1 extra-large egg

½ teaspoon cooking oil

½ cup sliced almonds

The Junior's Way—Cake crumbs are rolled inside these Danish to give them extra filling and flavor. To make the crumbs, process slices of pound cake from your local bakery or supermarket into fine crumbs in a food processor. If you have extra crumbs left over, don't worry; they freeze well.

1. Preheat the oven to 350°F and butter 2 baking sheets. Make the Danish Dough and roll it out into an 18-inch square.

2. Make the Smear and spread it over the dough from edge to edge. Mix the sugar and cinnamon and sprinkle over the dough. Sprinkle with the cake crumbs. Roll up jelly-roll-style into a roll 18 inches long and about 3 inches in diameter.

3. Cut the dough crosswise into 15 slices, each a little more than 1 inch thick. Place the rolls cut-side-down on the baking sheets, about 2 inches apart, forming Danish swirls. Whisk the egg with the oil and brush on the rolls. Top each Danish generously with the almonds.

4. Let the rolls rise until doubled in size, about 45 minutes. Bake the Danish until golden and set in the center, 15 to 18 minutes. Let the rolls cool on the baking sheet for 5 minutes, then transfer them to a rack to cool.

Smear

THE BAKERS KEEP talking about this "Smear." It pops up inside many of the coffeebreads and Danish that come out of Junior's ovens. It adds an interesting design to Almond Cinnamon Danish and sugar 'n' spice to individual coffee sticks called Cigars.

The best part—it adds that signature Junior's touch.

MAKES 1 CUP

6 tablespoons (¾ stick) margarine, at room temperature
¾ cup canned almond filling
1 tablespoon sugar

Using an electric mixer, cream all of the ingredients together in a large bowl on high until light and creamy, about 3 minutes. Use as directed in Almond Cinnamon Danish (page 260) or Cigars (below).

The Junior's Way—
The secret to this Smear is the canned almond filling. It's made from corn syrup, almonds, and other flavorings and spices. Look for it in your local supermarket or gourmet food store.

Cigars

NOT UNTIL THE third visit to Junior's did I see these fat Danish sticks. You have to come early, real early, before they're all sold out. The "Regulars" know. These cigars are usually stacked up at the take-out counter, but if you don't see them, ask. Cigars are long, slightly chunky, and overflowing with the same almond-cinnamon filling Junior's is known for.

Unless you're really hungry, share with a friend.

continued

½ recipe Danish Dough (page 258)

1 recipe Smear (page 261)

⅔ cup sugar

3 tablespoons ground cinnamon

⅔ cup cake crumbs

1 extra-large egg

½ teaspoon cooking oil

½ cup sliced almonds

The Junior's Way—When rolling each pastry strip, roll the dough out on the diagonal, pressing down slightly to give a tight roll. This helps the Danish keep their shape even as they rise and bake. This is very important in order to prevent the filling from oozing out in the oven.

1. Preheat the oven to 350°F and butter 2 baking sheets. Make the Danish Dough and divide it into two equal pieces. Roll out each piece of dough into a 12-inch square.

2. Make the Smear and spread half of it over the dough from edge to edge. Mix the sugar with the cinnamon and sprinkle half over the dough. Sprinkle with half the cake crumbs. Cut into 6 equal strips, each 12 inches long and 2 inches wide. Roll each strip up jelly-roll-style, slightly on the diagonal, making a pastry strip resembling the shape of a cigar, about 6 inches long and 2 inches in diameter. Repeat with the other piece of dough, making 12 cigars.

3. Place the rolls end-side-down on the baking sheets, about 2 inches apart. Whisk the egg with the oil and brush on the rolls. Generously top each roll with the almonds.

4. Let the rolls rise until doubled in size, about 45 minutes. Bake cigars until golden and set in the center, 15 to 18 minutes (watch carefully, as they should bake only until they are golden brown and set). Let the cigars cool on the baking sheet for 5 minutes, then transfer them to a rack to cool.

Apple Turnovers

AS I EXPECTED, these aren't just *any* apple turnovers. They are probably the biggest, juiciest, most delicious ones I can ever remember tasting. But just because they're overflowing with goodness, it doesn't mean they're not the perfect sweet thing to pack to go anywhere. These little totable pies slip perfectly into picnic baskets, lunch bags, even briefcases.

I like to make one recipe of the Danish dough, then use half of it for these turnovers.

MAKES 1 ½ DOZEN LARGE TURNOVERS

1 recipe Danish dough (page 258)

FOR THE APPLE FILLING

2 cups apple cider

1 cup sugar

1 teaspoon ground cinnamon

⅛ teaspoon salt

3 pounds firm red apples, peeled, cored, and cut into ½-inch chunks (6 cups)

¼ cup cornstarch

3 tablespoons cold water

2 teaspoons pure vanilla extract

¼ teaspoon lemon extract

FOR THE TURNOVERS

1 cup cake crumbs

½ cup (1 stick) unsalted butter, melted

FOR THE FROSTING

2 cups sifted confectioners' sugar

2 tablespoons heavy cream

1 teaspoon pure vanilla extract

The Junior's Way—
Be sure to let the filling cool at least fifteen minutes before placing it on the dough. The heat can cause the dough to become too soft and even melt the butter layered throughout the dough.

continued

1980s—When Brooklyn . . . Came Back!

1. Make the dough, fold into layers, wrap in plastic wrap, and refrigerate for 1 hour.

2. While the dough chills, make the Apple Filling: Combine the cider, sugar, cinnamon, and salt in a heavy saucepan. Bring to a full boil over high heat and boil for 5 minutes. Add the apples, reduce the heat to medium, and continue to simmer until the apples are tender, about 15 minutes. Watch closely, stirring occasionally to keep the apples from sticking.

3. To thicken the filling: Mix the cornstarch and water together in a cup until the cornstarch thoroughly dissolves. Stir in a little hot apple-cider sauce, then drizzle this cornstarch mixture into the apple-cider sauce in the saucepan, stirring constantly. Bring the mixture to a full boil and let the mixture continue to boil until it thickens, about 2 minutes. Remove the filling from the heat and stir in the vanilla and lemon extracts. Set the filling aside to cool to lukewarm, about 15 minutes. You will have about 4½ cups of filling.

4. Meanwhile, butter 2 baking sheets. Roll out half of the chilled Danish dough into an 18-inch square. Cut into nine 6-inch squares. Sprinkle each square with 2 heaping teaspoons of crumbs. Spoon a scant cup of filling onto half of the turnover in a triangular shape, leaving a half-inch border. Bring the other half of the pastry up over the filling, making a triangular pocket. Press the edges together with your fingers to seal. Repeat with the rest of the pastry, making 18 turnovers in all. Place the turnovers 2 inches apart on the baking sheets and brush them with melted butter. Let the turnovers rise until doubled in size, about 45 minutes.

5. Preheat the oven to 350°F. Bake the turnovers until golden and crisp, 15 to 18 minutes. Let the turnovers cool on the baking sheet for 5 minutes, then transfer them to a rack to cool.

6. To frost, stir all of the ingredients of the frosting together in a small bowl until smooth. When the turnovers have cooled, drizzle a little frosting on top of each.

Welcome to Junior's!

Fresh Peach Pie

*N*OTHING TASTES MORE **homemade and delicious than a slice of fresh peach pie. You'll know you're eating it the Junior's Way if the peach filling is still slightly warm and runny, the peach slices are plump and juicy, and the crust is buttery and flaky.**

MAKES ONE OVERSTUFFED 9-INCH PIE

1 recipe Pie Pastry, enough for a double-crust pie (page 40)

FOR THE PEACH FILLING

¾ cup granulated sugar

¾ cup packed light brown sugar

½ cup quick-cooking tapioca

3 to 4 tablespoons flour (depending on the juiciness of the peaches)

1 teaspoon ground cinnamon

¼ teaspoon salt

5 pounds juicy ripe fresh peaches, preferably freestone

2 tablespoons fresh lemon juice

2 tablespoons unsalted butter, cut into small pieces

FOR THE GLAZE

1 extra-large egg yolk

¼ teaspoon vegetable oil

The Junior's Way—
Shop for the peaches very carefully. Pick the ripest, sweetest ones you can find. If fresh peaches aren't in the market, you can use dry-pack frozen peach slices. Just thaw them and pat them dry on paper towels before tossing them with the cinnamon-sugar mixture.

1. Butter a 9-inch deep-dish pie plate. Make the Pie Pastry, roll out half of it ⅛ inch thick on a lightly floured surface, and trim to a 15-inch circle. Transfer the pastry to the pie plate, leaving a 1½-inch overhang. Place the pastry shell and the rest of the pastry in the refrigerator while you make the filling.

2. Mix the granulated sugar, the brown sugar, tapioca, flour, cinnamon, and salt together in a medium-size bowl. Set aside.

3. Peel, pit, and slice the peaches ¼ inch thick into a large bowl (you need 6 cups of peaches). Drizzle the peaches with the lemon juice and stir to mix. Sprinkle

1980s—When Brooklyn . . . Came Back!

the cinnamon-sugar mixture over the peaches and toss until all of the peach slices are well coated.

4. Place a rack in the center of the oven and preheat the oven to 425°F. Spoon the peach filling into the pie shell, mounding it high in the center. Dot with the butter.

5. Roll out the remaining pastry ⅛ inch thick and trim to a 13-inch circle. Using the tip of a paring knife, cut out a ½-inch circle of pastry in the center of the pastry round for the steam vent. Transfer the pastry circle to the top of the pie. Moisten the edges of the pastry with a little ice water, fold the edges under, and pinch them to seal. Shape the edge of the pastry to stand up 1 inch high, then flute.

6. To make the glaze, whisk the egg yolk with the oil and brush on the top of the pie. Bake the pie for 10 minutes at 425°F.

7. Reduce the oven temperature to 350°F and continue baking until the crust is golden, the peaches are tender, and the filling is bubbly, 50 minutes to 1 hour. If the top crust browns before the pie is done, lay a piece of foil loosely over the top of the pie for the rest of the baking time. Cool the pie on a wire rack for at least 2 hours before serving.

Fresh Blueberry Pie

*A*NY SEASON IS blueberry season at Junior's. It just seems that the bakers are able to find delicious berries all year long. You usually can too, thanks to fruit importers and purveyors supplying these beautiful berries from different corners of the earth month after month. But if for some reason your fruit market isn't stocking them the day you're baking, try the dry-pack frozen berries, not the ones packed in a sugar syrup. They bake up juicy and wonderful too.

MAKES ONE 9-INCH DEEP-DISH PIE

1 recipe Pie Pastry, enough for a double-crust pie (page 40)

FOR THE BLUEBERRY FILLING
1¼ cups granulated sugar
¾ cup packed light brown sugar

½ cup quick-cooking tapioca

3 tablespoons cornstarch

1 teaspoon ground cinnamon

¼ teaspoon ground nutmeg

¼ teaspoon salt

8 cups fresh blueberries, picked over for stems and
　　　　bruises

2 tablespoons fresh lemon juice

3 tablespoons unsalted butter, cut into small pieces

FOR THE GLAZE

1 extra-large egg yolk

¼ teaspoon vegetable oil

The Junior's Way—
To substitute frozen blueberries for the fresh ones, measure out the same amount of berries. Spread the frozen berries out on paper towels. Let them defrost at room temperature, about thirty minutes. Then pat them dry before tossing them with the lemon juice and cinnamon-sugar mixture.

1. Butter a 9-inch deep-dish pie plate. Make the Pie Pastry, roll out half of it ⅛ inch thick on a lightly floured surface, and trim to a 15-inch circle. Transfer the pastry to the pie plate, leaving a 1½-inch overhang. Place the pastry shell and the rest of the pastry in the refrigerator while you make the filling.

2. Mix the granulated sugar, brown sugar, tapioca, cornstarch, cinnamon, nutmeg, and salt together in a medium-sized bowl. Set aside.

3. Mix the blueberries and lemon juice together in a large bowl. Sprinkle the cinnamon-sugar mixture over the berries and toss until all of the berries are well coated.

4. Place a rack in the center of the oven and preheat the oven to 425°F. Spoon the berry filling into the pie shell, mounding it high in the center. Dot with the butter.

5. Roll out the remaining pastry ⅛ inch thick and trim to a 13-inch circle. Using the tip of a paring knife, cut out a ¾-inch circle of pastry in the center of the pastry round for the steam vent. Transfer the pastry circle to the top of the pie. Moisten the edges of the pastry with a little ice water, fold the edges under, and pinch them to seal. Shape the edge of the pastry to stand up 1 inch high, then flute.

6. To make the glaze, whisk the egg yolk with the oil and brush on the top of the pie. Bake the pie for 10 minutes at 425°F.

continued

7. Reduce the oven temperature to 350°F and continue baking until the crust is golden and the filling is bubbly, 50 minutes to 1 hour. If the top crust browns before the pie is done, lay a piece of foil loosely over the top of the pie for the rest of the baking time. Cool the pie on a wire rack for at least 2 hours before serving.

Pumpkin Pie

*E*VER SINCE THE Pilgrims' second Thanksgiving in 1623, pumpkin pie has been on the Thanksgiving menu. You know the holidays are here when the pumpkin pies begin marching out of the Junior's bakery. Folks line up for hours just to get one to take home.

They make this holiday favorite the old-fashioned way—from a pumpkin custard whipped up from fresh cream, milk, eggs, and lots of fresh pumpkin. Each pie is gently spiced with cinnamon, nutmeg, and ginger, then with a splash of vanilla to bring out all of the festive flavors. Once you've tried Junior's Pumpkin Pie, you'll never want to use any other recipe.

MAKES ONE 9-INCH DEEP-DISH PIE

½ recipe Pie Pastry, enough for a single-crust pie (page 40)

FOR THE PUMPKIN FILLING

1 2-pound pie pumpkin (such as sugar baby) or one 15-ounce can solid-pack pumpkin

2 extra-large eggs

1 cup sugar

1 tablespoon cornstarch

1 teaspoon ground cinnamon

½ teaspoon ground ginger

½ teaspoon ground nutmeg

½ teaspoon salt

1 cup heavy cream

The Junior's Way—For the freshest-tasting pumpkin pies, start with a fresh pie pumpkin, just like they do for their holiday pies at Junior's. It does take a little extra time to steam and purée the pumpkin pulp, but it's well worth it. (Of course, as the bakers say, one can always substitute canned solid pack pumpkin, if your time is limited.) To make a creamy filling, be sure to whip the eggs at the beginning until they are light yellow and thickened (this usually takes about 5 minutes). From this point on, beat all of the remaining ingredients just until they are well blended into the filling. Do not overbeat.

Welcome to Junior's!

½ cup milk

1 tablespoon pure vanilla extract

1. Preheat the oven to 425°F and butter a 9-inch deep-dish pie plate. Make the Pie Pastry, roll it out ⅛ inch thick on a lightly floured surface, and trim to a 15-inch circle. Transfer the pastry to the pie plate, leaving a 1½-inch overhang. Fold under the edge to stand up 1 inch high and flute. Do not prick the crust. Place in the refrigerator while you make the filling.

2. Make the fresh pumpkin purée: Cut the pumpkin into large pieces, discarding the stem, seeds, and pith. Cook the pumpkin in boiling water until tender and transfer it with a slotted spoon to paper towels to drain and cool. Now scrape the pulp into a medium-sized bowl and beat with an electric mixer until smooth (you need 1¾ cups of pumpkin purée).

3. Using an electric mixer set on high, beat the eggs until frothy, about 5 minutes. Mix the sugar, cornstarch, cinnamon, ginger, nutmeg, and salt together in a small bowl. Reduce the speed of the mixer to low and beat in this sugar mixture.

4. With the mixer still running, add the pumpkin purée, then the cream, milk, and vanilla. Beat only until the filling is well blended. Pour the filling into the chilled crust.

continued

1980s—When Brooklyn . . . Came Back!

5. Bake the pie for 10 minutes at 425°F. Lower the oven temperature to 350°F and continue baking the pie until the filling is golden and puffy and no longer jiggles in the center, about 45 minutes. The pie is ready to come out of the oven when a knife inserted into the center comes out clean. Cool the pie on a wire rack for 1 hour. Serve the pie at room temperature or refrigerate until it's cold. Store any leftover pie in the refrigerator.

Lemon Coconut Cake

*I*T'S ALWAYS THERE . . . you can spot it right away. It's one of the tallest cakes Junior's bakes and it's showered with lots of coconut. This is a buttery sponge cake filled with a lemony custard and built up into four towering layers. And consistent with Junior's generous philosophy, there's nothing skimpy about this cake. The lemon filling is thick and rich, the frosting is buttery and creamy, the coconut is sprinkled lavishly and lovingly.

MAKES ONE FOUR-LAYER 9-INCH CAKE, ABOUT 8 INCHES HIGH

1 recipe Sponge Cake (page 94)
1 recipe lemon filling (from Lemon Meringue Pie,
   page 36)

FOR THE VANILLA BUTTERCREAM FROSTING

8 cups (2 pounds) sifted confectioners' sugar
½ teaspoon salt
1½ cups (3 sticks) unsalted butter, at room temperature
½ cup margarine, at room temperature
2 tablespoons light corn syrup
2 tablespoons pure vanilla extract
½ cup heavy cream

FOR DECORATING

2 cups angel flake coconut

The Junior's Way—
Before frosting this cake, brush the layers with a soft pastry brush to remove the crumbs. Be sure to brush all the crumbs off the sides of the layers, too. This prevents crumbs getting into the frosting and creating a bumpy unprofessional look.

2 tablespoons angel flake coconut, tossed in a little green food coloring

1 long-stemmed red cherry

1. The day before or the morning of the day you plan to serve this cake, preheat the oven to 350°F. Butter two 9-inch layer cake pans and line the bottoms with wax paper. Make and bake the Sponge Cake batter and divide it evenly between the 2 pans. Bake each cake layer just until the center springs back when lightly touched, about 25 minutes. Let the cakes cool on a wire rack for 30 minutes (do not worry if they settle a little). Turn them upside down onto a cooling rack. Carefully peel off the paper liners. Let the cakes cool completely, at least 4 hours or overnight. (If keeping overnight, be sure to wrap the cooled cakes in plastic wrap.)

2. Meanwhile, about 2 hours before it's time to frost the cake, prepare the lemon filling. Refrigerate the filling until it's cool to the touch, but not chilled and set (the filling should still be able to be spread).

3. Prepare the Vanilla Buttercream Frosting: Sift the confectioners' sugar and salt together and set aside. Cream the butter and margarine together in a large bowl with an electric mixer on high for 3 minutes or until light yellow. With the mixer still running, beat in the corn syrup and vanilla. Reduce the mixer to low and beat in the sugar mixture in two additions, beating well after each addition. Blend in the cream until the frosting is a spreading consistency, adding a little extra cream if needed. Spoon about 1 cup of frosting into a pastry bag fitted with a medium star tip and set aside.

4. To assemble the cake: Cut each cake layer horizontally with a serrated knife into 2 equal layers, giving 4 even layers. Spread the first layer with about one-fifth of the frosting, then about one-fourth of the filling. Repeat with the second and third layers. Top the cake with the fourth layer.

5. To decorate the cake, frost the sides, then generously pat the white coconut on the sides, reserving about ¼ cup of coconut. Frost the top of the cake with the remaining frosting. Spoon the rest of the lemon filling on the top and sprinkle with the rest of the white coconut.

6. Using the frosting in the pastry bag, pipe scrolls of frosting along the top edge of the cake. Add a large fancy frosting rosette in the center, sprinkle it with the green coconut, and decorate with the cherry. Refrigerate the cake until it's time to serve. Store any leftover cake in the refrigerator.

1980s—When Brooklyn . . . Came Back!

Chocolate Fudge Layer Cake

*T*HIS IS ONE of Junior's most popular towering cakes. It's three layers tall, like most of their cakes. It's iced with a thick coating of rich Chocolate Fudge Frosting, with extra swirls piped on top, and finished with a dusting of chocolate crumbs. Unlike many fudge cakes you may have tasted, this one has that deep dark fudge flavor with a moistness that actually does melt-in-your-mouth with each bite. It's plain chocolate . . . plain good . . . plain incredible.

MAKES ONE THREE-LAYER 9-INCH CAKE, ABOUT 8 INCHES HIGH

3 cups cake flour

1 tablespoon baking powder

1 teaspoon salt

½ teaspoon baking soda

½ cup (1 stick) unsalted butter, at room temperature

½ cup shortening

1½ cups granulated sugar

¾ cup packed light brown sugar

6 extra-large eggs

9 ounces bittersweet baking chocolate, melted and cooled

1 tablespoon pure vanilla extract

2¼ cups milk

FOR FROSTING AND DECORATING

1 recipe Chocolate Fudge Frosting (page 274)

½ cup chocolate cake crumbs (from leftover or store-bought chocolate cake)

2 tablespoons angel flake coconut, tossed in a little green food coloring

1 long-stemmed red cherry

The Junior's Way—To make the deep chocolate cake that Junior's is famous for, buy the best bittersweet baking chocolate that you can find. If you're near a baking supply house or gourmet bake store, try them first.

1. Arrange a rack in the middle of the oven and preheat it to 350°F. Butter three 9-inch cake pans and line the bottoms with parchment or wax paper. Sift the cake flour, baking powder, salt, and baking soda together into a medium-sized bowl and set aside.

2. Cream the butter, shortening, and both of the sugars in a large bowl with an electric mixer on high until light yellow, about 5 minutes. Then, with the mixer still running, add the eggs, one at a time, beating 2 minutes after adding each egg. Then beat in the chocolate and vanilla (don't worry if the batter looks a little curdled at this stage; that's just fine). The batter is ready after you've beaten it about 20 minutes.

3. Sift about one-fourth of the flour mixture over the batter and stir it in by hand (don't use the mixer for this), then stir in one-third of the milk. Repeat by adding one-fourth more flour, one-third more milk, another one-fourth of the flour, then the rest of the milk. Finally, stir in the rest of the flour. Stir after each addition until the ingredients are well blended.

4. Divide the batter equally among the 3 pans. Spread the batter out evenly, then lightly tap each pan on the countertop to release any air bubbles. Set the pans side by side in the oven, making certain the pans are not touching each other (depending on the size of your oven, it's best to bake the third layer separately, if necessary, instead of on a rack that's not in the middle of the oven).

5. Bake the cakes until the center of each cake springs back when lightly touched and a toothpick inserted into the center comes out with moist crumbs clinging to it (no batter), about 30 minutes. Let the cakes cool on a wire rack for 30 minutes before turning them upside down onto a cooling rack. Carefully peel off the paper liners. Let the cakes cool completely.

6. To fill and frost: Prepare the Chocolate Fudge Frosting. Fill and frost between the layers and on top of the cake. For that extra professional touch, comb the sides and top of the cake with thin narrow lines in a circular design, about ⅛ inch apart, using a cake comb or the tines of a fork. Sprinkle the bottom edge of the cake with chocolate cake crumbs, extending only about ½ inch up the sides.

7. Using a pastry bag fitted with a medium star tip, pipe 8 to 10 large scrolls of frosting on the top of the cake, starting from the outer edge and pointing into the center. Add a large fancy frosting rosette in the center, sprinkle it with the green coconut, and decorate with the cherry. Finish the cake by dusting a fine smattering (about a tablespoon) of chocolate cake crumbs over the top.

Chocolate Fudge Frosting

THIS IS *the frosting* whenever Junior's frosts a fudge layer cake, a brownie, a birthday cake, or one of their specialty cupcakes at Halloween time. It's creamy yet light, an intensely deep chocolate color, and it tastes just like rich fudge. The best part is that it's extremely easy to work with. It doesn't get grainy or set up too fast, thanks to the combination of both butter and margarine in the recipe.

**MAKES 8 CUPS FROSTING
(PLENTY TO FROST THE TOP AND SIDES OF A
THREE-LAYER CAKE)**

8 cups (2 pounds) sifted confectioners' sugar

1⅓ cups unsweetened cocoa powder

½ teaspoon salt

1½ cups (3 sticks) unsalted butter, at room temperature

½ cup (1 stick) margarine, at room temperature

¼ cup dark corn syrup

2 tablespoons pure vanilla extract

⅔ cup heavy cream

The Junior's Way—
Before frosting the layers, brush away any crumbs from the top and sides of the cake layers with a soft pastry brush. After filling between the layers, refrigerate the cake to set the frosting before frosting the sides and top (usually about an hour is needed).

1. Sift the confectioners' sugar, cocoa, and salt together and set aside.

2. Cream the butter and margarine together in a large bowl with an electric mixer on high until light yellow and slightly thickened, about 3 minutes. With the mixer still running, beat in the corn syrup and vanilla.

3. Reduce the mixer speed to low and beat in the sugar mixture in two additions, beating well after adding each. Blend in the cream until the frosting is a spreading consistency, adding a little extra cream if needed.

4. Return the mixer speed to high and whip the frosting until extra light and creamy, about 2 minutes more. Use immediately or place a piece of plastic wrap directly on the frosting and chill until ready to frost the cake. Great for icing Chocolate Fudge Layer Cake (page 272), German Chocolate Layer Cake (page 275), and even Brownies (page 278).

German Chocolate Layer Cake

*L*EGEND HAS IT that Samuel German, a food developer at the General Foods Company in the late nineteenth century, developed a sweet chocolate, which he became so famous for that it was soon known as German chocolate. In 1957, a Texan baked a layer cake with this chocolate and topped it with a coconut-pecan frosting. A Dallas newspaper published the recipe, causing the sale of German chocolate to soar. The company perfected the recipe and created a tradition. Junior's bakes its own version—a towering three-layer cake of fudge, instead of the lighter sweet chocolate. The bakers fill and top the cake with the traditional frosting of coconut and chunky pecans, then add the finishing touch of chocolate fudge frosting on the sides. If you want to add the final Junior's touch, pipe swirls of extra frosting around the edge.

MAKES ONE 3-LAYER 9-INCH CAKE, ABOUT 8 INCHES HIGH

1 recipe Chocolate Fudge Layer Cake (page 272)

½ recipe Chocolate Fudge Frosting (page 274)

FOR THE COCONUT-PECAN ICING

4 extra-large egg yolks

2 cups sugar

1 cup heavy cream

1 cup milk

1 cup (2 sticks) unsalted butter

1 tablespoon pure vanilla extract

5 cups angel flake coconut (14 ounces)

2 cups chopped pecans

The Junior's Way—
Originally this cake was left unfrosted on the sides. But the bakers at Junior's always spread the sides with rich fudge frosting, then finish off their masterpiece with generous spoonfuls of extra coconut-pecan icing on top, plus swirls of more fudge frosting around the edge.

1980s—When Brooklyn . . . Came Back!

1. Preheat the oven to 350°F and butter a 9-inch springform pan. Make and bake the Chocolate Fudge Layer Cake in three 9-inch layer cake pans. Cool the cakes in the pans on a rack for 10 minutes, then remove the cakes from the pan and cool completely.

2. While the cake layers are cooling, make the coconut-pecan icing: Beat the egg yolks and sugar together in a large bowl with an electric mixer on high for 3 minutes or until light yellow and slightly thickened. Beat in the cream and milk, then transfer this mixture to a large saucepan and add the butter.

3. Cook and stir the icing on medium heat until the butter melts, the mixture thickens, and the icing turns a light golden brown. Remove from the heat and stir in the vanilla, then the coconut and pecans. Let the icing cool while you make the Chocolate Fudge Frosting.

4. To frost the cake, spread one-third of the coconut-pecan icing between the layers and on the top of the cake. Frost the sides with the Chocolate Fudge Frosting, then pipe extra swirls around the top edge if you wish. Let the cake stand for about an hour at room temperature before serving. To store any leftover cake, cover with plastic wrap and refrigerate.

Carrot Cake with Cream Cheese Frosting

*A*S I WALKED past the bakery counter one morning, I heard someone asking: "What's that huge white cake? It looks delicious . . . whatever it is, I'll take a slice." That huge cake is Junior's carrot cake, and you can always have a slice, for every day carrot cake after carrot cake is sent down from the bakery. Each one is three layers high and frosted with the creamiest, richest, smoothest cream cheese frosting I have ever tasted.

MAKES ONE 3-LAYER 9-INCH CAKE, ABOUT 8 INCHES HIGH

Welcome to Junior's!

FOR THE CARROT CAKE

3 cups all-purpose flour

1 tablespoon baking powder

1 tablespoon ground cinnamon

1 teaspoon baking soda

1 teaspoon salt

1⅓ cups dark raisins

6 extra-large eggs

3 cups granulated sugar

1⅓ cups vegetable oil

1 tablespoon pure vanilla extract

1 pound carrots, peeled and finely grated (3 cups)

1 cup minced apples (about 1 pound)

1 cup chopped walnuts (optional)

FOR THE CREAM CHEESE FROSTING

4 packages (8 ounces each) pure cream cheese (the regular variety, not light
    Neufchâtel cream cheese), at room temperature

½ cup (1 stick) unsalted butter, at room temperature

½ cup (1 stick) margarine, at room temperature

¼ cup light corn syrup

1 tablespoon pure vanilla extract

8 cups sifted confectioners' sugar (2 pounds)

The Junior's Way—
Grate the carrots very fine. If you have a food processor with a grating disk, use this. If not, use the grater with the smallest holes you can find.

1. Preheat the oven to 325°F and butter three 9-inch layer cake pans, then line the bottoms with wax paper. Sift the flour, baking powder, cinnamon, baking soda, and salt onto a piece of wax paper and set aside. Place the raisins in a saucepan, cover them with boiling water, cover the pan, and let the raisins soak until they are plump, about 15 minutes. Drain them well.

2. Meanwhile, beat the eggs in a large bowl with an electric mixer on high until light yellow, about 5 minutes. Gradually add the granulated sugar, about ¼ cup at a time, beating well, at least a minute, after each addition. With the mixer running, slowly drizzle in the oil, then the vanilla. You should beat the batter a total of about 20 minutes; it will become light golden and airy.

continued

3. Sprinkle the flour mixture over the batter and stir it in by hand until no more white flecks appear. Stir in the carrots, raisins, and apples, plus the walnuts, if you wish.

4. Divide the batter evenly among the 3 layer cake pans. Bake each cake layer just until the center springs back when lightly touched and a toothpick inserted into the center comes out almost clean, about 40 minutes. Let the cakes cool in the pans on a wire rack for 15 minutes before turning them out onto the rack to cool completely.

5. While the cakes are baking, make the frosting: Beat the cream cheese, butter, and margarine together in a large bowl with an electric mixer on high until light yellow and creamy, about 3 minutes. With the mixer still running, beat in the corn syrup and vanilla.

6. Reduce the mixer to medium low and beat in the confectioners' sugar in two additions, beating well after each addition. Place a piece of plastic wrap directly on the frosting and chill until ready to use.

7. To frost the cake, spread a thick layer of frosting between the layers, on the sides and on the top of the cake. Using your fingers, make high peaks in the frosting on the top of the cake. Store any extra leftover cake in the refrigerator.

Brownies

AS YOU MIGHT imagine, Junior's brownies are at least three inches square and almost as high. They are chock-full of chunks of walnuts and swirled with creamy fudge, then crowned with a cluster of a few more walnuts in the center. They're brimming with that deep chocolate flavor, moist and fudgy with every bite. There's only one drawback to these brownies—it's almost impossible to eat just one.

**MAKES A DOZEN LARGE BROWNIES, 3 INCHES SQUARE
(THIS RECIPE DOUBLES EASILY)**

2 cups (4 sticks) unsalted butter

10 ounces bittersweet baking chocolate

3¼ cups all-purpose flour

2 teaspoons salt

9 extra-large eggs

4 cups sugar

2 tablespoons pure vanilla extract

4 cups chopped walnuts

½ recipe Chocolate Fudge Frosting (page 274)

The Junior's Way—

For these fudgy, moist brownies, start with good bittersweet baking chocolate. Shop for it in a gourmet store or a good supermarket. Bake the brownies just until they are almost set in the center—no longer.

1. Preheat the oven to 325°F and generously butter a 13 × 9 × 2-inch baking pan.

2. Melt the butter and chocolate over low heat in a large heavy saucepan, then remove from the heat. Mix the flour and salt together in a large bowl and set aside.

3. Beat the eggs in a large bowl with an electric mixer on high for 3 minutes or until light yellow and slightly thickened. With the mixer still running, beat in the sugar. Reduce the mixer to low and blend in the butter-chocolate mixture and the vanilla.

4. Stir in the flour mixture with a spoon just until the flour disappears (do not overmix). Fold in the walnuts.

5. Pour the batter into the baking pan and bake *just* until the brownies are almost set in the center, about 40 minutes (do not overbake). The brownies are ready to come out of the oven when a toothpick inserted into the center of the brownies comes out almost clean. Let the brownies cool in the pan on a rack for 1 hour, then spread with the fudge frosting. To make cutting easier, refrigerate the brownies about 30 minutes before slicing.

Pure Butter Cookies

*Y*OU KNOW THESE little cookies—rich, buttery, often shaped in small buttons with fancy little peaks. In Germany, they're called *Spritz*, from the German word *spritzen*, which means to squirt or spray. The shape comes from the dough being squirted or pushed through a pastry tube or cookie press into fancy shapes. In many bake shops, spritz butter cookies appear only around the December holidays. But not at Junior's. You can buy a batch of these heavenly butter cookies any day you like. They're ideal for serving alongside a bowl of ice cream.

MAKES 8 DOZEN COOKIES

4½ cups all-purpose flour

½ teaspoon salt

¼ teaspoon baking powder

2 cups (4 sticks) unsalted butter, at room temperature

1⅓ cups sugar

2 extra-large eggs

1 tablespoon pure vanilla extract

2 teaspoons lemon extract

Candied red cherries, quartered, or multicolored sparkling sugar (optional)

The Junior's Way—
Chill the dough first, just until it's cold to the touch, yet still pliable. Then force it through a pastry bag fitted with a large fluted tip.

1. Preheat the oven to 375°F and butter some baking sheets (3 if you have them). Mix the flour, salt, and baking powder in a medium-size bowl and set aside.

2. Cream the butter in a large bowl with an electric mixer on high for 2 minutes. Then, with the mixer still running, gradually add the sugar, then the eggs, one at a time. Continue beating until the mixture is creamy and light yellow. Beat in the vanilla and lemon extracts.

3. With a spoon, stir in the flour mixture, just until it's mixed (do not overmix the batter at this stage, as the protein in the flour might become overdeveloped and cause the cookies to be tough). Chill the batter for 30 minutes or until dough is cold to the touch but not firm.

4. Force the dough through a pastry bag fitted with a medium-size fluted tip into 1½-inch fluted rounds, about 2 inches apart. Top each cookie with a cherry or sprinkle with sparkling sugar, if you wish (especially if it's the holiday season).

5. Bake the cookies just until golden and set (but not brown), about 8 minutes. Let the cookies cool on the baking sheets for 5 minutes, then slide them onto a cooling rack and let them cool for at least 1 hour before storing in airtight containers. These cookies also freeze great in zipper-closing plastic freezer bags (best when used within a month).

Chocolate Chip Cookies

ROWS AND ROWS of cookies are always lined up in the glass bakery cases, welcoming you every time you walk inside Junior's.

As you might expect, chocolate chip cookies are one of the most popular. But these aren't the kind that you taste and forget. These are so chunky with pecans and chips of rich chocolate that you'll find yourself eating a handful, whether you intended to or not.

MAKES 10 DOZEN COOKIES
(THIS RECIPE DOUBLES EASILY)

2 cups all-purpose flour

1½ cups cake flour

1½ teaspoons baking soda

1½ teaspoons salt

1½ cups (3 sticks) unsalted butter, at room temperature

1¼ cups packed light brown sugar

1 cup sugar

3 extra-large eggs

1 tablespoon pure vanilla extract

4 cups chocolate chips (2 12-ounce packages)

3 cups chopped pecans

The Junior's Way— Drop the cookie batter by heaping teaspoons for each cookie, not tablespoons. Cookies bake out 2 to 2½ inches wide and extra chunky.

continued

1980s—When Brooklyn . . . Came Back!

1. Preheat the oven to 375°F and butter some baking sheets (4 if you have them). Mix both flours, baking soda, and salt in a medium-sized bowl and set aside.

2. Cream the butter in a large bowl with an electric mixer on high for 2 minutes. Then, with the mixer still running, gradually add both of the sugars, then the eggs, one at a time. Continue beating the mixture until it is creamy and light yellow. Beat in the vanilla.

3. With a spoon, stir in the flour mixture, just until it's mixed (do not overmix the batter at this stage, as the protein in the flour might become overdeveloped and cause the cookies to be tough). Stir in the chocolate chips and the pecans.

4. Drop the batter by heaping teaspoons onto the baking sheets, about 2 inches apart. Bake the cookies until golden and firm, 9 to 11 minutes (watch carefully and do not let them get too brown). Let the cookies cool on the baking sheets for 10 minutes, then slide them onto a cooling rack. Let the cookies cool for at least 1 hour before storing in airtight containers. These cookies also freeze great, for up to 1 month, in zipper-closing plastic freezer bags.

Welcome to Junior's!

Coconut Macaroons

OFTEN, **MACAROON COOKIES** come small and dainty. But not at Junior's. These are over 3 inches in diameter and chock-full of coconut. Biting into one is a treat—golden crispy on the outside, white and chewy on the inside.

MAKES 2 DOZEN MACAROONS
(THIS RECIPE DOUBLES EASILY)

3 tablespoons cake flour

¼ teaspoon salt

3 extra-large egg whites

1 cup sugar

1 teaspoon pure vanilla extract

½ teaspoon almond extract

¼ teaspoon orange extract

2 cups shredded or flaked coconut

The Junior's Way—
Bake the macaroons on ungreased baking sheets lined with parchment or brown paper. After baking, slide the paper liners with cookies still on them to cooling racks lined with damp towels. Let the macaroons cool then peel away from the paper liners.

1. Preheat the oven to 325°F and line 2 baking sheets with parchment or brown paper. Line cooling racks with damp towels. Mix the flour and salt together and set aside.

2. Beat the egg whites in a large bowl with an electric mixer on high until soft peaks begin to form, about 3 minutes. While the mixer is still running, gradually add the sugar, about a tablespoon at a time, and continue beating until the mixture stands up in stiff glossy peaks, about 5 minutes of beating in all.

3. Reduce the speed of the mixer to low and blend in the flour mixture and the vanilla, almond, and orange extracts. (Do not overmix the batter at this stage, as the protein in the flour might become overdeveloped, which can result in chewy cookies.)

4. Drop the batter by heaping tablespoons onto the lined baking sheets about 2 inches apart (you will have about 24 cookies). Bake the cookies just until they are golden and set, about 15 minutes. Slide the paper liners, still with the macaroons attached to them, to the lined cooling racks. Let the cookies cool completely, then peel away the paper. Store the macaroons in an airtight container. Do not refrigerate or freeze macaroons.

1980s—When Brooklyn . . . Came Back!

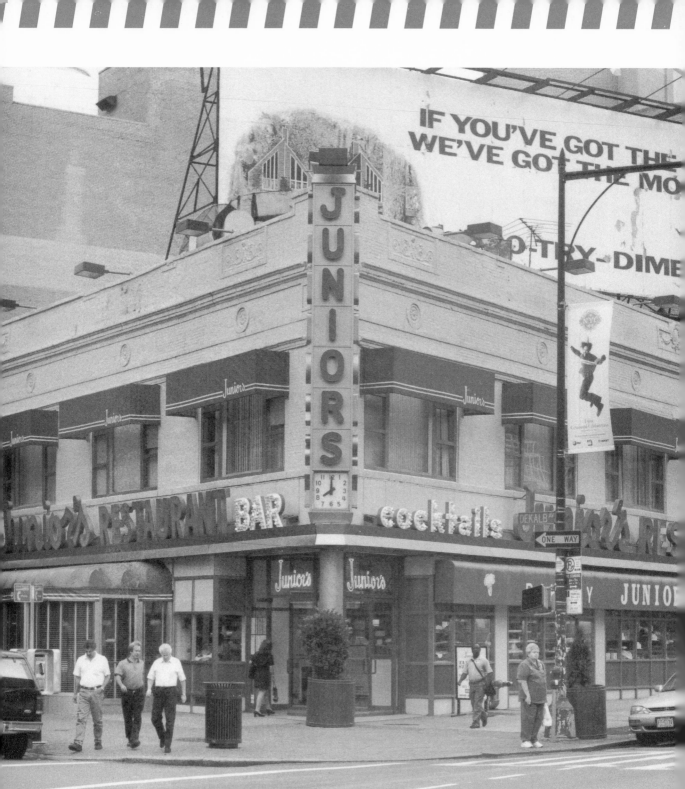

At the corner of Flatbush and DeKalb, Junior's is a home away
from home for everybody who walks through these doors—from
neighborhood residents to travelers, politicians, businesspeople,
movie stars, sports teams, families, celebrities, and friends.

CHAPTER SEVEN

1990s—Brooklyn! Still the World!

P RESIDENT BUSH MOVED into the Oval Office in 1990 and

that same year New Yorkers elected David Dinkins our first

African-American mayor. Dinkins was a popular candidate

in Brooklyn and ran a gentlemanly no-smear campaign that

promised to focus on community prosperity. But with the

huge population flux in the late 1980s, he might as well have

promised to hold a wave on the sand.

Common Underground

The 1990 census revealed that the majority of New York residents were people of color—60 percent Hispanic, black, Asian, and other nonwhites. In that Brooklyn was the largest borough with about 2.5 million people, we didn't need a census to tell us that the whole world had moved here. Any subway ride at any time of day could prove that point. On the BMT to Coney Island, the IRT to Utica or Lefferts Boulevard or the IND to Far Rockaway, one rode with the United Nations—literally. There might have been someone from each of thirty-some countries on one subway car alone.

The trains are the last equalizer/galvanizer in Brooklyn and the best way to get a sense of who we all are. We come together in transit, on our way somewhere, packed inside a subway car. There are laborers, young couples, old couples, mothers with babies, men and women with briefcases, backpacks, shopping bags. There are schoolkids and Wall Street professionals. It's the most integrated experience anyone can find anywhere in New York—and that includes Mets, Knicks, Liberty, and Yankee games. Get on the IRT Express at Times Square or Grand Central and head toward Brooklyn. I'll bet you ten-to-one that you're riding with people who were born, or whose parents were born, in Nigeria, Guyana, Mexico, Peru, Ecuador, Bolivia, Guatemala, the Dominican Republic, Puerto Rico, Poland, Trinidad, Jamaica, Haiti, Lebanon, India, Pakistan, Israel, Ireland, Russia, Sri Lanka, Vietnam, Cambodia, Ukraine, Egypt, Yemen, Shanghai, Japan, Hong Kong, North Carolina, Laguna Beach, California, Whitefish, Montana, Salt Lake City, Utah, Maplewood, New Jersey, and/or Poughkeepsie, New York.

The New Neighborhoods

There are problems and benefits that come from packing such diverse cultures together in one borough. In a neighborhood such as Crown Heights in 1991, the West Indians and African Americans clashed with the Orthodox Jews. These two different populations had shared the neighborhood for years and the tension of living together sparked a violent eruption after two young black boys were hit by a car. Then a young Jewish man was stabbed in the melee that followed. The rioting

Welcome to Junior's!

Ethnicity is strong in Brooklyn and neighborhood merchants' associations are thriving. This shot is from the Fifth Avenue Festival in Sunset Park. *Courtesy of the Brooklyn Historical Society*

between the blacks and the Jews was the first ever in Brooklyn and it was so intense that a curfew was needed to shut the area down. Neighborhood coalitions since then have kept the lines of communication open between the two groups so as to relieve tension before it builds. A lot of healing has happened there since '91.

In other neighborhoods new minority-owned restaurants and retail shops were rising out of the ashes of burned buildings and crack houses. Urban coalitions and neighborhood action partnerships were beginning to revitalize streets in still beleaguered areas, giving help to young entrepreneurs who had grown up in these neighborhoods and wanted to open businesses and stay.

What Dinkins couldn't do as mayor was to take a bite out of crime. The numbers of serious crimes rose on his watch, which left a big opening for a contender in the new mayoral race. Rudolph Giuliani, a Republican, promised a safer city. He took office in 1994 and—what do you know? Crime went down; property values went up; loans and mortgages were more accessible, too.

By the latter half of the 1990s, some neighborhoods had peaked in the well-off department. In Brooklyn Heights, for example, it'd take more than a million dollars to purchase a home, and nearly that much for a condo. Some other

"It is the proximity that makes [New York neighborhoods] unique. If you gathered up from a suburban town all the people and put them together in a small space and made them live next to one another, it would change their lives dramatically. They would know one another better, probably resent one another more. They would irritate one another more and learn to love more profoundly."

—Mario Cuomo

neighborhoods have just begun to see their revivals. One cherished neighborhood, East New York, where George and Ira Gershwin grew up, now has many well-kept streets with perfectly maintained houses where abandoned properties used to be. By 1998, in East New York and Brownsville, places which had taken such a nosedive in the 1960s and 1970s, it was possible for a Haitian immigrant cab driver, for example, to buy a well-maintained house with a yard and a rental for extra income for about $165,000. He then had a shot at raising his family in an upwardly mobile environment.

A New Downtown Dawning

There were big strides in the early 1990s to pull off years of plans to revitalize downtown. Bruce Ratner's brainchild MetroTech Center is a twenty-five-block complex that has rejuvenated downtown with a commercial mall, a three-acre park, and business service to 150 stores and restaurants downtown. The MetroTech flagship, the Chase building, went up in 1992 and is a twenty-four-hour facility with six thousand employees. The new buildings, the landscaping, the added workers, all give downtown a new feel of progressive forward movement.

Brooklyn's first new hotel since the long-closed St. George dominated the Brooklyn Heights scene in the 1930s and 1940s opened downtown, too. In 1998, as part of the MetroTech revival, the Renaissance Plaza Marriott Hotel opened its doors onto Adams Street across from Borough Hall.

Down the street from Junior's toward the Manhattan Bridge—under the bridge actually—an artist's colony is beginning to thrive. Hundreds of sculptors and painters have moved into the warehouse lofts to take advantage of the river view and the light. They have affectionately named the area DUMBO (down under the Manhattan Bridge Overpass). We have no hopes that it will become a TriBeCa or SoHo. We hope it doesn't. The fact that artists are being beckoned by the creative energy of Brooklyn and are colonizing waterfront properties is a sign of health in and of itself.

Meanwhile Fulton Street Mall, which was once the Fifth Avenue of downtown Brooklyn, is more like the old Coney Island boardwalk, "a honky-tonk esthetic," our Chamber of Commerce president Ken Adams calls it. It's a spirited mix of electronics stores, sneaker shops, fast-food places, gold jewelry stores, and street vendors of all kinds—more like the old Times Square before Disney moved in. The stately Macy's building, which for years was A&S, seems patiently out of place amid the bright fast-food marquees and the noisy hustle. Still, a hundred thousand pedestrians traverse the mall every day and business is very good. Fulton Mall is one of the city's highest-grossing commercial streets.

Junior's 1990s Highlights

The 1990s have seen a change of management at Junior's. Alan and Kevin are the third generation of Rosens to be making the day-to-day decisions. Walter still keeps his eye on the kitchens, cooks, and quality control. Marvin's eye falls on the front of the house— service and customer comfort. But Kevin and Alan are in charge of taking Junior's into the twenty-first century.

AH-H-H! THE PRICE OF FAME	
1956 SLICE OF JUNIOR'S CHEESE PIE	$.35
1972 SLICE OF JUNIOR'S CHEESECAKE	.90
1982	1.50
1992	2.10
1998	3.95

If the 1990s are a good indication, then the 2000s should be thriving! As of now, Junior's is doing great business in downtown Brooklyn but we're also selling at least two thousand cheesecakes weekly via overnight mail order. About once a month, too, Alan makes an appearance on a cable-TV shopping network. His first show netted orders for twenty-four hundred Junior's cheesecakes—all guaranteed to arrive at the caller's home within ten days (naturally, ovens were baking twenty-four hours a day and everyone got their cakes!). A few shows later down the road and Alan's appearances were producing twenty-seven thousand orders! Because of the new demand, Alan and Kevin have hired more bakers to satisfy the countrywide appetite for Junior's cheesecake.

"I have to tell you . . . I got engaged in front of Junior's three years ago. My boyfriend bought a cheesecake and said, 'Let's go home and eat it.' As we were walking home, he said, 'Open the box.' Inside a dollop of whipped cream was my engagement ring! I grew up in Brooklyn and all I ever loved was Junior's cheesecake. Now, all I ever want and get is Junior's, Junior's, Junior's."

—Stephanie, on the telephone, during one of
Alan Rosen's appearances on TV

Meanwhile, here on the corner of Flatbush Avenue Extension and DeKalb, business is better than ever. Holidays especially are busy in the bakery. The day before Thanksgiving, for example, our bakers put in many extra hours producing Pumpkin Cheesecakes, and customers line up around the corner waiting to buy them. Other holidays such as Christmas, Valentine's Day, Easter, Mother's Day, Memorial Day, and the Fourth of July are the same. At one point we petitioned to have our stretch of DeKalb Avenue renamed Cheesecake Alley, but the powers-that-be said it sounded a little risqué.

Junior's continues to grow, too, as we look to expand into Manhattan. Plans are afoot to become part of the revival of Grand Central Terminal by putting up a kind of mini-Junior's there, plus a bakery counter for cheesecake-to-go.

Almost any day of the year, there's a family at Junior's celebrating a birthday, an anniversary, First Communion, graduation, a homecoming, a bon voyage, Easter, Mother's Day—you name it! Courtesy of the Rosen family

Let's Go to the Videotape

As the decade has rolled by, so has lots of video footage featuring Junior's. It seems that we've been in the news a lot. Cameras have always followed dignitaries through Junior's front door. Mayors Lindsay, Beame, Koch, Dinkins, and Giuliani have all been videotaped and photographed shaking hands inside Junior's. In 1992, Bill Clinton campaigned here amid photographers and cameramen, too. That night the TV news reported that Clinton ordered a pastrami on rye sandwich, cheesecake, cheese blintzes, and a diet Coke to go.

FAHGEDABOUTIT!

"Maybe my English ain't poifect but I 'aven't got a Brooklyn accent. Besides, what's wrong wid a Brooklyn accent?"

—Anonymous customer at Junior's

When Bill Clinton was the presidential candidate in 1992, his campaign trail led him to Junior's. Before he left, Marvin's daughter, Sheri Rosen, presented him with sandwiches and cheesecake for the road. Courtesy of the Rosen family

This is Alan Rosen with the cake we sent to Judge Ito, who had said some disparaging words about the so-called Brooklyn accent during the O. J. Simpson trial in L.A. Photo by Susan May Tell, courtesy of the Rosen family

In 1995, when Judge Lance Ito, who was presiding over the O. J. Simpson trial in Los Angeles, complained about attorney Peter Neufeld's Brooklyn accent and asked him to slow down so that he could be understood by the jurors, there was an uprising in the New York papers. Brooklynites especially did not appreciate the condescending remarks by Ito. The next day, news crews were here at Junior's to get customers' opinions of Ito and to get a look at the cake we had baked for the judge. It was inscribed, *Brooklyn to Ito: Bite Me*. And, yes, we sent it.

Later that same year the media also did a story when we offered to host Santa for the Christmas season. When Macy's found it too much of a budgetary problem to provide Santa for Christmas wishes, a Junior's waiter who was also an actor, a guy by the name of William Williams, put on the white beard and red suit and stepped in. On the far wall here in the restaurant we set up a big red chair on a decorated platform, complete with toy soldiers. From December 15 through Christmas Eve, between the hours of four and seven, kids lined up to sit on Santa's knee and recite their wish lists.

Welcome to Junior's!

"No Grinch is going to steal Christmas in downtown Brooklyn this year. Santa can't stop his sleigh at the old A&S on Fulton Street because it's now a Santa-free Macy's. So Junior's Restaurant down the block has invited Santa to set up shop there."

—*News 4 New York,* December 1995

We provided a fine home for Santa in 1994 when Macy's on Fulton Street had to downsize him. Courtesy of the Rosen family

In 1996 Mayor Giuliani promised to send a Junior's cheesecake to Atlanta's mayor if the Braves won the World Series against the Yankees. Well, we sent one anyway, even as the Yankees were enjoying their victory ticker-tape parade. For us in Brooklyn, it was a particularly proud day when the Yankees won, even though the team had always been the nemesis of the Brooklyn Dodgers. Joe Torre, the winning manager of the Yanks, was one of our own—born and raised here in Brooklyn.

ONE MAN'S OPINION

"What makes Brooklyn food different? It's the ayembeeance!"

—Customer at Junior's take-out counter

Mayor Giuliani and Alan and Kevin Rosen pose with the Junior's cheesecake that Giuliani had promised Atlanta's mayor if Atlanta could manage to take the World Series. They lost; we won! In victory, we sent it anyway. Photo by Diane Bondareff, Mayor's Photo Unit, courtesy of the Rosen family

In 1998 we joined the whole city in marking the final episode of *Seinfeld* by offering a *Seinfeld* TV dinner for two. For $23.95, *Seinfeld* fans got a chef's salad, Manhattan clam chowder, tuna or pastrami on marble rye, black-and-white cookies, and of course, cheesecake. The price also included Junior Mints. That same year of 1998, when New York Yankee outfielder Darryl Strawberry came out of cancer surgery, he told the press he was craving cheesecake. Kevin, Alan, and Alan's wife, Leslie, immediately went to the hospital and personally delivered Darryl's favorite—fresh strawberry cheesecake from Junior's.

Welcome Back to Brooklyn

Even as people have moved away, they tell us they yearn to return to Brooklyn. The huge variety of ethnic foods that has come to be called *Brooklyn food* is one magnet. Nowhere can you find such variety in eight square miles: Jamaican jerk chicken on

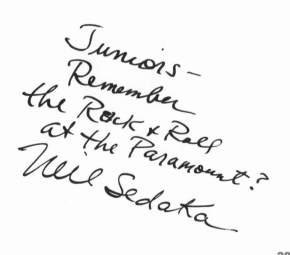

Hi ♡ Kim Coles!

I miss the cheesecake yum yum!!!

VOTED NO. 1 "THE BEST CHEESE CAKE IN N.Y." NEW YORK MAGAZINE

Junior's MOST FABULOUS RESTAURANT CATERERS

To all My Friends at Junior's— I love you + adore you all! What would I do without the Best cheesecake in the World! XXX Wendy "the Snapple Lady"

Famous people can always be spotted at Junior's. Courtesy of the Rosen family

Flatbush Avenue, fajitas in Windsor Terrace, sweet plantains and rice in Sunset Park, knishes in Brighton Beach, Nathan's hot dogs in Coney Island, specialty bagels and muffins in countless neighborhood diners, deli in Bensonhurst and Williamsburg, freshly made pita, hummus, and baba ganoush in the shops along Atlantic Avenue, freshly baked brick-oven breads in Greenpoint, coffee shops featuring blue plate specials, and of course Junior's cheesecake, blintzes, pastrami, and specials of the day.

Another magnet that pulls people back is the energy. Still there's a feeling that anything and everything's possible in Brooklyn. You can't really find it anywhere

Junior's— Remember the Rock + Roll at the Paramount? Neil Sedaka

1990s—Brooklyn! Still the World!

else. Emotion, too. Brooklynites are not afraid to express sadness as well as anger as well as joy. On the day Frank Sinatra died, for example, May 16, 1998, workers in the streets, house painters, and delivery guys were playing Sinatra tunes on radios and tape decks, as if the sadness could be contained only by listening to his songs.

The need to come back and touch, smell, walk around, and connect with Brooklyn was the impetus behind the Welcome Back to Brooklyn Festival which began in 1982 and usually takes place on the first weekend in June. Brooklyn businesses and neighborhoods take part. Junior's always decorates a huge cake for the festival. In '97 a great number of restaurants and chefs baked birthday cakes for the fifteen-year-old homecoming party.

It's an all-day event that gathers all those Brooklyn-born or -raised under the arch at Grand Army Plaza. The entire Eastern Parkway is closed off between the Brooklyn Museum and the arch. People come by the thousands, including hundreds of celebrities. It feels great to see someone who has "gone off and made good" come home. Richard Dreyfus, Woody Allen, Elliott Gould, Brenda Vaccaro, Paul Sorvino, Mel Brooks, Mary Tyler Moore, Neil Simon, Al Lewis, Rhea Perlman, Jimmy Smits, Gabe Kaplan, Jim Brooks, Dom DeLuise, Buddy Hackett, Joan Rivers, Jerry Stiller, Rodney Dangerfield, Lena Horne, Gregory Hines, Carole King, Wendy Wasserstein, Neil Diamond, Steve Lawrence, Joe Garagiola, Joe Torre, Neil Sedaka, Vic Damone, *Monday Night Football*'s Al Michaels, Joe Paterno, Lee Mazzilli, and John Franco are just a few who have come from Brooklyn. Each year all are welcome to come back. Most recently, Lainie Kazan, who grew up in Flatbush, and Tony Lo Bianco, who grew up in Sunset Park, were crowned homecoming king and queen.

Meanwhile . . .

Junior's continues as a landmark downtown restaurant seven days a week. The list of notable "Regular" customers goes back as far as Jack Dempsey and Leo Durocher and as recent as Spike Lee, who has business meetings at the back table once a week or so. Ed

Evander Holyfield adds his autograph to our collection. Courtesy of the Rosen family

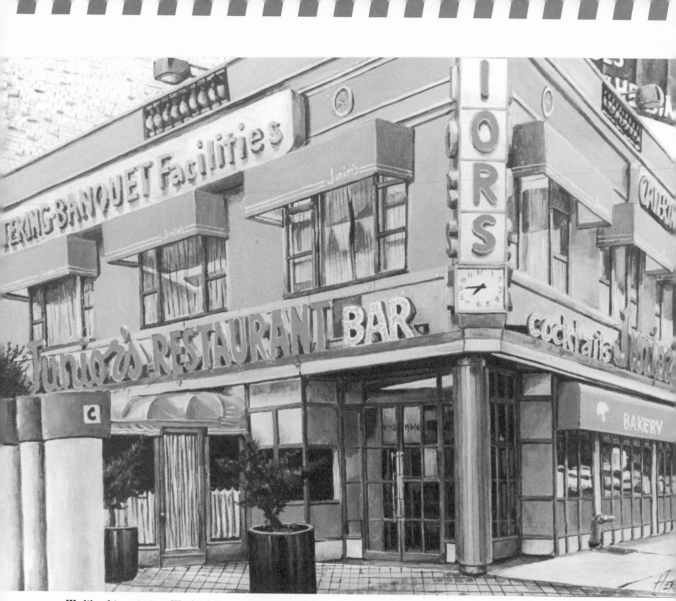

We like this painting. We think it represents the life and excitement of Junior's. It draws you inside. Courtesy of the Rosen family

Koch still comes in, as do newsman Gabe Pressman, Borough President Howard Golden, and Al Sharpton. LL Cool J stops in, too.

An infamous "Regular," Frank Gerarro, the one man who leapt from the stands during a Dodgers game at Ebbets Field to pummel an unpopular umpire, found and courted and dined the love of his life here at Junior's.

"When I walk into Junior's I'm immediately reminded of my high school years. We'd go to the movies at the Paramount, then afterwards rush over and pile into a booth for burgers and milk shakes. The basics haven't changed. You still get great quality and quantity for your dollar at Junior's. And the cheesecake! In my time, I've had Reuben's and Lindy's. I've had them all. Junior's truly is the best in the world."

—Clare Rich, Junior's customer since 1954

The corner of DeKalb and Flatbush, two steps from the D-train. Photo by Amos Chang

We enjoy all our "Regulars" and we enjoy the new ones—those tourists who arrive via the New York Apple double-decker buses (also an addition in the late nineties) or the ones who find their way by themselves on the D-Train. But whether the tourists come or not, we are still likely to see Norman Mailer every once in a while, as well as city attorneys, Democrats, Republicans, religious leaders, families celebrating together, and young lovers on a date.

For as long as we can imagine, Junior's will be everybody's place for good food, good service, good people—good times!

Up front and behind the scenes at Junior's—late 90s. Photos by Amos Chang

1990s—Brooklyn Food

EVERYTHING OLD IS new again. People who once left Brooklyn are coming back. "We can do anything" is back . . . things are once again possible in Brooklyn. Better than ever. Especially the food.

From Flatbush to Coney Island, from Jamaican jerk chicken to hot dogs, Brooklyn has re-created its own cuisine. Once again, it's freshly baked breads, blue plate specials, freshly roasted coffee, homemade blintzes.

But now, fried chicken comes in small chicken fingers with honey mustard . . . the daily specials might be flounder one day, shrimp scampi the next . . . potato salad's made from little red new potatoes . . . fries are made from yams. And of course at Junior's the menu reflects the nationalities, the flavors, the traditions of yesterday, today, tomorrow.

All you want of what you want and how you want it keeps "Regulars" coming back to Junior's. Photo by Amos Chang

Homemade Cheese Blintzes

UNDER ANY OTHER name, blintzes are simply thin pancakes resembling the French crêpes that are filled, folded, and fried into a delectable specialty. They use an authentic crêpe pan to make them at Junior's. It's about six inches across the bottom with sloping sides and a long handle. But if you don't have one, a small skillet will work, too. Try to use one with sides that are on an angle, not straight.

**MAKES A DOZEN 6-INCH BLINTZES
(THIS RECIPE DOUBLES EASILY)**

FOR THE CRÊPES

1 cup all-purpose flour

3 tablespoons sugar

1 tablespoon cornstarch

4 extra-large eggs

1 cup water

2 tablespoons unsalted butter,

   melted, plus 2 to 3 tablespoons for baking crêpes and filled blintzes

1 tablespoon vegetable oil

FOR THE CHEESE FILLING

1 pound cream cheese (the regular variety, not light Neufchâtel cream cheese)

1 cup large-curd cottage cheese (pot style)

⅔ cup sugar

1 teaspoon pure vanilla extract

FOR THE GO-ALONGS—TAKE YOUR PICK

Applesauce

Sour Cream

Fresh Strawberry Sauce (page 98)

The Junior's Way—Success in making blintzes is all in the folding. Spoon the filling in the center of the crêpe, then fold the ends of the crêpe over like an envelope: first the top edge, then the left side, next the right side, and finally the bottom edge. Be sure the filling is tightly enclosed. Place the crêpe folded-ends-down in the skillet. As the crêpe fries, the heat seals the edges shut.

continued

1. Use a crepe pan, about 6 inches across the bottom, or set out a small skillet with sloping sides. Mix the flour, sugar, and cornstarch together in a small bowl and set aside.

2. Using an electric mixer set on high, beat the eggs, water, butter, and oil together until light yellow. Reduce the speed to low and blend in the flour mixture all at once, just until the white disappears. (Do not overbeat at this stage, as this can make the crepes tough.)

3. Preheat a crepe pan, over medium-high heat until a droplet of water sprinkled on the bottom of the pan sizzles. Brush the preheated crepe pan or skillet with butter, coating it well.

4. For each crepe, pour about ¼ cup of the batter into the pan and immediately tilt the pan so the batter, completely but lightly, coats the bottom (don't worry if some of the batter moves up the sides of the pan about ¼ inch). Cook about 30 seconds until the bottom of the crepe is golden brown (just lift the edge to see).

5. Loosen the crepe by shaking the pan, then gently turn the crepe over with a spatula, being careful not to tear it. If you're adventuresome, you might even try flipping one over, just like the chefs do, by tossing it slightly in the air and catching it back in the pan. Cook the crepe on the underside for only about 15 seconds, just until it's set. Turn the crepes, light underside-up, onto a cooling rack. Refrigerate the crepes for up to 2 days or freeze for up to 1 month.

6. To make the filling: Stir all of the ingredients for the cheese filling together in a small bowl until blended. To fill each crepe, spoon 3 tablespoons of filling in the center on the underside of the crepe, then fold the edges over like an envelope.

7. To fry the blintzes, melt 2 to 3 tablespoons butter in a large skillet over medium heat. Place the filled blintzes in the skillet, folded-ends-down. Fry the blintzes until golden and hot on both sides, turning once, about 5 minutes total. Serve hot with applesauce, sour cream, or Fresh Strawberry Sauce.

Belgian Waffles

ANY RESTAURANT AS famous for giving you all you can eat as Junior's is would naturally have giant-sized Belgian waffles for breakfast. But once again, these are different. First of all, they're nowhere on the menu, but there's often a tent card on your table announcing they're a daily special. These waffles come out piping hot, not just lukewarm, with a little ramekin of hot melted butter alongside. And there's always another little dish sitting on the plate that's filled with a warm and spicy apple-and-raisin creation (they call it preserves, although it's not overly sweet). Even Mondays get off to a great start when you sink your teeth into one of these!

MAKES 4 CUPS OF WAFFLE BATTER, ENOUGH FOR EIGHT 8-INCH WAFFLES

2 cups all-purpose flour

¼ cup sugar

1 tablespoon baking powder

1 teaspoon salt

4 extra-large eggs

1 cup milk

¾ cup heavy (whipping) cream

6 tablespoons (¾ stick) unsalted butter, melted

1 tablespoon plus 1 teaspoon pure vanilla extract

Extra unsalted butter, melted and kept warm

1 recipe Apple and Raisin Preserves (page 126)

The Junior's Way—Use a Belgian waffle iron, which makes thick waffles, if you have one. But if not, the batter cooks up just as good in a standard waffle iron. The vanilla in the batter not only gives off a wonderful aroma as the waffles cook, but also brings out all of the flavors in the waffle, bite after bite.

1. Preheat your waffle iron according to the manufacturer's directions.

2. Mix the flour, sugar, baking powder, and salt together in a large bowl. Make a well in the center of the dry ingredients with your hands or a large spoon.

continued

1990s—Brooklyn! Still the World!

3. Beat the eggs in a large bowl with an electric mixer on high until light yellow and slightly thickened, about 3 minutes. Beat in the milk, cream, 6 tablespoons melted butter, and the vanilla until well combined.

4. Pour this egg mixture all at once into the well in the dry ingredients. Using a spoon, stir the dry ingredients into the wet ones until the batter is well blended (do not overmix and do not worry if a few white specks of flour remain).

5. Cook the waffles according to your waffle-iron manufacturer's directions. Serve the waffles piping hot, with small ramekins of warm melted butter, plus a helping of warm Apple and Raisin Preserves alongside.

Buffalo Wings with Bleu Cheese Sauce

*I*T'S ONE OF my favorite lunches," says Alan Rosen with a smile as he bites into a Buffalo wing. "The sauce is one of the best . . . talk to the chef, he'll tell you how he makes it." So I found the chef and was delighted to see how really simple these spicy wings are to make.

The secret ingredient? A splash of hot pepper sauce, naturally, as much or as little as you like.

MAKES A DOZEN BUFFALO WINGS

Vegetable oil for frying
12 chicken wings (about 2 pounds)

FOR THE SPICY COOKING SAUCE

2 cups tomato juice
1 cup ketchup
⅓ cup distilled white vinegar
2 tablespoons sugar

The Junior's Way—
Deep-fry the wings in medium-hot oil, about 370°F. If the oil is hotter, it will smoke and fry the wings too fast, before they are done on the inside.

¼ teaspoon ground white pepper, or to taste

3 to 4 drops Tabasco (hot pepper sauce), or to taste

FOR THE BLEU CHEESE DIPPING SAUCE (OPTIONAL)

1 cup Hellmann's Real Mayonnaise (not the light variety)

½ cup blue cheese, crumbled (2 ounces)

1. Heat the oil in a deep-fat fryer according to the manufacturer's instructions. Or, if you're using a skillet (an iron one is great), pour in about 1 inch of oil and heat over medium-high heat to 370°F. Add the chicken wings and cook them until golden brown and crisp on both sides, about 8 minutes in all. Using a slotted spoon, transfer the wings to paper towels to drain off any excess oil.

2. Combine all of the ingredients for the sauce in a large saucepan and stir over medium-high heat until the sauce begins to simmer. Reduce the heat to low and add the chicken wings. Simmer the dish until it's hot throughout, about 10 minutes.

3. To make the Bleu Cheese Dipping Sauce: Stir the mayonnaise and the bleu cheese together. Use right away or chill until serving time.

1990s—Brooklyn! Still the World!

Chicken Fingers

*I*T WAS BOUND to happen. Any food as popular as Junior's fried chicken is likely to command more than one spot on the menu. And this is it—another form of their popular Golden Fried Chicken, Southern Style.

This time, only skinless, boneless white meat is cut into long thin pieces that resemble fingers. They're dipped, breaded, and fried till they're golden and crispy. You'll find them under "Appetizers" on the menu (Number 571), but just serve extra helpings, as I do, and call it dinner.

MAKES 8 APPETIZER SERVINGS OR 4 MAIN-DISH SERVINGS

1 recipe Dipping Batter (page 188)

1 recipe Honey Mustard Sauce (page 307)

2 pounds boneless, skinless chicken breasts
(about 2 whole breasts or 4 halves)

Vegetable oil

FOR THE POULTRY BREADER

1¾ cups all-purpose flour

¼ cup yellow cornmeal

2 tablespoons cornstarch

2 tablespoons fried chicken seasonings (look in the spice rack in your supermarket
or gourmet store)

1 tablespoon paprika

1 tablespoon dried thyme leaves

1 teaspoon ground white pepper

> *The Junior's Way—*
> Buy boneless, skinless chicken breasts and cut into fingers about 4 inches long and ¾ inch wide.

1. Make the Dipping Batter and let it stand for 15 minutes. Make the Honey Mustard Sauce and refrigerate.

2. Meanwhile, rinse the chicken, pat it dry with paper towels, and cut into finger shapes, about 4 inches long and ¾ inch wide.

Welcome to Junior's!

3. Mix all of the ingredients for the poultry breader in a large shallow dish.

4. Dip the chicken fingers in the batter, then roll them in the poultry breader, coating each piece evenly. Place in the refrigerator for 15 minutes to set the coating.

5. Meanwhile heat about 1 inch of oil in a large skillet (an iron skillet is great), or use a deep-fat fryer according to the manufacturer's directions. Fry the chicken, in 2 or 3 batches, until golden brown and the juices run clear when pierced with a fork, turning each piece one time, 8 to 10 minutes total. Transfer the chicken to a cooling rack to drain. Best when served piping hot or at room temperature.

Honey Mustard Sauce

FRIED CHICKEN FINGERS are one of Junior's most popular appetizers. "Regulars" often order a plateful for the table, while everyone is reading the menu. Whenever a batch of chicken fingers arrives, this dipping sauce just automatically appears—sweet, sparkling, and spicy, all at the same time.

It's the perfect complement for fried shrimp, fish, or chicken.

MAKES 1 CUP MUSTARD SAUCE

⅔ cup Dijon mustard
2 tablespoons honey
1 tablespoon cider vinegar

The Junior's Way—Some mustard sauces require long, slow cooking. This one starts from a prepared country mustard, so you can mix it up in minutes.

Mix all of the ingredients together in a small bowl. Cover and store any leftover sauce in the refrigerator. Whenever you're serving fried chicken, seafood, or fish, whip up this sauce—it's delicious!

Manhattan
Clam Chowder

*I*T'S FRIDAY— and Junior's large soup pots are bubbling with this red clam chowder. "Unlike the white creamy one, this chowder has no cream, bell peppers, or carrots—but clam juice, chicken broth, and tomato paste instead," explained the chef as he stirred the simmering soup.

It's thick, filling, and is plenty for lunch or a late supper.

MAKES 2 QUARTS CHOWDER

½ cup (1 stick) unsalted butter

1 cup peeled and finely chopped carrots

1 cup finely chopped celery

1 cup finely chopped green bell pepper

1 cup finely chopped onions

2 tablespoons minced garlic

2 cups chicken broth

1 6-ounce can tomato paste (¾ cup)

2 cups clam broth

2 large boiling potatoes, peeled and cut into 1-inch cubes (2 cups)

2 teaspoons dried thyme

¼ teaspoon ground white pepper

2 bay leaves

1 quart minced fresh chowder clams, in their own juice (4 cups)

2 tablespoons cooking sherry

The Junior's Way—
Never drain the clams when you're making this chowder. Their juice adds an important flavor to the soup.

1. Melt the butter in a large stockpot over medium-high heat. Add the carrots, celery, bell pepper, onions, and garlic. Sauté until the vegetables are golden and tender, about 7 minutes.

Welcome to Junior's!

2. Whisk the chicken broth and tomato paste until blended; stir into the stockpot with the clam broth, the potatoes, thyme, white pepper, and bay leaves. Bring the soup to a full boil.

3. Reduce the heat to medium-low and simmer the soup, without covering the pot, until the potatoes are tender and the soup has thickened slightly, about 20 minutes. Stir the soup occasionally to prevent any possible sticking, adding a little more chicken broth if needed.

4. Stir in the fresh clams and their juices. Return the heat to medium-high and cook just until the clams turn opaque and are cooked through (do not overcook at this stage, as the fresh clams can become tough, about 5 minutes). Remove the soup from the heat. Discard the bay leaves and stir in the sherry. Serve steaming hot.

Homemade Black Bean Soup

*H*ERE'S ANOTHER SOUP that is always on the menu at Junior's. And is it ever popular! Maybe it's because of its unique flavor, coming from the simmering of the black beans with a ham bone and several fresh vegetables. Or perhaps it's because this bowl of soup becomes an easy meal in itself, for it's always served with rice on-the-side. These are the same beans that are often called turtle beans and are very popular throughout the Caribbean and South America. But these days, they are readily available in most supermarkets.

MAKES 2 QUARTS SOUP

continued

2 cups dried black beans (1 pound)

8 cups water (2 quarts)

FOR THE SOUP

½ cup (1 stick) unsalted butter, preferably clarified (page 314)

2 cups finely chopped celery

2 cups finely chopped onions

1 ham shank or ham bone

2 tablespoons minced garlic

½ teaspoon ground white pepper

7 cups boiling water

2 cups cooked sugar-cured ham, cut into bite-size
   chunks

FOR GO-ALONGS

Chopped white onions to top each serving

Cooked white rice

The Junior's Way—
While Black Bean Soup is cooking, a foam or skin might form on the top. Just check the pot frequently and skim it off. Check the amount of water in the pot occasionally too and add more if needed. These beans often need more water than other dried beans and peas.

1. Either soak the beans overnight in 8 cups of cold water, then rinse and drain, or cover the beans with 8 cups of boiling water, bring to a full boil over high heat, and boil for 2 minutes. Cover the pot and let the beans stand in the hot water for 1 hour, then rinse them well and drain. You will now have 5 cups of soaked beans.

2. Melt the butter in a large stockpot over medium-high heat. Add the celery, onions, ham shank or bone, garlic, and pepper. Sauté until the vegetables are golden and tender, about 7 minutes. Stir in the soaked beans, then pour in the boiling water. Bring to a full boil.

3. Reduce the heat to medium-low and simmer the soup, without covering it, until the beans are tender and the soup has thickened, about 45 minutes. After 30 minutes of cooking, add the chunks of ham. Stir the soup occasionally to prevent any possible sticking and add a little more water if needed.

4. When the soup is ready to serve, remove it from the heat and ladle into soup dishes. Sprinkle with chopped onions and serve the cooked rice on the side.

BAR-B-Q Baby Back Ribs

*T*HESE BARBEQUED RIBS are some of the juiciest and tenderest ones I have ever bitten into. In fact, they practically fall off the bones as you're eating them. The best part is that they seem to cook on their own with little watching from you.

First parboil them in a pot, then let them simmer in their own sauce in the oven—no watching's needed.

MAKES 6 SERVINGS

2 racks baby back ribs (about 6 pounds)
1 tablespoon salt
1 tablespoon minced garlic
1 bay leaf
1 recipe BAR-B-Q Sauce (page 312)

The Junior's Way—After baking the ribs until nice and tender, baste them again with sauce and place on the grill or under the broiler just until glazed and browned, about 3 minutes on each side. Watch closely, as the ingredients in the sauce can cause them to brown quickly. This extra grilling makes them nice and crispy.

1. Place the ribs in a large stockpot with the salt, garlic, and bay leaf. Add enough water to cover the ribs. Cover the pot and bring to a boil over high heat.

2. Reduce the heat to low and simmer the ribs until they are tender, about 1 hour. Check occasionally and add more water if necessary to keep the ribs completely covered with the cooking liquid.

3. Preheat the oven to 350°F. Transfer the ribs to a large baking pan, placing them in a single layer if possible. Discard the bay leaf. Pour the BAR-B-Q Sauce over the ribs and let them stand for 15 minutes to soak up some of the sauce.

4. Bake the ribs, without covering them, until the ribs are hot, browned, and bubbly, about 25 minutes.

5. If you wish, baste the ribs with extra sauce, then glaze and brown them under the broiler or over a hot charcoal grill for 3 to 4 minutes on each side, just like they do at Junior's. Heat any extra sauce in a small saucepan and serve as a dipping sauce.

1990s—Brooklyn! Still the World!

BAR-B-Q Sauce

*B*AR-B-Q AND JUNIOR'S are almost synonymous—"Regulars" don't think of one without the other. And no wonder—Junior's is famous for its barbeque. Customers just keep coming back time and again for BAR-B-Q chicken . . . BAR-B-Q Baby Back Ribs . . . the BAR-B-Q Ribs & Chicken Combo.

Whatever you choose, you'll be glad you did. It all has a lot to do with this delicious slightly sweet and just-spicy-enough sauce.

MAKES 3 CUPS SAUCE

1 28-ounce can tomato purée

¾ cup distilled white vinegar

¼ cup bottled chili sauce

1 tablespoon corn syrup

1 teaspoon salt

1 teaspoon freshly ground black pepper

⅓ cup cold water

2 tablespoons cornstarch

The Junior's Way—Tomato purée is one of the secrets of this sauce. It not only thickens the sauce to the right consistency, but also helps it stick to whatever you brush it on. The corn syrup is another reason it works so well as a basting sauce. On the grill, the corn syrup puts a shiny glaze on any meat you brush the sauce on.

1. Combine the tomato purée, vinegar, chili sauce, corn syrup, salt, and pepper in a heavy saucepan. Stir over medium heat until the mixture comes to a full boil. Reduce the heat to low and let the sauce simmer in the open pan for 10 minutes, stirring the sauce occasionally to keep it from sticking.

2. Mix the water and cornstarch together in a cup until the cornstarch thoroughly dissolves. Stir in a little of the hot tomato mixture, then drizzle this cornstarch mixture into the simmering sauce.

3. Return the heat to medium and bring the mixture to a full boil. Stirring constantly, let the mixture boil until it thickens slightly, about 2 minutes. Remove the sauce from the heat. Great for brushing on BAR-B-Q Baby Back Ribs (page 311), or try it the next time you grill chicken.

Broiled Shrimp Scampi

FOR THAT SPECIAL supper in a hurry—Junior's Shrimp Scampi is it! Go ahead and splurge on the largest jumbo shrimp you can find. Then take a few extra moments to butterfly them, so they spread out big and beautiful, even after cooking.

The Scampi Butter works fabulously on broiled sea scallops too. You'll find both on Junior's regular menu. Serve with Junior's famous Yellow Rice, as they go together perfectly.

MAKES 4 SERVINGS OF 4 SHRIMPS EACH

1 recipe Scampi Butter (page 314)
1 recipe Yellow Rice (page 88) (optional)
16 jumbo shrimps in shells (about 1½ pounds)
Wedges of fresh lemon

The Junior's Way—To butterfly the shrimps, use a sharp-pointed paring knife to cut down the back outer curved edge of the shrimps—almost through but not completely. Open the shrimps like a book, remove any veins you see, and lay them out flat, cut-side-up, with the tails pointing up in the air.

1. Prepare the Scampi Butter and set aside. Make the Yellow Rice, if you wish.

2. Preheat the broiler and smear a broiling pan or shallow baking pan with butter (use one that has 1-inch sides).

3. Peel the shrimps (leave the tails on). Using a sharp-pointed paring knife, butterfly the shrimps, slitting along the back curved edge of the shrimps, cutting almost through them but not completely. Remove any veins you see. Brush the shrimps generously on both sides with the Scampi Butter. Lay the shrimps cut-side-up on the baking pan and drizzle them generously with more of the butter.

4. Broil the shrimps about 6 inches from the broiler until they turn opaque, about 6 to 8 minutes (watch carefully, as the shrimps can become tough if they overcook). Since the shrimps are butterflied and are spread out thinly, there's no need to turn them while they're broiling. Just be sure to baste the shrimps frequently during cooking with extra Scampi Butter. Garnish the shrimps with the lemon wedges and serve immediately, with Yellow Rice, if you wish, like they do at Junior's.

1990s—Brooklyn! Still the World!

Scampi Butter

AS WITH MOST specialties, Junior's has its own recipe for this popular butter. Many scampi butter recipes have only butter or oil and garlic; some have vermouth too. The chef at Junior's uses a delicate dry white wine to make this Scampi Butter.

It's the ideal basting sauce for broiling all kinds of fish fillets and most seafood, such as fresh sea scallops and jumbo shrimps.

MAKES 1 CUP

¾ cup (1½ sticks) unsalted butter,
      clarified (see The Junior's Way)

1 tablespoon minced garlic

1 teaspoon paprika

2 tablespoons dry white wine

The Junior's Way—To clarify butter, melt the butter in a saucepan and let it stand for about fifteen minutes to let the foam rise to the top and the whey and milky solids sink. Carefully spoon off and discard the foam. Spoon out the clear yellow clarified butter in the pan, leaving the solids behind.

1. Clarify the butter in a small saucepan.

2. Add the garlic to the butter (if you really like garlic, use 2 tablespoons instead of only one). Heat the butter just until the garlic begins to wilt. Whisk in the paprika and wine. Use for basting Broiled Shrimp Scampi (page 313) and Broiled Fresh Sea Scallops (page 315).

Broiled Fresh Sea Scallops with Garlic Butter

*F*OR SOME REASON, scampi garlic butter is usually served *only* with shrimps—but not at Junior's. They always use it for cooking broiled scallops, too. And often the scallops arrive with a great big helping of Yellow Rice.

The next time your fishmonger has fresh sea scallops for sale, serve them the Junior's Way.

MAKES 4 SERVINGS

1 recipe Scampi Butter (page 314)

1 recipe Yellow Rice (page 88) (optional)

1½ pounds sea scallops

Wedges of fresh lemon

The Junior's Way—For this dish, choose the larger sea scallops, not the small bay scallops. As they broil, turn them frequently to keep them cooking evenly. Cook them just until they turn opaque—no longer.

1. Prepare the Scampi Butter and set aside. Make the Yellow Rice, if you wish.

2. Preheat the broiler and smear a shallow baking pan with butter (one that has 1-inch sides).

3. Wash the scallops under cold running water, being sure you wash away any sand in the crevices, then drain them on paper towels. Place the scallops on the baking pan and drizzle them generously with the Scampi Butter.

4. Broil the scallops about 5 inches from the broiler until they turn opaque, about 6 to 7 minutes, turning them once (watch carefully, as scallops can become tough if they overcook).

5. After the top sides of the scallops turn opaque, turn the scallops over once, being sure to baste them frequently with extra Scampi Butter as they cook. Serve the scallops immediately with Yellow Rice, if you wish, plus plenty of fresh lemon wedges.

1990s—Brooklyn! Still the World!

Chicken on a Bun

*L*EAVE IT TO Junior's to serve Chicken on a Bun *not* on a bun but really on thick slices of grilled Challah bread. This sandwich is filled not only with a juicy charbroiled chicken cutlet, but also with two crispy strips of bacon and some slices of melted American cheese.

No wonder this sandwich is found on the menu under the section labeled "Sensational Sandwiches." It really *is* sensational!

MAKES 1 SANDWICH

2 tablespoons unsalted butter

2 slices Challah bread, at least 1 inch thick (page 32)

1 boneless skinless chicken breast half (4 to 5 ounces)

2 thick strips bacon, cooked crisp

3 slices American cheese (3 ounces)

2 leaves curly leaf lettuce

2 thick slices ripe tomato

French fries (optional)

> *The Junior's Way—*
> Grill the bread in butter in a skillet or on a hot griddle until it's golden and slightly crispy. This keeps the bread sturdy, not soggy, when the grilled chicken is placed on top.

1. Preheat the broiler. Melt half the butter on a hot grill or in a large skillet. Grill the 2 slices of bread on both sides, adding more butter as you need it.

2. At the same time, charbroil or grill the chicken until the juices are clear, about 3 to 4 minutes on each side. Place the chicken on one slice of bread, top it with the cooked bacon, and cover with the cheese. Pop this slice of bread with the chicken and cheese under the broiler to melt the cheese (watch carefully as it takes only a few seconds), then transfer to a plate.

3. Place the second slice of grilled bread on an angle, covering one end of the sandwich slightly, leaving the sandwich mostly open-faced. Add the lettuce leaves to the plate and top them with the tomato slices. Stack up thick-cut French fries, if you like, covering the rest of the plate.

Welcome to Junior's!

Yam Fries

*T*HERE'S ALWAYS A heap of reddish-brown fries ready to go into the fryers at Junior's. Folks call them yam fries—and all the "Regulars" know to order them, even though they're nowhere on the menu. These fries can be made either from yams or the dark-orange-skinned sweet potatoes, which grow in the United States and are often misnamed "yams." The true yam is a different plant variety grown mostly in South and Central America, the West Indies, and Africa, slightly sweeter than the sweet potato and more moist. Every time I visit Junior's at lunchtime, there are plates and plates of these yummy-looking Yam Fries marching out of the kitchen. Evidently the word is out that these are a specialty that's not to be missed.

MAKES 4 CUPS FRIES

2 pounds yams

2 extra-large egg whites

1 tablespoon cold water

2 tablespoons fines herbes

1 tablespoon Creole or Cajun seasoning (look on the spice
        rack of your supermarket or gourmet store)

1 tablespoon salt

½ teaspoon ground white pepper

¼ cup (½ stick) unsalted butter, cut into small pieces

¼ cup vegetable oil

The Junior's Way—
Buying the right yams or sweet potatoes is the first important step toward making Yam Fries like they're served at Junior's. Look for yams with dark orange skin and deep vivid orange flesh. These are sweet and moist and ideal for this recipe.

1. Wash, scrub, and peel the yams. Cut the yams in half lengthwise, then into thick sticks as long as the potatoes, usually about 5 inches long and ½ inch thick (no thinner, as they can break apart during frying). You will have about 8 cups of potato sticks. Place the potatoes in a bowl of ice water for 15 minutes—no longer, as this can make them watery. Using a slotted spoon, transfer the yams to paper towels and pat them dry.

continued

1990s—Brooklyn! Still the World!

2. Preheat the oven to 400°F. Line a baking sheet with foil and lay out the potatoes on the sheet in a single layer.

3. Whisk the egg whites with the water and brush on all sides of the yam sticks. (Don't worry if you don't use all of the egg-white mixture; just be sure the yams are well coated all over.)

4. Mix together the fines herbes, Creole seasoning, salt, and pepper. Sprinkle the spices on the yam sticks, using all of the spice mixture and turning the yam sticks as you go.

5. Bake the yams for 10 minutes, tossing them 2 or 3 times during baking.

6. Meanwhile, heat the butter and oil in a skillet over medium-high heat to 375°F. Fry the yam sticks until golden and tender, about 10 minutes, turning them frequently. Serve these fries immediately while they're still piping hot.

Spicy Fries

ORDER A STEAK sandwich at Junior's and you'll quickly hear the question "Regular or spicy?" Well, before arriving at Junior's, I had never heard of Spicy Fries, and had certainly never eaten them. But now I'm a fan. These fries are chunky and thick-cut, with their skins still on. Go ahead, try them.

They're crunchy on the outside, soft on the inside; spicy as their name implies, but not overpowering.

Probably just better than any fried potatoes you have ever eaten.

MAKES 4 CUPS FRIES

2 pounds russet baking potatoes (Idahos)

2 extra-large egg whites

1 tablespoon cold water

1 tablespoon Creole or Cajun seasoning (look on the spice rack of your supermarket or gourmet store)

Welcome to Junior's!

1 tablespoon salt

1 teaspoon freshly ground black pepper

¼ to ½ teaspoon red pepper flakes (depending on how much pepper you like)

¼ cup (½ stick) unsalted butter, cut into small pieces

¼ cup vegetable oil

The Junior's Way—

Choose Idaho russet baking potatoes for making these fries. They're high in starch and low in moisture, which helps the potato sticks hold their shape in the hot oil. Pick out the potatoes that are long and flat, instead of the short and round ones (they're easier to cut).

1. Wash and scrub the potatoes well, but do not peel. Cut the potatoes in half lengthwise, then into thick sticks as long as the potatoes, usually about 5 inches long and ½ inch thick (no thinner, as they can break apart during frying). You will have about 8 cups of potato sticks. Place the potatoes in a bowl of ice water for 15 minutes—no longer, as this can make them watery. Using a slotted spoon, transfer the potatoes to paper towels and pat them dry.

2. Preheat the oven to 400°F. Line a baking sheet with foil and lay out the potatoes on the sheet in a single layer.

3. Whisk the egg whites with the water and brush on all sides of the potato sticks. (Don't worry if you don't use all of the egg-white mixture; just be sure the potatoes are well coated all over.)

4. Mix together the Creole seasoning, the salt, black pepper, and red pepper flakes. Sprinkle the spices on the potato sticks, using all of the mixture and turning the potato sticks as you go.

5. Bake the potatoes for 10 minutes, tossing them 2 or 3 times during baking.

6. Meanwhile, heat the butter and oil in a skillet over medium-high heat to 375°F. Fry the potato sticks until golden and tender, about 10 minutes, turning them frequently. Serve hot!

Something Different

WHEN YOU'RE HUNGRY for a sandwich and you want something different, try this Something Different special from Junior's. Two golden-brown crispy potato pancakes are overstuffed with slices of freshly roasted beef brisket.

It's found under "Sensational Sandwiches" on the menu—truly one of those sandwiches made only at Junior's, as far as I have been able to find out, and only for those with hearty appetites.

MAKES 1 HEARTY SANDWICH

2 Homemade Potato Pancakes, hot, golden-brown, and
   crispy (page 127)
4 to 6 thin slices hot Fresh Brisket of Beef (page 82) or
   roast beef
Applesauce

1. Place one hot pancake on a plate and mound the slices of hot beef brisket on top.

2. Cover with the second pancake and spear the sandwich closed with a long toothpick. Serve with a bowl of applesauce on the side.

The Junior's Way—

Look for the extra-long sandwich picks in a gourmet store. The ones used at Junior's are red plastic, topped with a small red anchor. The long picks with frilly paper ends may be easier to find and work just as well.

Red Potato Salad

*E*VEN POTATO SALAD at Junior's is a treat. It's made from red potatoes that still have their skins on. There are small bites of hard-boiled eggs, shreds of crisp carrots, sprigs of parsley, and bits of green onion.

And as you might expect, the dressing is not just mayonnaise but has sour cream and a little Dijon mustard folded in. Luckily, potato salad is a daily entry, always available as a "special" on-the-side.

MAKES 2 QUARTS POTATO SALAD

FOR THE SALAD

1 teaspoon fresh lemon juice

1 teaspoon salt

2½ pounds red-skinned potatoes (leave skins on)

3 extra-large eggs

½ cup finely chopped green onions

⅓ cup chopped fresh parsley

¼ cup shredded carrots

1 tablespoon chopped fresh dill

FOR THE DRESSING

¾ cup *Hellmann's Real Mayonnaise* (not the light variety)

⅓ cup sour cream

2 tablespoons Dijon mustard

1 teaspoon salt

1 teaspoon sugar

½ teaspoon garlic powder

½ teaspoon ground white pepper

The Junior's Way—
When cooking the potatoes, add a little lemon juice to the water. This little bit of acid keeps the potatoes white while they are cooking by neutralizing any hard alkaline salts that might be in the water.

1. Fill a large saucepan half-full with water and add the lemon juice and salt. Slice the potatoes ¼ inch thick, drop them into the water, and bring to a boil over high heat.

continued

2. Reduce the heat to medium and simmer the potatoes until they are tender when tested with a fork, 10 to 15 minutes depending on how big they are. Be sure to remove the potatoes from the heat before they start breaking apart.

3. Transfer the potatoes to a colander and rinse with cold water. Drain the potatoes well and place them in a large bowl.

4. While the potatoes are cooking, place the eggs in a small saucepan, cover with cold water, and bring to a full rolling boil over medium heat. Reduce the heat to low and simmer in the pan until the eggs are hard-cooked, about 10 minutes. Rinse the eggs under cold running water and peel them. Coarsely chop the eggs and add to the potatoes. Add the green onions, parsley, carrots, and dill and toss until the ingredients are mixed well.

5. To make the dressing: Mix all of the ingredients for the dressing together in a small bowl. Spoon the dressing over the potato mixture and gently stir in the dressing until all of the ingredients are well coated. Cover the salad with plastic wrap and chill until it's time to serve. Refrigerate any leftovers.

Sweet Potato Pie

EVER SINCE THE 1950s, sweet potato pie has been a favorite at Junior's. The bakers start baking them before Thanksgiving and continue baking them every day, right through the Christmas holidays.

Though most folks think of sweet potatoes as only vegetables, they whip up deliciously into this pie, too. They turn into a pie that's very similar to pumpkin but usually with more spice. If you've never had sweet potato pie, this is the recipe!

MAKES ONE 9-INCH DEEP-DISH PIE

½ recipe Pie Pastry, enough for a single-crust pie (page 40)

1½ pounds fresh sweet potatoes or 3 cups drained canned sweet potatoes

4 extra-large eggs

1 cup granulated sugar

Blintzes and Dairy

(81) Homemade Potato Pancakes with Sour Cream or Applesauce	127
(83) Homemade Cheese Blintzes with Strawberry Sauce and Sour Cream	301

Eggs and Omelettes

(96) Western Omelette	122

French Toast and Griddle Cakes

(103) Old-Fashioned French Toast with Apple and Raisin Preserves	123
(108) Griddle Cakes with Apple and Raisin Preserves	124

Side Orders

(113) Lettuce and Tomatoes with Russian Dressing	89
(116) Red Potato Salad	321
(117) Creamy Cole Slaw	138
(118) French Fried Onion Rings	175
(128) Cornbread	133
(128) Blueberry Muffins	128
(128) Golden Corn Muffins	132
(129) Spaghetti with Chef's Marinara Sauce	178

Appetizers

(130) Jumbo Shrimp Cocktail	71
(139) Buffalo Wings with Bleu Cheese Sauce	304
(571) Chicken Fingers with Honey Mustard Sauce	306

Homemade Soups—Chili

(145) New England Clam Chowder	74
(145) Split Pea Soup	27
(145) Manhattan Clam Chowder	308
(147) Wine from Water	25
(147) Matzoh Ball Soup	26

Welcome to Junior's!

Hot Open Sandwiches

Delicatessen Sandwiches

Combination Sandwiches

Junior's Fabulous Desserts at the Bake Shoppe

Skyscraper Ice Cream Sodas

Junior's Mountain High Sundaes

Beverages

Welcome to Junior's!

Specialties of the House—But Nowhere on the Menu

Some of Junior's specials are almost always being made in the kitchen, just 'cause they're so popular. But they're nowhere on the menu! You just need to be "in the know" and *know* that you can order them. The "Regulars" at Junior's know. Just ask them about the spicy Yam Fries, the heavenly Cornbread that melts-in-your-mouth, the Yellow Rice that often appears even if you don't order it. As I've heard so often, "Just ask for it . . . if we have it, we'll make it, you'll get it."

And that's the way it is with the popular foods on this list.

Belgian Waffles	303
Tea Biscuits	256
Cigars	261
Home Fries	144
Mashed Potatoes	75
Pickled Beets	140
Spicy Fries	318
Yam Fries	317
Yellow Rice	88
Big Meatballs with Spaghetti and Chef's Marinara Sauce	176
Baked Virginia Ham	179
Mac and Cheese Pie	141
Pecan Pie	194
Pumpkin Pie	268
Sweet Potato Pie	322
Lemon Coconut Cake	270
Brownies	278
Coconut Macaroons	283
Mountain High Vanilla Sundae	45
Chocolate Egg Cream	43

Bibliography

Abel, Allen. *Flatbush Odyssey: A Journey Through the Heart of Brooklyn*. Toronto: McClelland & Stewart, Inc., 1995.

Bisogno, Frank. *"Is Anyone Here from Brooklyn?"* New York: Fradon Publishing, 1990.

Capote, Truman. "A House on the Heights," from *Selected Writings by Truman Capote*. New York: Curtis Publishing, 1959.

Daly, Margaret. *Brooklyn Eats*. New York: City & Company, 1998.

Fischler, Stan. *Confessions of a Trolley Dodger from Brooklyn*. Flushing, N.Y.: H&M Productions II, Inc., 1995.

Frommer, Myrna Katz, and Harvey Frommer. *It Happened in Brooklyn*. Orlando, Fla.: Harcourt Brace & Co., 1993.

Gordon, Mary. "The Winds Were Warm, Then Bitter." *The New York Times*, January 25, 1998.

Guare, John. "My Dinner with Donald and Other Happenings." *The New York Times*, January 25, 1998.

Harney, James, and Thomas Hanrahan. "Fire Hits Junior's in Brooklyn." *New York Daily News*, August 17, 1981.

Ing, David. "Famed B'klyn Restaurant Eighty-Sixed by Big Blaze." *New York Post*, August 18, 1981.

Kappstatte, Bob. "Wishful Thinking for the New Year." New York *Daily News*, December 31, 1981.

Lipsyte, Robert. "Land of Giants, Bums and Bombers." *The New York Times*, January 25, 1998.

"Memories of Junior's: The Heart, Soul and Pulse of Downtown." *The Phoenix*, August 27, 1981.

Monti, Ralph. *I Remember Brooklyn*. New York: Birch Lane Press, 1991.

Paley, Grace. "Tough Times for a City of Tenants." *The New York Times*, January 25, 1998.

Prince, Carl E. *Brooklyn's Dodgers*. New York: Oxford University Press, Inc., 1996.

Reid, Mark A. *Spike Lee's Do the Right Thing*. New York: Cambridge University Press, 1997.

Roma, Thomas. *Found in Brooklyn*. New York: W. W. Norton & Company, Inc., 1996.

Rosenbaum, Ron. "The Best Cheesecake in New York." *The Village Voice*, July 26, 1973.

Sheraton, Mimi. "Touring the Heart's Own Brooklyn." *The New York Times,* May 8, 1998.

Silvers, Phil, with Robert Saffron. *This Laugh Is on Me.* New York: Prentice-Hall, 1973.

Snider, Duke, with Bill Gilbert. *The Duke of Flatbush.* New York: Kensington Publishing, 1988.

Snyder-Grenier, Ellen M. *Brooklyn: An Illustrated History.* Philadelphia, Pa.: Temple University Press, 1996.

Stallworth, Lyn, and Rod Kennedy, Jr. *The Brooklyn Cookbook.* New York: Alfred A. Knopf, Inc., 1993.

Stern, Jane, and Michael Stern. *Road Food and Good Food.* New York: Alfred A. Knopf, Inc., 1986.

Willensky, Elliot. *When Brooklyn Was the World.* New York: Crown Publishers, Inc., 1986.

Wyatt Sexton, Andrea, and Alice Leccese Powers. *The Brooklyn Reader: Thirty Writers Celebrate America's Favorite Borough.* New York: Crown Publishers, Inc., 1994.

Younger, William Lee. *Old Brooklyn in Early Photographs.* New York: Dover Publications, Inc., 1978.

Youngman, Henny, with Carroll Carroll. *Take My Wife . . . Please!* Putnam/Berkley, 1973.

Index